The Pillsbury
BAKE-OFF®
Cookbook

Pictured top to bottom: Choco-Peanut Toppers, page 112; Marshmallow Cookie Tarts, page 119

The Pillsbury
BAKE-OFF®
Cookbook

Doubleday
New York • London • Toronto • Sydney • Auckland

The Pillsbury Company
Pillsbury Publications

Managing Editor: Diane B. Anderson
Associate Editor: Elaine Christiansen
Recipe Copy Editor: Susanne Mattison
Home Economists: Bake-Off® Contest, Pillsbury Consumer Service and
  Publications
Nutrition Coordinators: Patricia Godfrey, R.D., Indra Mehrotra, R.D., Diane
  Christensen
Contributing Editor: S. J. Thoms & Associates, Inc.
Art Direction and Design: Lynne Dolan, Tad Ware & Company, Inc.
Food Stylists: Lynn C. Boldt, JoAnn Cherry, Sharon Harding, Barb Standal

Front Cover Photograph: Topsy Turvy Apple Pie, p. 162

Bake-Off® Contest, Poppin' Fresh® figure, Classic® Cookbooks, Pillsbury's
BEST®, Hungry Jack®, Green Giant®, Niblets®, Valley Combinations®, Rice
Originals®, Harvest Fresh®, Mexicorn® and LeSueur® are registered
trademarks of The Pillsbury Company.

PUBLISHED BY DOUBLEDAY
a division of Bantam Doubleday Dell Publishing Group, Inc.
666 Fifth Avenue, New York, New York 10103

DOUBLEDAY and the portrayal of an anchor with a dolphin are trademarks of
Doubleday, a division of Bantam Doubleday Dell Publishing Group, Inc.

Library of Congress Cataloging-in-Publication Data
The Pillsbury Bake-Off® cookbook. — 1st ed.
      p.   cm.
    Includes index.
    1. Baking.   I. Pillsbury Company.   II. Bake-Off® (Contest)
  TX765.P518   1990
  641.7′1 — dc20   89-34418
                                                      CIP

ISBN 0-385-23868-1

Quality printing and binding by:

Arcata Graphics/Hawkins
Press Road
New Canton, TN 37642
U.S.A.

Contents

America's Premier Baking and Cooking Contest

The Bake-Off® Contest began modestly enough as an opportunity for women to share their treasured recipes. At the same time, the contest was intended to recognize the creativity of homemakers, paying them special honor for their baking skills.

Created by executives from Pillsbury's advertising agency, that first event—held in 1949—was called the Grand National Recipe and Baking Contest. Almost immediately media people dubbed it the Bake-Off® Contest. Contest finalists became overnight celebrities for skills they had honed to perfection in their own kitchens. So popular was the contest that Pillsbury executives decided to repeat it the next year, and the next year, until it became an institution. Today it is described as the granddaddy of cooking contests.

The Bake-Off® Contest remains popular today because it has kept pace with the changing needs and interests of American consumers. Entry rules and judging criteria have been revised often over the years. In 1966, the Bake-Off® Contest recognized the growing trend to convenience cooking by adding the theme "Busy Lady." Two years later, categories for convenience mixes and refrigerated fresh dough were introduced. And in 1973, the "Bake It Easy" theme stressed the need for simple recipes with strong family appeal.

For many people, the Bake-Off® Contest is a continuing source of fascination and intrigue. How do people become finalists? Who are they, and how do they come up with prizewinning recipes? What happens at the contest? How does it happen?

The pages that follow offer a peek into the intricate inner workings of the Bake-Off® Contest—how it began, how it has changed and what it is all about today.

In the Beginning

Eleanor Roosevelt was the honored guest at that first contest in 1949 and called it "an important part of the American scene." It was and has been ever since!

Held at New York's Waldorf-Astoria, an oversight almost kept the contest from happening. Just hours before the event, the staff discovered that the hotel's private electrical system was direct current, while the

From The First Pillsbury Grand National Baking Contest in 1949:

Above: Judges sampling cakes.

Above: Celebrities sharing the excitement.

Left: Winners enjoying top honors and checks.

electric ranges for the contest required alternating current. As the finalists slept, a hole was cut in the hotel's wall and a cable was dropped four stories to the street below. From there it descended via a manhole to the New York Central Railroad. A power cord was tapped into the railway's alternating current line, and the 100 ranges were ready to go in time.

With so many years of history, the Bake-Off® Contest is a treasury of funny anecdotes and poignant memories. And the unique charm of the contest is created by the finalists themselves, like . . .

- The farm housewife who, distrustful of city ways, brought eggs from her own chicken house to prepare her recipe.
- The Texas teenage finalist who hauled out a hammer to crack peppermint candy for her dessert entry.
- The contestant who sighted along a carpenter's level before committing her cake to the oven.

Stories like these reflect the depth and character of this remarkable event. It's about food, but more important, it's about people. It's a cherished vignette of Americana.

A Window on the Kitchens of America

Bake-Off® recipes are widely recognized as reflecting and even setting trends in American-style cooking. When the contest began, cooking was primarily the work of women, many of whom spent hours in the kitchen baking elaborate recipes. Homemakers who had experienced the rationing and shortages of World War II were taking new interest in cooking.

For Americans of the 1950s, home and family were all-important. The idea of "the good life" was evident in rich, filling meals topped off with sweet, often glamorous desserts and treats. Typical of these fancy mealtime finales were Snappy Turtle Cookies and "My Inspiration" Cake. Grand Prize winner in 1952, the cookies were cleverly shaped to look like turtles and featured the popular flavor combination we now know in turtle candy. "My Inspiration" Cake, the top winner just one year later, was layer upon layer of cake, chocolate and nuts.

As America moved into the 1960s, convenience of preparation became a greater concern than it had been previously. Women were entering the work force in larger numbers and needed recipes that could be made quickly. Reflecting this, entries included many one-step cakes, press-in-the-pan pie crusts, bar cookies and all-in-one main dishes. America—and its meals—went casual with quick and easy main dishes like Crafty Crescent Lasagne, a 1968 Bake-Off® favorite featuring refrigerated crescent dinner rolls. Good cooks also looked to the Bake-Off® Contest for new desserts that were inviting yet easy to make, such as the famous Tunnel of Fudge Cake and Magic Marshmallow Crescent Puffs.

In the 1970s, society's emphasis on nutrition was evident in the contestants' use of fruits and vegetables for everything from main dishes to desserts. Whole grain flours and cereals, nuts and seeds, plus honey and maple syrup for sweetening, became staple ingredients. Adventuresome cooks began to experiment with more herbs, spices and flavorings. Whole Wheat Raisin Loaf and other back-to-scratch baked goods were in vogue. Alongside were recipes like Chocolate Cherry Bars and Potato-Beef Quick Meal that made creative use of new convenience products like cake mixes and dried potato products.

What was trendy in the 1970s became a way of life in the 1980s—fresh vegetables, whole grain products and light, nutritious fare. Ethnic cuisine with an American twist became popular, as evidenced by such entries as Puffy Chiles Rellenos snacks, Streamlined Hungarian Torte and Italian Cheese Rustica Pie. Contestants also reached into their own heritage to prepare family heirloom recipes as well as regional favorites like Santa Fe Corn and Cheese Bake.

With the emphasis on fast meals, microwave cooking came into its own. Finalists used the new oven to prepare part or all of their recipes in a matter of minutes. They also continued to use small appliances, such as electric mixers, food processors and blenders, to help speed preparation of recipes.

Today's recipe entries combine the best of each Bake-Off® era. The ready availability of a wide variety of fresh ingredients makes it possible for American cooks to prepare virtually anything they desire any time of the year. Dishes like Italian Spinach Torta and Polish Poppy Swirl Loaf feature ethnic ideas adapted for American tastes. The concern about nutrition is reflected in light meal and mini-meal alternatives, such as Garden Chicken Salad and Ham and Cheese Biscuit Pockets. However, Americans still "pull out the stops" on cost, time and calories when it comes to desserts and sweet snacking, as evidenced by Chocolate Praline Layer Cake, the glamorous grand prize winner from 1988.

There is a new awareness of attractive food presentation, probably because of more frequent dining out. Main dishes, soups and side dishes might call for a special herb sprinkle or fresh vegetable garnish. And Bake-Off® dessert recipes often incorporate fancy pipped frosting or whipped cream plus chocolate curls.

Ask tens of thousands of creative cooks from around the country to share their favorite recipes, and you will get a good look at how America cooks today. That is the unique picture presented by entries in the Bake-Off® Contest.

Choosing the Bake-Off® Finalists

Have you ever wondered what happens to a Bake-Off® entry once it is dropped into a mailbox? How the recipes are selected for the finals?

To get a true picture, it's really necessary to back up about a year, to the time when the entry rules and judging criteria for the upcoming contest are written. In 1949, one rule was that all recipes had to use at least ½ cup of flour. During the 1960s, convenience mix and refrigerated dough categories were added. Over the years, various contest themes and recipe groups have been created to keep the contest in tune with the way Americans are cooking. They have covered ideas from Regional American Foods and Family Favorites to Quick and Easy Recipes and Ethnic Recipes.

About nine months before the contest, a promotional campaign is launched. Information begins to appear in supermarkets, magazines and newspapers throughout the country. The goal: to encourage America's best cooks to enter their favorite innovative recipes in the Bake-Off® Contest.

The Mailbags Arrive

Entries journey through the mail system and eventually arrive at the office of an independent judging agency. The agency's job is to screen all recipes, making sure the official rules and judging criteria are met. These judges also review the recipes for trends in food interests, which are incorporated into a report at the conclusion of the entry phase and used by Pillsbury home economists and marketing people, as well as newspaper and magazine food editors.

Eligible recipes are assigned a special code number, and the entrants' names and addresses are removed. This is a vitally important step in maintaining the integrity of the contest. Hundreds of these coded recipes are forwarded to Pillsbury test kitchens, where home economists read through them again. They continue the search for the most interesting food ideas, eliminating recipes that appear inaccurate or too involved, or that require unusual equipment or ingredients.

Test and Taste

Kitchen testing is the next step. Seasoned home economists sample and evaluate every possible detail of each recipe. Does it have family appeal? Is it a recipe most cooks would make often? Is it easy to prepare? Is the presentation appealing? And most important of all, does it taste good?

Meanwhile, a research team of home economists pore over a library of food publications. Their job is to make sure recipes have not been previously published by

Pillsbury home economists test and taste to assure reliable recipes.

national cookbooks, magazines or food companies nor chosen as winners in national contests.

The process of selecting the best 100 recipes is long and rigorous. Thousands of recipes are forwarded by the independent judging agency to Pillsbury, and each is read carefully for its special merits. Hundreds are prepared and evaluated by professional home economists in taste-test panels. The best are tested further, and finally, after months of work, the 100 winning entries are selected. Not until this time does the independent judging agency reveal the names and addresses of the people who submitted the recipes.

Next Step, Contest Preparations

As soon as the 100 recipes are selected, 100 finalists must be contacted and preparations for the Bake-Off® Contest begun. Countless details must be handled in order to make this "the experience of a lifetime" and to assure that every finalist has an equal opportunity to win prize money.

Calling All Finalists

A team of Pillsbury people goes to work contacting all finalists by phone to let them know of their newfound celebrity status. Locating the finalists can sometimes turn into a detective hunt. One contestant was traveling the country with no itinerary or plans to call home. So the highway patrols from several states, forest rangers and park officials joined in the chase! Another finalist without a phone in her home luckily "had her ears on" and responded to a CB message broadcast by her community's postmistress.

One by one, each of the finalists is contacted and congratulated. Certain papers must be signed and biographical information completed. Reading the biographies is like viewing a cross section of the American population. Bake-Off® finalists often seem familiar— like next-door neighbors. At the same time, they are all unique individuals.

- In addition to cooking and baking, their hobbies have ranged from "baby-sitting" orphaned sea otters to weight lifting.
- Many enjoy traveling and trying out the cuisine of exotic lands like Nepal, Poland, Monaco and the Fiji Islands. Still others have visited nearly every U.S. state.
- Among the finalists have been homemakers, students, physicians, teachers, military officers, bus drivers and musicians.
- Many men have counted among the finalists, with three qualifying for the earliest contest.
- The youngest to win the Grand Prize was a seventeen-year-old woman. A ten-year-old was the youngest finalist ever to compete in the contest.

With finalists coming from all corners of the United States, travel arrangements for the free trip to the contest site have involved a mix of transporation methods. Most fly, but a few have requested rail travel. Some simply drive from their nearby homes. The most unusual: a dogsled used for the first leg of the trip by a finalist living in a remote region of Alaska.

The World's Longest Shopping List

Once the finalists arrive at the contest site, Pillsbury supplies all of the groceries and cooking equipment needed for recipe preparation. Gathering these supplies is an immense organizational feat that involves a team of home economists. They call finalists to check and double-check the "shopping lists" so that everyone has exactly what they would use at home to prepare their winning recipe.

As with the recipes, the grocery and equipment lists reflect current cooking styles. For example, early contest recipes were prepared "by hand," but many contemporary finalists use microwave ovens, food processors, blenders and other small appliances. As part of their recipes, today's finalists even call for ingredients to add fancy garnishing, such as chocolate leaves or filigree or piped toppings.

How the Grocery List Has Changed!

With 3,000 items in a typical grocery store of 1949, the shopping list for the first contest was a relatively short one of 120 different ingredients.

Now this list contains more than 225 ingredients as Bake-Off® finalists choose from over 15,000 items in today's supermarket.

There's Nothing Like the Bake-Off® Contest

One hundred mini-kitchens in one great ballroom! Whether it's in Los Angeles, New York, Houston, or one of the many other sites chosen for the Bake-Off® Contest, the atmosphere is a marvelous melding of anticipation, excitement and fun combined with earnest and skilled competition for thousands of dollars in prize money.

Each contestant has an assigned work area complete with a range and preparation area plus ingredients and utensils. As finalists step to their areas to begin cooking, their "assistants" stand by. Chosen by Pillsbury, these assistants run errands for the finalists and escort them to the judges' area and to photography. They even help out with the dishwashing.

For each contest, 100 cooks in 100 mini-kitchens vie for prize money.

The Bake-Off® floor is a flurry of activity. Magazine and newspaper food editors as well as photographers and TV cameras record the action. Show business celebrities and dignitaries are on hand to greet the contestants and cheer them on. Special guests from the supermarket industry observe the hubbub. And Pillsbury officials roam the floor to ensure absolute integrity on the part of everyone involved.

Finalists work painstakingly to prepare their recipes. Even so, disasters can occur. One contestant accidentally dropped her finished cake just as she was taking it to the judges' area. Another set her fresh-baked pie on a chair to cool—and absentmindedly sat on it.

Other finalists seem totally unaffected by the near-chaos of the contest floor. A contestant from Hawaii danced the hula for photographers while she waited for her recipe to bake. One finalist was observed reading a book and commented that the setting was really quite peaceful compared to her kitchen at home with five children underfoot.

Some have likened the situation to a people traffic jam. Yet despite the commotion, finalists turn out wonderful foods—beautifully decorated and consistently delicious.

Great Cooks of America

On the Bake-Off® floor, finalists become celebrities for skills they have honed to perfection in their own kitchens. Many are uniquely talented cooks, enjoying all types of baking and cooking. Others have developed specialties, such as cake or bread baking as an all-consuming avocation. And there are novice cooks who have just recently discovered their own innate knack with food.

There's really no way to predict who will become a Bake-Off® contestant. Many enter multiple recipes, hoping that one will become a prizewinner. Some make the finals on their very first try, with only one recipe entry. At the 33rd contest, one of the first-time finalists was a senior citizen who had entered every Bake-Off® Contest since 1949. One woman entered many times but was never named a finalist. Then her husband entered and became a finalist on his first try.

Among the finalists are those who have made a "career" of entering all types of cooking contests. They join clubs and subscribe to newsletters that offer tips on how to win contests.

There are others for whom the Bake-Off® Contest is a family affair. Grandmothers and mothers pass along a heritage of Bake-Off® lore to the younger generations.

Many contestants express a long-standing love for food—an interest that endures beyond the excitement of the Bake-Off® experience. Young finalists have gone on to college to study food science. Other finalists have started bakeries and restaurants. Still others are now cookbook authors and food writers for magazines and newspapers.

The Tastes of Success

The inspirations for winning recipes are as varied and interesting as the finalists themselves. Sometimes the recipes are created specifically for the Bake-Off® Contest. One woman said that she sleeps with pen and paper next to her bed in case she gets a new recipe idea before going to sleep at night.

Many finalists draw inspiration from their own food heritage. They start with hand-me-down recipes and add a creative new twist. Newer citizens of the U.S. use American ingredients to re-create the essence of foods from their homelands. Well-traveled finalists develop recipes that replicate dishes from favorite restaurants of the world.

Choosing the Winners

Being part of the Bake-Off® Contest is reward enough, according to many finalists. But it also is an opportunity to win thousands of dollars in prize money. Therefore, the finalists are serious about their work on Bake-Off® day.

In years past, there was a rule stating that "you must be able to prepare the recipe in a day." Now, however, finalists are given six hours, and some are finished in less than an hour.

Finalists are supplied enough ingredients to prepare their recipes three times, and many do. They make one for photography, one to share with their newfound friends on the Bake-Off® floor and the best one for the judges.

Working in secrecy, the judges conduct their evaluation in a well-guarded room away from the contest area. Chosen for their knowledge of good food, the judges include newspaper and magazine food editors, cookbook authors and other noted food authorities.

The judges sample and discuss each recipe thoroughly, weighing the merits with no idea of the finalists' names or hometowns. Foods are taste-tested at their freshest best—hot foods are judged when hot and cold foods are kept chilled. Judging 100 wonderful recipes may seem like great duty, but it can be tiring. To prevent fatigue, the judges sip water, tea and clam broth and clear their palates with celery and carrot sticks.

Maintaining the secrecy of the judging process is vital to the integrity of the contest. So, finalists, media representatives, other Bake-Off® guests and Pillsbury personnel alike—all must await the judges' final decisions.

Esther Tomich WINS Grand Prize in 1978 for Nutty Graham Picnic Cake!

And the Winners Are . . .

The day after the official contest, finalists gather with other Bake-Off® guests for the awards ceremony. All are dressed in their Sunday best. The tables are graced with colorful flowers. As the music plays, a celebrity mounts the grand stage for the big moment—to announce who has won the top prizes in the nation's most famous cooking contest. The atmosphere is charged with eager anticipation, and as the winners are announced, cheers of congratulations go up from the crowd.

$ Prizes Galore $

Nearly $2,500,000 in prize money has been awarded to Bake-Off® finalists since 1949, the first contest.

Only a privileged few are among the big money winners but all finalists are celebrities. Their photos are in the newspapers. They appear on local and sometimes national television. Whole families, employer-companies and towns share in the excitement. Returning to her hometown, one finalist was greeted at the airport with crowd commotion like that for a winning football team returning from the Super Bowl. Another finalist said she was so busy making public appearances that she might not have time to return to her job.

Some Recipes Become Classics

Bake-Off® recipes gain celebrity status as well, and many have become culinary classics. These are recipes that have withstood the test of time, remaining popular for years and even decades. They have been incorporated into personal recipe collections across America and are enjoyed by literally thousands of families, who pass them on from one generation of good cooks to the next.

Some of the Bake-Off® recipes that have become favorites won the top prizes, but others are simply great recipes appreciated for their perfect fit with the way American families cook and eat. Among them are recipes like Cherry Wink Cookies, Peanut Blossoms and Dilly Casserole Bread, which have become so commonplace that their origins in the Bake-Off® Contest are often forgotten.

Also ranking as classics are recipes that caused quite a commotion in the marketplace when they became top prize winners. The 1954 Grand Prize winner, Open Sesame Pie, featured sesame seed in the crust. During the week that followed publication of the recipe, grocery stores around the country sold out their stock of this exotic little seed.

Many people puzzled over the selection of Magic Marshmallow Crescent Puffs as the top prize winner

in 1969. "It's so simple—just a marshmallow wrapped in dough," they said. The Puffs became a winner precisely because of this very simple way to achieve good taste. Each triangle of refrigerated crescent dough was wrapped around a marshmallow that "magically" melted during baking to create a hollow-centered sweet roll.

Product Inspirations

Certain recipes from among the "classics" have gone on to inspire new Pillsbury products. None is better-known than the 1966 prize winner, Tunnel of Fudge Cake, a rich, moist chocolate cake with a soft, fudgy center. So popular was the recipe that Pillsbury created a convenient mix version featuring the same delicious taste that made the original recipe a classic.

Great Recipes Made Better Than Ever

Pillsbury home economists return to the Bake-Off® files for often requested recipes and recipes they know are "winners." The best are retested and revised to ensure their appeal to today's consumers.

All of the recipes in this book have been thoroughly tested in the Pillsbury kitchens. And many of the old-favorite recipes have been updated so that contemporary consumers can enjoy the great tastes all over again. Here are some of the ways that the recipes have been retested and updated:

- Ingredients no longer made are replaced with readily available products.
- From-scratch steps are replaced with timesaving mixes as well as refrigerated and frozen products.
- Easy-to-follow preparation instructions and cooking terms are used.
- Oven temperatures and ingredient amounts are adjusted to ensure greater success.
- Fats and salt are reduced to suit current preferences.
- Flour sifting is eliminated.
- Microwave preparation is incorporated when it is a proven timesaver.

America's Fascination with Good Food

The best of Bake-Off® recipes are presented here for you to enjoy . . . to read and recall from your own memory . . . to prepare and share with family and friends. If you've never made these recipes, now is the time to try them out. They're guaranteed to become part of your family's collection of Bake-Off® favorites.

Harvest Fresh® Spinach Soup, page 14; Savory Crescent Chicken Squares, page 28

Soups, Sandwiches and Snacks

❦

The easy-to-prepare soups and stews, baked sandwiches and intriguing snacks of this chapter seem especially fitting for a nation on the go. You'll find hearty and wholesome fare as well as many foods for lighter eating and the increasingly popular mini-meals. Tuna Cheese Flips and Cheese Steak Crescent Braid demonstrate the versatility of refrigerated biscuit and crescent roll doughs, used by savvy finalists to wrap all manner of ingredients. And Italian Spinach Torta features all-ready pie crust, a wonderfully convenient way to make appetizers that look and taste as if they came from the best catering shop in town.

Everyday, off-the-shelf staples are combined with a new ingredient or two for deliciously wholesome yet quick meals. Frozen or canned vegetables are teamed with meats and seasonings for savory soups like Zesty Chicken Vegetable Bisque and Harvest Fresh® Spinach Soup. The microwave oven, the blender and other small appliances add to the convenience of these recipes.

While easy preparation is essential for today's meals-on-the-run, good taste, wholesomeness and imaginative presentation are qualities that set these Bake-Off® favorites apart from other "fast" food. Quesadilla Quiche is served with sour cream, salsa, chopped tomato and sliced ripe olives — ideal for a family supper and fine enough for a company meal. Chicken 'n Artichoke Crescent Sandwiches borrow an ingredient combination from gourmet cooking for a quick and neat-to-eat meal.

Creative touches like these make the recipes in this collection so appealing and so right for the way we cook and eat today. They're sure to be winners on your table, too!

Harvest Fresh® Spinach Soup

Harvest Fresh®
Spinach Soup
~ᴑ᎑ᴑᏭ~

After entering every Bake-Off® Contest since the first one in 1949, this contestant finally became a finalist with this recipe for a delicately flavored, easy cream soup. It is delicious served hot or cold.

Olga Jason, Massachusetts
Bake-Off® 33, 1988

¼ cup chopped onion
¼ cup margarine or butter, melted
¼ cup all purpose or unbleached flour
1 teaspoon salt, if desired
½ teaspoon dry mustard
¼ teaspoon nutmeg
10¾-ounce can condensed chicken broth
½ cup shredded carrots
9-ounce package frozen chopped spinach in a pouch
2½ cups milk
Lemon slices, if desired

In 2-quart saucepan over medium heat, cook onion in margarine until tender. Remove from heat; blend in flour, salt, dry mustard and nutmeg. Gradually stir in chicken broth. Bring to a boil, stirring constantly. Add carrots and spinach. Reduce heat to medium; simmer uncovered 10 minutes or until carrots are tender and spinach is thawed, stirring occasionally.* Cool to lukewarm. In blender container or food processor bowl with metal blade, puree spinach mixture until smooth. Stir in milk. Cover; refrigerate until thoroughly chilled. Garnish each serving with lemon slice. **5 (1-cup) servings.**

MICROWAVE DIRECTIONS: In 8-cup microwave-safe measuring cup or large bowl, combine onion and margarine. Microwave on HIGH for 45 to 60 seconds or until onion is tender. Blend in flour, salt, dry mustard and nutmeg; gradually stir in chicken broth. Microwave on HIGH for 4 to 5 minutes or until mixture comes to a boil, stirring once halfway through cooking. Add carrots and spinach. Microwave on HIGH for 8 to 9 minutes or until carrots are tender and spinach is thawed, stirring twice during cooking.* Continue as directed above.

TIP: *To serve soup warm: puree *hot* spinach mixture in blender container or food processor bowl with metal blade until smooth. Transfer mixture to saucepan; stir in milk. Heat gently, stirring frequently. Or, transfer mixture to 8-cup microwave-safe measuring cup. Microwave on HIGH for 2 to 3 minutes or until thoroughly heated.

NUTRIENTS PER 1/5 OF RECIPE

Calories	210	Protein	15% U.S. RDA
Protein	9g	Vitamin A	90% U.S. RDA
Carbohydrate	16g	Vitamin C	10% U.S. RDA
Fat	12g	Thiamine	8% U.S. RDA
Cholesterol	10mg	Riboflavin	20% U.S. RDA
Sodium	1160mg	Niacin	10% U.S. RDA
Potassium	570mg	Calcium	20% U.S. RDA
Dietary Fiber	2g	Iron	6% U.S. RDA

'Tater Tuna Chowder
~ᴑ᎑ᴑᏭ~

Lorraine Blahnik, Michigan
Bake-Off® 25, 1974

6 slices bacon
½ cup chopped onion
1 package au gratin or cheese scalloped potato mix
2 cups hot water
1½ cups milk
1¼ cups chicken broth
17-ounce can whole kernel corn, undrained
1 bay leaf, if desired
1 to 2 (6½-ounce) cans tuna, drained
5.33-ounce can (⅔ cup) evaporated milk or ⅔ cup half-and-half

In large saucepan or skillet, cook bacon until crisp. Remove bacon from saucepan; drain, reserving 2 tablespoons drippings in saucepan. Add onion; cook until tender. Add potato slices, contents of seasoning mix envelope, water, milk, chicken broth, corn and bay leaf. Simmer uncovered 15 to 20 minutes or until potatoes are tender, stirring occasionally. Crumble bacon over potato mixture. Add tuna and evaporated milk; mix well. Heat gently, stirring frequently. *Do not boil.* Remove bay leaf before serving. **6 (1½-cup) servings.**

NUTRIENTS PER 1/6 OF RECIPE

Calories	280	Protein	40% U.S. RDA
Protein	27g	Vitamin A	8% U.S. RDA
Carbohydrate	27g	Vitamin C	15% U.S. RDA
Fat	7g	Thiamine	10% U.S. RDA
Cholesterol	50mg	Riboflavin	20% U.S. RDA
Sodium	1160mg	Niacin	50% U.S. RDA
Potassium	640mg	Calcium	20% U.S. RDA
Dietary Fiber	1g	Iron	10% U.S. RDA

'Tater Tuna Chowder

Mexican Vegetable Soup

Mexican Vegetable Soup

Nancy Hindenach, Michigan
Bake-Off® 33, 1988

1 pound ground beef
1.25-ounce package taco seasoning
    mix
   46-ounce can (6 cups) tomato juice
   16-ounce package frozen mixed
       vegetables
   15-ounce can chili hot beans
   12-ounce can tomato paste
    2 cups crushed corn chips
    8 ounces (2 cups) shredded
       Cheddar cheese

In 5-quart Dutch oven, brown ground
beef; drain. Add taco seasoning mix,
tomato juice, vegetables, chili beans
and tomato paste; mix well. Bring just
to a boil. Reduce heat; simmer uncovered 20 to 25 minutes or until vegetables are tender, stirring occasionally.
Top each serving with corn chips and
cheese. **11 (1-cup) servings.**

NUTRIENTS PER 1/11 OF RECIPE

Calories	340	Protein	25% U.S. RDA
Protein	18g	Vitamin A	50% U.S. RDA
Carbohydrate	29g	Vitamin C	45% U.S. RDA
Fat	17g	Thiamine	10% U.S. RDA
Cholesterol	45mg	Riboflavin	15% U.S. RDA
Sodium	1210mg	Niacin	20% U.S. RDA
Potassium	840mg	Calcium	25% U.S. RDA
Dietary Fiber	6g	Iron	25% U.S. RDA

Creole Gumbo

Elaine Thornton, Mississippi
Bake-Off® 6, 1954

GUMBO
   ¾ cup chopped celery
   ⅓ cup chopped green bell pepper
   ⅓ cup chopped onion
    2 garlic cloves, minced
    3 tablespoons olive oil
   ¼ cup all purpose or unbleached
       flour
    3 cups water
   16-ounce can tomatoes, undrained,
       cut up
    1 tablespoon chopped parsley
    1 teaspoon salt
   ⅛ teaspoon pepper
    1 cup diced canned, frozen, or
       fresh okra
   6-ounce can crab meat, drained

CROUTONS
   10-ounce can refrigerated flaky
       biscuits
    1 tablespoon margarine or butter,
       melted
    2 tablespoons grated Parmesan
       cheese
       Paprika

In large saucepan, cook celery, green pepper, onion and garlic in oil 5 minutes. Blend in flour; cook over medium heat about 10 minutes or until mixture browns, stirring constantly. Gradually add water and tomatoes, stirring constantly. Stir in remaining gumbo ingredients. Bring to a boil. Reduce heat, cover and simmer 1 hour.

Heat oven to 400°F. Separate dough into 10 biscuits; cut each into 4 pieces. Place on ungreased cookie sheet. Brush with margarine; sprinkle with Parmesan cheese and paprika. Bake at 400°F. for 6 to 9 minutes or until golden brown. Remove from cookie sheet immediately; cool on wire racks. Pour gumbo into individual serving bowls; top each serving with croutons.

4 (1¼-cup) servings.

NUTRIENTS PER 1/4 RECIPE

Calories	460	Protein	20% U.S. RDA
Protein	13g	Vitamin A	50% U.S. RDA
Carbohydrate	48g	Vitamin C	50% U.S. RDA
Fat	24g	Thiamine	30% U.S. RDA
Cholesterol	35mg	Riboflavin	20% U.S. RDA
Sodium	1850mg	Niacin	25% U.S. RDA
Potassium	600mg	Calcium	10% U.S. RDA
Dietary Fiber	4g	Iron	25% U.S. RDA

Zesty Chicken Vegetable Bisque

Taylor Arnold, Texas
Bake-Off® 33, 1988

3 whole chicken breasts, skinned, boned, halved
3 tablespoons margarine or butter
1 cup sliced onions
3 garlic cloves, minced
2 tablespoons all purpose or unbleached flour
2 (14½-ounce) cans (3½ cups) chicken broth
16-ounce can whole tomatoes, undrained, cut up
1 tablespoon chopped fresh parsley
1 teaspoon thyme leaves
½ to 1½ teaspoons salt
1 teaspoon hot pepper sauce
2 bay leaves
2 cups chopped green bell peppers
1 cup frozen whole kernel corn
1 cup frozen sweet peas
4.5-ounce jar sliced mushrooms, undrained
3 cups hot cooked rice

In large, deep skillet over medium heat, brown chicken breasts in margarine. Remove chicken breasts from skillet. Add onions and garlic; cook over medium heat until onions are tender, about 3 minutes. Remove from heat. Stir in flour. Add chicken broth, tomatoes, parsley, thyme, salt, hot pepper sauce and bay leaves; blend well. Add browned chicken breasts; cook over low heat 30 minutes, stirring occasionally. Add green peppers; cook an additional 10 minutes. Add corn, peas and mushrooms; cook 10 to 15 minutes more or until chicken is tender. Remove bay leaves before serving. To serve, place ½ cup rice in each individual serving bowl. Top with chicken breast half and generous 1 cup of bisque. **6 servings**

NUTRIENTS PER 1/6 OF RECIPE

Calories	420	Protein	50% U.S. RDA
Protein	34g	Vitamin A	20% U.S. RDA
Carbohydrate	45g	Vitamin C	100% U.S. RDA
Fat	10g	Thiamine	25% U.S. RDA
Cholesterol	70mg	Riboflavin	15% U.S. RDA
Sodium	1370mg	Niacin	80% U.S. RDA
Potassium	780mg	Calcium	8% U.S. RDA
Dietary Fiber	6g	Iron	25% U.S. RDA

Zesty Chicken Vegetable Bisque

This spicy chicken and vegetable one-dish meal is like Brunswick stew. Large pieces of boneless chicken, a variety of vegetables and a well-seasoned broth are spooned over rice in individual serving bowls.

Creole Gumbo

Tomatoes, crab meat and okra team up for a winning flavor combination in this marvelous gumbo from the '50s. It has been updated to use refrigerated flaky biscuit dough to speed up the preparation time for the cheesy crouton toppers.

Cheese Steak Crescent Braid

Cindy Joy, California
Bake-Off® 33, 1988

Cheese Steak Crescent Braid

This attractive sandwich braid has flavors like the popular Philadelphia cheese steak sandwich.

Bacon Tomato Open-Faced Rounds

The popular BLT takes a new twist in this baked version that has a tender, flaky biscuit crust.

4 portions frozen, thinly sliced sandwich steaks, cut crosswise into 1/2-inch strips
2 tablespoons margarine or butter
1/2 cup chopped onion
1 large green bell pepper, cut into strips (1 1/2 cups)
Salt and pepper to taste
2 (8-ounce) cans refrigerated crescent dinner rolls
4 ounces (1 cup) shredded mozzarella cheese
1 egg, beaten, if desired

Heat oven to 350°F. In large skillet over medium-high heat, stir-fry steak strips in margarine until no longer pink; remove from skillet. Add onion and green pepper; cook until crisp-tender, about 5 minutes. Return cooked steak to skillet; season with salt and pepper.

Unroll 1 can dough into 2 long rectangles. Place on ungreased cookie sheet with long sides overlapping 1/2 inch; firmly press edges and perforations to seal. Press or roll out to form 13 × 7-inch rectangle. Spoon heaping cupful of meat mixture in 2-inch strip lengthwise down center of dough to within 1/4 inch of each end. Sprinkle 1/2 cup of the cheese over meat mixture. Make cuts 1 inch apart on longest sides of rectangle just to edge of filling. To give braided appearance, fold strips of dough at an angle halfway across filling, alternating from side to side. Fold ends of braid under to seal. On second ungreased cookie sheet, repeat, using remaining can of dough, meat mixture and cheese. Brush braids with beaten egg. Bake at 350°F. for 16 to 22 minutes or until golden brown. Cool slightly; remove from cookie sheet. Cool 5 minutes before serving. **6 servings.**

NUTRIENTS PER 1/6 OF RECIPE

Calories	440	Protein	35% U.S. RDA
Protein	22g	Vitamin A	8% U.S. RDA
Carbohydrate	32g	Vitamin C	40% U.S. RDA
Fat	25g	Thiamine	20% U.S. RDA
Cholesterol	50mg	Riboflavin	20% U.S. RDA
Sodium	960mg	Niacin	20% U.S. RDA
Potassium	360mg	Calcium	15% U.S. RDA
Dietary Fiber	2g	Iron	20% U.S. RDA

Bacon Tomato Open-Faced Rounds

Helen Bridges, California
Bake-Off® 31, 1984

10-ounce can refrigerated flaky biscuits
10 slices bacon, cut into thirds, crisply cooked
10 thin slices tomato*
1/2 cup mayonnaise or salad dressing
1/2 cup chopped onion
2 ounces (1/2 cup) shredded Swiss cheese
1 teaspoon basil leaves

Heat oven to 400°F. Separate dough into 10 biscuits. On ungreased cookie sheets, press or roll out each biscuit to 4-inch circle, forming 1/4-inch rim around edge of each circle. Arrange 3 bacon pieces on each circle; top each with tomato slice. In small bowl combine mayonnaise, onion, cheese and basil. Spoon rounded tablespoonful of mayonnaise mixture over each tomato slice, spreading slightly. Bake at 400°F. for 11 to 16 minutes or until edges of biscuits are golden brown.
10 sandwiches.

TIP: *If tomato slices are juicy, drain on paper towel before using.

To reheat, wrap loosely in foil; heat at 350°F. for 15 to 20 minutes or until warm.

NUTRIENTS PER 1 SANDWICH

Calories	240	Protein	8% U.S. RDA
Protein	6g	Vitamin A	4% U.S. RDA
Carbohydrate	14g	Vitamin C	6% U.S. RDA
Fat	18g	Thiamine	10% U.S. RDA
Cholesterol	20mg	Riboflavin	6% U.S. RDA
Sodium	490mg	Niacin	6% U.S. RDA
Potassium	100mg	Calcium	6% U.S. RDA
Dietry Fiber	1g	Iron	6% U.S. RDA

Bacon Tomato Open-Faced Rounds

Pictured top to bottom: Broccoli Ham and Swiss Rolls, Tex-Mex Biscuit Sandwiches

Broccoli Ham and Swiss Rolls

Angela Schlueter, California
Bake-Off® 33, 1988

2 tablespoons margarine or butter
2 tablespoons flour
½ cup milk
9-ounce package frozen cut broccoli in a pouch, thawed, drained
¼ cup dairy sour cream
1 teaspoon lemon juice
¼ teaspoon hot pepper sauce
4 (4-inch) Kaiser rolls, unsliced
4 thin slices cooked ham
4 tomato slices, ¼ inch thick
4 thin slices Swiss cheese

In medium saucepan over low heat, melt margarine. Stir in flour; cook until mixture is smooth and bubbly, stirring frequently. Gradually stir in milk. Cook over medium heat until mixture thickens and boils, stirring constantly. Add broccoli, sour cream, lemon juice and hot pepper sauce. Cook until thoroughly heated, stirring occasionally.

Using sharp knife, remove about ½-inch slice from top of each roll; set aside. Remove bread from inside of rolls, leaving about ½-inch shell. Spoon about ⅓ cup of hot broccoli mixture into each roll. Place on ungreased cookie sheet or broiler pan. Top each with 1 slice ham, 1 slice tomato and 1 slice cheese. Broil 6 to 8 inches from heat for about 2 minutes or until cheese is melted. (Watch carefully.) Cover each with top of roll.
4 sandwiches.

NUTRIENTS PER 1 SANDWICH

Calories	440	Protein	35% U.S. RDA
Protein	22g	Vitamin A	20% U.S. RDA
Carbohydrate	40g	Vitamin C	40% U.S. RDA
Fat	21g	Thiamine	30% U.S. RDA
Cholesterol	50mg	Riboflavin	25% U.S. RDA
Sodium	970mg	Niacin	15% U.S. RDA
Potassium	330mg	Calcium	40% U.S. RDA
Dietary Fiber	3g	Iron	10% U.S. RDA

Tex-Mex Biscuit Sandwiches

Elaine Schultz, Florida
Bake-Off® 33, 1988

2½ ounces (½ cup) deli roast beef, chopped
¼ cup taco sauce
¼ cup barbecue sauce
¼ cup sliced green onions
¼ cup sliced ripe olives, drained
2 ounces (½ cup) shredded Cheddar cheese
10-ounce can refrigerated flaky biscuits
2 tablespoons cornmeal
½ cup dairy sour cream
10 pimiento slices
10 ripe olive slices

Heat oven to 350°F. In medium bowl, combine roast beef, taco sauce, barbecue sauce, green onions, ¼ cup olives and cheese; set aside.

Separate dough into 10 biscuits. Dip both sides of each biscuit in cornmeal. Press or roll out each to 5-inch circle. Place 5 circles on ungreased cookie sheet. Spoon about ¼ cup of roast beef mixture onto center of each circle. Brush edges lightly with water. Place remaining 5 biscuit circles over roast beef mixture. Press edges with fork to seal. Using back of tablespoon, make indentation in center of each sandwich. Sprinkle sandwiches with remaining cornmeal.

Bake at 350°F. for 14 to 22 minutes or until golden brown. Remove from oven; gently repeat indentation if necessary. Fill each with heaping tablespoonful of sour cream. Garnish each with 2 pimiento slices and 2 ripe olive slices. **5 sandwiches.**

NUTRIENTS PER 1 SANDWICH

Calories	340	Protein	20% U.S. RDA
Protein	12g	Vitamin A	10% U.S. RDA
Carbohydrate	31g	Vitamin C	8% U.S. RDA
Fat	19g	Thiamine	15% U.S. RDA
Cholesterol	35mg	Riboflavin	15% U.S. RDA
Sodium	950mg	Niacin	10% U.S. RDA
Potassiuim	200mg	Calcium	15% U.S. RDA
Dietary Fiber	2g	Iron	15% U.S. RDA

Against all odds—

Although a few contestants have not been able to compete at the last minute—two had babies and two had serious health problems—many have competed under trying circumstances. One woman whose husband's dying wish was to have her attend the Bake-Off® did so the day after his funeral. Needless to say, when her indomitable spirit and creativity brought her a $2,000 prize for her efforts, the applause was long and from the hearts of admiring peers.

Pictured top to bottom: Chicken and Cheese Crescent Chimichangas, page 31, Quesadilla Quiche

Quesadilla Quiche

꙳꙳

Laurie Keane, California
Bake-Off® 33, 1988

15-ounce package refrigerated pie
  crusts
1 teaspoon flour

FILLING
  1 cup coarsely chopped onions
  1 tablespoon margarine or butter
  1 cup coarsely chopped tomatoes,
    drained
  4-ounce can sliced ripe olives,
    drained
  1/4 teaspoon garlic powder or salt
  1/4 teaspoon cumin
  1/8 teaspoon pepper
  4-ounce can chopped green
    chiles, drained
  2 eggs, beaten
  2 to 3 drops hot pepper sauce
  4 ounces (1 cup) shredded
    Monterey jack cheese
  4 ounces (1 cup) shredded
    Cheddar cheese
    Dairy sour cream, if desired
    Salsa or picante sauce, if desired

Prepare pie crust according to package directions for *two-crust pie* using a 10-inch tart pan with removable bottom or a 9-inch pie pan. Place 1 prepared crust in pan; press in bottom and up sides of pan. Trim edges if necessary. Place oven rack at lowest position. Heat oven to 375°F.

In medium skillet, cook onions in margarine until tender. Reserve 1 tablespoon each tomatoes and olives. Stir remaining tomatoes and olives, garlic powder, cumin, pepper and chiles into cooked onions. In small bowl, beat eggs with hot pepper sauce; reserve 2 teaspoons of mixture. To remaining egg mixture, stir in 1/2 cup of the Monterey jack cheese and 1/2 cup of the Cheddar cheese. Sprinkle remaining cheeses over bottom of pie crust-lined pan. Spoon onion mixture evenly over cheese. Carefully pour egg mixture over onion mixture; spread to cover. Top with second crust; seal edges. With sharp knife, slit crust in decorative design in several places. Brush with reserved egg mixture.

Bake at 375°F. on lowest oven rack for 45 to 55 minutes or until golden brown. Let stand 5 minutes; remove sides of pan. Serve warm with sour cream, salsa and reserved tomatoes and olives. **6 servings.**

NUTRIENTS PER 1/6 OF RECIPE

Calories	600	Protein	20% U.S. RDA
Protein	15g	Vitamin A	50% U.S. RDA
Carbohydrate	39g	Vitamin C	20% U.S. RDA
Fat	43g	Thiamine	4% U.S. RDA
Cholesterol	140mg	Riboflavin	15% U.S. RDA
Sodium	1120mg	Niacin	2% U.S. RDA
Potassium	280mg	Calcium	35% U.S. RDA
Dietary Fiber	2g	Iron	6% U.S. RDA

Poppin' Fresh® Barbecups

꙳꙳

Peter Russell, Kansas
Bake-Off® 19, 1968

1 pound ground beef
1/2 cup barbecue sauce
1 tablespooon instant minced
  onion or 1/4 cup chopped onion
1 to 2 tablespoons brown sugar
10-ounce can refrigerated flaky
  biscuits
2 ounces (1/2 cup) shredded
  Cheddar or American cheese

Heat oven to 400°F. Grease 10 muffin cups. In large skillet, brown ground beef; drain. Stir in barbecue sauce, instant minced onion and brown sugar. Cook 1 minute to blend flavors, stirring constantly. Separate dough into 10 biscuits. Place 1 biscuit in each greased muffin cup; firmly press in bottom and up sides, forming 1/4-inch rim. Spoon about 1/4 cup of meat mixture into each biscuit-lined cup. Sprinkle each with cheese. Bake at 400°F. for 10 to 12 minutes or until edges of biscuits are golden brown. Cool 1 minute; remove from pan. **10 servings.**

TIP: To make ahead, prepare, cover and refrigerate up to 2 hours; bake as directed above.

NUTRIENTS PER 1/10 OF RECIPE

Calories	220	Protein	15% U.S. RDA
Protein	11g	Vitamin A	2% U.S. RDA
Carbohydrate	17g	Vitamin C	<2% U.S. RDA
Fat	12g	Thiamine	6% U.S. RDA
Cholesterol	35mg	Riboflavin	8% U.S. RDA
Sodium	460mg	Niacin	15% U.S. RDA
Potassium	150mg	Calcium	4% U.S. RDA
Dietary Fiber	<1g	Iron	8% U.S. RDA

Quesadilla Quiche

꙳꙳

Cheese and chiles melted in a tortilla characterize quesadillas, a spicy Mexican cheese sandwich. That great combination becomes a main-dish pie in this recipe.

Poppin' Fresh® Barbecups

꙳꙳

This Junior Prize-winning recipe was created by a twelve-year-old boy. He and his sister prepared this great-tasting, simple-to-do recipe for dinner on the nights his mother and dad worked late. Since its creation, Pillsbury has promoted many versions of this recipe.

Chicken 'n Artichoke Crescent Sandwiches

June Grayson, Oklahoma
Bake-Off® 33, 1988

- 1 whole chicken breast, skinned, boned, cut into bite-sized pieces*
- 1/2 teaspoon salt
- 1/8 teaspoon pepper
- 2.5-ounce jar sliced mushrooms, drained
- 1 tablespoon margarine or butter, melted
- 1 tablespoon oil
- 1/3 cup mayonnaise or salad dressing
- 1/8 to 1/4 teaspoon garlic powder
- 1/8 teaspoon hot pepper sauce
- 6-ounce jar marinated artichoke hearts, drained, chopped
- 2-ounce jar chopped pimiento, drained
- 8-ounce can refrigerated crescent dinner rolls
- 1 egg white, slightly beaten
- 1 tablespoon sesame seed
- Dairy sour cream, if desired

Heat oven to 375°F. Sprinkle chicken with salt and pepper. In large skillet over medium heat, cook chicken and mushrooms in margarine and oil 3 to 5 minutes or until chicken is tender and slightly brown, stirring occasionally. Remove from heat.

In medium bowl, combine mayonnaise, garlic powder and hot pepper sauce. Stir in artichoke hearts, pimiento and chicken mixture; blend well. Separate dough into 4 rectangles; firmly press perforations to seal. Spoon about 1/2 cup of chicken mixture on half of each rectangle to within 1/4 inch of edges. Fold dough in half over filling; place on ungreased cookie sheet. Press edges with fork to seal. Brush beaten egg white over sandwiches; sprinkle with sesame seed. Bake at 375°F. for 15 to 20 minutes or until centers of sandwiches are golden brown. Serve warm with sour cream. **4 sandwiches.**

TIP: *Use about 1/2 pound skinned, boned chicken.

NUTRIENTS PER 1 SANDWICH			
Calories	540	Protein	30% U.S. RDA
Protein	19g	Vitamin A	10% U.S. RDA
Carbohydrate	28g	Vitamin C	10% U.S. RDA
Fat	39g	Thiamine	15% U.S. RDA
Cholesterol	60mg	Riboflavin	15% U.S. RDA
Sodium	1010mg	Niacin	35% U.S. RDA
Potassium	390mg	Calcium	6% U.S. RDA
Dietary Fiber	3g	Iron	15% U.S. RDA

Reuben in the Round Crescents

Irene Dunn, Ohio
Bake-Off® 27, 1976

- 2 (8-ounce) cans refrigerated crescent dinner rolls
- 8-ounce package thinly sliced pastrami or corned beef
- 6-ounce package (4 slices) Swiss or mozzarella cheese
- 8-ounce can (1 cup) sauerkraut, drained
- 1/2 teaspoon caraway seed
- 1/2 teaspoon sesame seed

Heat oven to 400°F. Separate 1 can of dough into 4 rectangles. Place in ungreased 12-inch pizza pan or 13 × 9-inch pan; firmly press over bottom and 1/2 inch up sides to form crust. Seal perforations. Arrange pastrami, cheese and sauerkraut in layers over dough. Sprinkle with caraway seed. Separate remaining can of dough into 8 triangles. Arrange triangles spoke-fashion over filling with points toward center. Do not seal outer edges of triangles to bottom crust. Sprinkle with sesame seed. Bake at 400°F. for 15 to 25 minutes or until golden brown. Serve immediately. **6 to 8 servings.**

TIPS: To make ahead, prepare, cover and refrigerate up to 2 hours; bake as directed above.

To reheat, cover loosely with foil; heat at 375°F. for 15 to 18 minutes or until warm.

NUTRIENTS PER 1/8 OF RECIPE			
Calories	380	Protein	25% U.S. RDA
Protein	15g	Vitamin A	4% U.S. RDA
Carbohydrate	24g	Vitamin C	4% U.S. RDA
Fat	25g	Thiamine	10% U.S. RDA
Cholesterol	50mg	Riboflavin	15% U.S. RDA
Sodium	1000mg	Niacin	15% U.S. RDA
Potassium	240mg	Calcium	20% U.S. RDA
Dietary Fiber	2g	Iron	10% U.S. RDA

Reuben in the Round Crescents

Chiles 'n Ham Cups

Chiles 'n Ham Cups

Audeen Faller, Colorado
Bake-Off® 32, 1986

10-ounce can refrigerated flaky biscuits
3-ounce package cream cheese, softened
1 cup cubed cooked ham
¼ cup sliced ripe olives
4 ounces (1 cup) shredded Cheddar cheese
4-ounce can chopped green chiles, drained*
10 small pitted ripe olives, if desired

Heat oven to 375°F. Grease 10 muffin cups. Separate dough into 10 biscuits. Place 1 biscuit in each greased muffin cup; firmly press in bottom and up sides, forming ¼-inch rim.

In large bowl, combine cream cheese, ham, ¼ cup sliced olives, cheese and chiles; blend well. Spoon about ¼ cup of ham mixture into each biscuit-lined cup. Bake at 375°F. for 20 to 25 minutes or until edges of biscuits are golden brown. Cool 1 minute; remove from pan. Garnish each with pitted olive. If desired, serve with salsa or sour cream. **10 servings.**

TIPS: *For a milder flavor, use ¼ cup of the chopped green chiles.

To reheat, wrap loosely in foil; heat at 350°F. for 20 to 25 minutes or until warm.

NUTRIENTS PER 1/10 OF RECIPE

Calories	190	Protein	10% U.S. RDA
Protein	8g	Vitamin A	25% U.S. RDA
Carbohydrate	13g	Vitamin C	25% U.S. RDA
Fat	12g	Thiamine	15% U.S. RDA
Cholesterol	30mg	Riboflavin	8% U.S. RDA
Sodium	620mg	Niacin	6% U.S. RDA
Potassium	110mg	Calcium	10% U.S. RDA
Dietary Fiber	1g	Iron	6% U.S. RDA

Potato-Topped Burger Cups

Lillian Cymbala, Connecticut
Bake-Off® 33, 1988

1 pound ground beef
3 tablespoons finely chopped onion
1 garlic clove, minced
¼ to ½ teaspoon cayenne pepper
½ teaspoon salt, if desired
⅓ cup chili sauce
1 tablespoon vinegar
10-ounce can refrigerated flaky biscuits

TOPPING
1½ cups water
3 tablespoons margarine or butter
½ teaspoon salt
1½ cups mashed potato flakes
3-ounce package cream cheese, softened
½ cup coarsely crushed potato chips

Heat oven to 375°F. Grease 10 muffin cups. In large skillet, brown ground beef with onion, garlic and cayenne pepper; drain well. Stir in ½ teaspoon salt, chili sauce and vinegar; cook 1 minute to blend flavors, stirring constantly. Set aside. Separate dough into 10 biscuits. Place 1 biscuit in each greased muffin cup; firmly press in bottom and up sides forming ¼-inch rim.

In medium saucepan, combine water, margarine and ½ teaspoon salt; bring to a rolling boil. Remove from heat. Using fork, stir in potato flakes until well blended. Add cream cheese; beat until mixture is smooth. (Mixture will be very thick.)

Spoon about ¼ cup of meat mixture into each biscuit-lined cup. Spoon topping mixture over each filled cup; press to cover completely. Sprinkle each with potato chips. Bake at 375°F. for 25 to 30 minutes or until edges of biscuits are golden brown. Cool 1 minute; remove from pan. **10 servings.**

NUTRIENTS PER 1/10 OF RECIPE

Calories	300	Protein	15% U.S. RDA
Protein	11g	Vitamin A	8% U.S. RDA
Carbohydrate	23g	Vitamin C	6% U.S. RDA
Fat	18g	Thiamine	10% U.S. RDA
Cholesterol	40mg	Riboflavin	10% U.S. RDA
Sodium	740mg	Niacin	15% U.S. RDA
Potassium	320mg	Calcium	2% U.S. RDA
Dietary Fiber	2g	Iron	10% U.S. RDA

Savory Salmon-Filled Crescents

Carol DuVall, New York
Bake-Off® 26, 1975

16-ounce can salmon or 2 (6½-ounce) cans tuna, drained, flaked
1½ cups seasoned croutons
½ cup chopped onion
2 tablespoons chopped fresh parsley or 2 teaspoons parsley flakes
1 teaspoon dill weed
½ teaspoon garlic salt
¼ teaspoon pepper
½ cup mayonnaise or salad dressing
½ cup dairy sour cream
4 hard-cooked eggs, coarsely chopped
2 (8-ounce) cans refrigerated crescent dinner rolls
1 to 2 tablespoons margarine or butter, melted
Parsley, if desired

Heat oven to 350°F. In medium bowl, combine salmon, croutons, onion, 2 tablespoons parsley, dill weed, garlic salt, pepper, mayonnaise, sour cream and eggs; toss lightly. Separate dough into 8 rectangles; firmly press perforations to seal. Spoon about ½ cup of salmon mixture onto center of each rectangle. Pull 4 corners of dough to center of salmon mixture; twist firmly. Pinch edges to seal. Place on ungreased cookie sheets. Brush each with margarine; sprinkle with parsley. Bake at 350°F. for 18 to 28 minutes or until golden brown. Serve immediately. **8 sandwiches.**

TIP: To reheat, wrap loosely in foil; heat at 350°F. for 15 to 20 minutes or until warm.

NUTRIENTS PER 1 SANDWICH

Calories	500	Protein	30% U.S. RDA
Protein	19g	Vitamin A	10% U.S. RDA
Carbohydrate	25g	Vitamin C	2% U.S. RDA
Fat	36g	Thiamine	15% U.S. RDA
Cholesterol	180mg	Riboflavin	20% U.S. RDA
Sodium	770mg	Niacin	30% U.S. RDA
Potassium	410mg	Calcium	20% U.S. RDA
Dietary Fiber	1g	Iron	15% U.S. RDA

Famous Faces at Bake-Off® since 1949

Bob Barker
Pat Boone
Joe E. Brown
Gary Collins
Duke and Duchess of Windsor
Irene Dunne
Greer Garson
Arthur Godfrey
Averell Harriman
Art Linkletter
Mary Ann Mobley
Garry Moore
Patricia Nixon
Tyrone Power
Ivy Baker Priest
Ronald Reagan
Eleanor Roosevelt
Red Skelton
Margaret Truman
Rudy Vallee
Tuesday Weld

Savory Crescent Chicken Squares

❧

Doris Castle, Illinois
Bake-Off® 25, 1974

Ham and Cheese Biscuit Pockets

❧

Carol J. Grass, Colorado
Bake-Off® 31, 1984

❧

Chaos or calm—

At one event, a very relaxed contestant sat quietly reading a book while she waited for her entry to bake. When queried about her calm demeanor, she said that the Bake-Off® floor was peaceful compared to her home kitchen filled with the exuberance of her five children. In contrast, another finalist, who was used to cooking with only her cat looking on, found it extremely difficult to concentrate on the task at hand and deferred all interviews until she finished.

3-ounce package cream cheese, softened
1 tablespoon margarine or butter, softened
2 cups cubed cooked chicken*
1 tablespoon chopped chives or onion
1/4 teaspoon salt
1/8 teaspoon pepper
2 tablespoons milk
1 tablespoon chopped pimiento, if desired
8-ounce can refrigerated crescent dinner rolls
1 tablespoon margarine or butter, melted
3/4 cup seasoned croutons, crushed

Heat oven to 350°F. In medium bowl, beat cream cheese and 1 tablespoon softened margarine until smooth. Add chicken, chives, salt, pepper, milk and pimiento; mix well. Separate crescent dough into 4 rectangles; firmly press perforations to seal. Spoon 1/2 cup of chicken mixture onto center of each rectangle. Pull 4 corners of dough to center of chicken mixture; twist firmly. Pinch edges to seal. Place on ungreased cookie sheet. Brush tops of sandwiches with 1 tablespoon melted margarine; dip in crushed croutons. Bake at 350°F. for 20 to 25 minutes until golden brown. **4 sandwiches.**

TIP: *Two 5-ounce cans chunk chicken, drained and flaked, can be substituted for cubed cooked chicken.

NUTRIENTS PER 1 SANDWICH

Calories	500	Protein	40% U.S. RDA
Protein	27g	Vitamin A	15% U.S. RDA
Carbohydrate	28g	Vitamin C	4% U.S. RDA
Fat	30g	Thiamine	15% U.S. RDA
Cholesterol	110mg	Riboflavin	15% U.S. RDA
Sodium	890mg	Niacin	40% U.S. RDA
Potassium	350mg	Calcium	4% U.S. RDA
Dietary Fiber	1g	Iron	15% U.S. RDA

1 cup cubed cooked ham
4 ounces (1 cup) shredded Swiss cheese
1/2 cup finely chopped peeled apple
10-ounce can refrigerated flaky biscuits
1 egg, slightly beaten
1 teaspoon water

Alfalfa sprouts, if desired
Chopped tomato, if desired

Heat oven to 375°F. Lightly grease large cookie sheet. In small bowl, combine ham, cheese and apple. Separate dough into 10 biscuits. On greased cookie sheet, press or roll out 5 biscuits to 4-inch circles. Place about 1/2 cup of ham mixture onto center of each circle. Press or roll out remaining 5 biscuits to 5-inch circles. Place each over filling. Press edges with fork to seal. Combine egg and water; brush over filled biscuits.

Bake at 375°F. for 13 to 18 minutes or until golden brown. Cut each in half to form pocket sandwiches. To serve, garnish with alfalfa sprouts and tomato. Serve warm. **5 servings.**

TIP: To reheat, wrap loosely in foil; heat at 350°F. for 12 to 15 minutes or until warm.

NUTRIENTS PER 1/5 OF RECIPE

Calories	320	Protein	25% U.S. RDA
Protein	17g	Vitamin A	4% U.S. RDA
Carbohydrate	27g	Vitamin C	8% U.S. RDA
Fat	16g	Thiamine	25% U.S. RDA
Cholesterol	90mg	Riboflavin	20% U.S. RDA
Sodium	1000mg	Niacin	15% U.S. RDA
Potassium	170mg	Calcium	25% U.S. RDA
Dietary Fiber	1g	Iron	10% U.S. RDA

Ham and Cheese Biscuit Pockets

Crescent Three Cheese Calzone

Crescent Three Cheese Calzone

Irene McEwen, Arizona
Bake-Off® 32, 1986

2 eggs
15-ounce carton (1³/₄ cups) ricotta cheese
2 ounces (¹/₂ cup) shredded mozzarella cheese
¹/₄ cup grated Parmesan cheese
¹/₂ teaspoon salt, if desired
¹/₂ teaspoon basil leaves
¹/₂ teaspoon oregano leaves
¹/₄ teaspoon pepper
1 garlic clove, minced or ¹/₈ teaspoon instant minced garlic
2 (8-ounce) cans refrigerated crescent dinner rolls

SAUCE
2 (8-ounce) cans tomato sauce with mushrooms*
2 to 4 tablespoons red table wine, if desired
¹/₄ teaspoon basil leaves
¹/₄ teaspoon oregano leaves

Heat oven to 375°F. In large bowl, beat eggs slightly. Add ricotta cheese, mozzarella cheese, Parmesan cheese, salt, ¹/₂ teaspoon basil, ¹/₂ teaspoon oregano, pepper and garlic; blend well. Separate dough into 8 rectangles; firmly press perforations to seal. Press or roll out each to 7 × 5-inch rectangle. Spoon scant ¹/₃ cup of cheese mixture onto half of each rectangle to within 1 inch of edges. Fold dough in half over filling; firmly pinch edges to seal. Place on ungreased cookie sheet. With sharp knife, cut 3 slits in top of each filled rectangle. Bake at 375°F. for 14 to 17 minutes or until deep golden brown.

In small saucepan, combine all sauce ingredients; bring to a boil. Reduce heat; simmer uncovered for 15 minutes to blend flavors. Spoon over each serving. **8 servings.**

TIPS: *An 8-ounce can tomato sauce and a 2.5-ounce jar sliced mushrooms, drained, can be substituted for the tomato sauce with mushrooms.

To reheat, wrap loosely in foil; heat at 375°F. for 15 to 20 minutes or until warm.

NUTRIENTS PER 1/8 OF RECIPE

Calories	350	Protein	25% U.S. RDA
Protein	15g	Vitamin A	20% U.S. RDA
Carbohydrate	30g	Vitamin C	8% U.S. RDA
Fat	19g	Thiamine	15% U.S. RDA
Cholesterol	100mg	Riboflavin	20% U.S. RDA
Sodium	1030mg	Niacin	10% U.S. RDA
Potassium	450mg	Calcium	25% U.S. RDA
Dietary Fiber	2g	Iron	15% U.S. RDA

Chicken and Cheese Crescent Chimichangas

Marlene Zebleckis, California
Bake-Off® 33, 1988

1/2 cup chopped onion
2 garlic cloves, minced
3 tablespoons oil
2 1/2 cups shredded cooked chicken
2 (8-ounce) cans refrigerated crescent dinner rolls
1/2 cup salsa
8 ounces (2 cups) shredded Cheddar cheese

Dairy sour cream
Salsa

Heat oven to 350°F. Grease large cookie sheet. In large skillet, cook onion and garlic in oil until onion is tender. Add chicken; cook over low heat until thoroughly heated, stirring occasionally. Remove from heat.

Separate dough into 8 rectangles; firmly press perforations to seal. Spread 2 teaspoonfuls of the salsa on each rectangle to within 1/2 inch of edge. Stir 1 cup of the cheese into chicken mixture. Spoon heaping 1/3 cup of chicken mixture onto half of each rectangle. Starting at shortest side of rectangle topped with chicken, roll up; firmly pinch ends to seal. Place seam side down on greased cookie sheet.

Bake at 350°F. for 16 to 21 minutes or until golden brown. Remove from oven; top each with about 2 tablespoonfuls of remaining cheese. Return to oven. Bake an additional 1 to 2 minutes or until cheese is melted. Serve with sour cream and additional salsa. **8 sandwiches.**

NUTRIENTS PER 1 SANDWICH

Calories	480	Protein	35% U.S. RDA
Protein	22g	Vitamin A	10% U.S. RDA
Carbohydrate	26g	Vitamin C	2% U.S. RDA
Fat	32g	Thiamine	15% U.S. RDA
Cholesterol	80mg	Riboflavin	20% U.S. RDA
Sodium	910mg	Niacin	25% U.S. RDA
Potassium	370mg	Calcium	25% U.S. RDA
Dietary Fiber	1g	Iron	10% U.S. RDA

Tuna Cheese Flips

Marilyn Belschner, Nebraska
Bake-Off® 27, 1976

2 (6 1/2-ounce) cans tuna, drained, flaked
1/8 teaspoon lemon pepper seasoning
1/3 cup sliced ripe or green olives, drained
1/3 cup mayonnaise or salad dressing
2 ounces (1/2 cup) shredded Monterey jack or Cheddar cheese
10-ounce can refrigerated flaky biscuits
1 egg, beaten, or 2 tablespoons milk
1 cup crushed potato chips

Heat oven to 375°F. In small bowl, combine tuna, lemon pepper seasoning, olives, mayonnaise and cheese. Separate dough into 10 biscuits. Press or roll out each to 5-inch circle. Spoon about 1/4 cup of tuna mixture onto center of each circle. Fold dough in half over filling; press edges with fork to seal. Brush both sides of each sandwich with egg; press both sides in chips. Place on ungreased cookie sheet. With sharp knife, make two or three 1/2-inch slits in top of each sandwich. Bake at 375°F. for 18 to 24 minutes or until deep golden brown. **10 sandwiches.**

TIP: To reheat, wrap loosely in foil; heat at 350°F. for 10 to 15 minutes or until warm.

NUTRIENTS PER 1 SANDWICH

Calories	250	Protein	20% U.S. RDA
Protein	14g	Vitamin A	2% U.S. RDA
Carbohydrate	16g	Vitamin C	2% U.S. RDA
Fat	14g	Thiamine	6% U.S. RDA
Cholesterol	60mg	Riboflavin	8% U.S. RDA
Sodium	460mg	Niacin	30% U.S. RDA
Potassium	210mg	Calcium	6% U.S. RDA
Dietary Fiber	1g	Iron	8% U.S. RDA

Chicken and Cheese Crescent Chimichangas

Chimichangas are made with a flour tortilla wrapped around a seasoned filling and fried until crisp. In this recipe, chimichangas are made easier when light, flaky crescents replace the tortilla and they are baked in the oven.

Crescent Chick-Be-Quicks

Rosemarie Berger, North Carolina
Bake-Off® 33, 1988

Crescent Chick-Be-Quicks

To create this hot chicken snack, fresh chicken pieces coated with french fried onions are baked in tiny crescent dough triangles. Serve them with sweet and sour sauce for dipping.

³/₄ cup crushed canned french fried onions
1 tablespoon flour
¹/₄ teaspoon seasoned salt
8-ounce can refrigerated crescent dinner rolls
1 whole chicken breast, skinned, boned, cut into 16 pieces*
1 egg, beaten
Sesame or poppy seed

Heat oven to 375°F. Lightly grease cookie sheet. In small bowl, combine french fried onions, flour and salt; blend well. Set aside. Separate dough into 8 triangles. Cut each in half lengthwise to make 16 long triangles. Dip chicken pieces in beaten egg; coat with onion mixture. Place one coated piece on wide end of each triangle; roll to opposite point. Place point side down on greased cookie sheet. Brush tops with remaining beaten egg; sprinkle with sesame seed. Bake at 375°F. for 12 to 15 minutes or until golden brown. Serve warm or cold. **16 snacks.**

TIP: *About ¹/₂ pound, skinned and boned chicken.

NUTRIENTS PER 1 SNACK

Calories	100	Protein	8% U.S. RDA
Protein	5g	Vitamin A	<2% U.S. RDA
Carbohydrate	7g	Vitamin C	<2% U.S. RDA
Fat	5g	Thiamine	4% U.S. RDA
Cholesterol	30mg	Riboflavin	2% U.S. RDA
Sodium	160mg	Niacin	10% U.S. RDA
Potassium	75mg	Calcium	<2% U.S. RDA
Dietary Fiber	<1g	Iron	2% U.S. RDA

Shrimp Cocktail Crescent Snacks

Carole Ann (Flieller) Aktines, Texas
Bake-Off® 26, 1975

2 tablespoons margarine or butter, melted
1 tablespoon prepared horseradish
1 tablespoon ketchup
1 teaspoon lemon juice
3¹/₂-ounce can shrimp, rinsed, drained
8-ounce can refrigerated crescent dinner rolls
1 tablespoon grated Paramesan cheese
Sesame seed

Heat oven to 375°F. In small bowl, combine 1 tablespoon of the margarine, horseradish, ketchup, lemon juice and shrimp; mix well. Separate dough into 8 triangles; cut each in half diagonally to make 16 triangles. Place rounded teaspoonful of shrimp mixture onto center of each triangle. Fold short end of each triangle over filling; fold long end over all. Place on ungreased large cookie sheet. Brush each with remaining margarine; sprinkle with Parmesan cheese and sesame seed. Bake at 375°F. for 15 to 18 minutes or until golden brown. Serve warm. **16 snacks.**

TIP: To make ahead, prepare, cover and refrigerate up to 2 hours; bake as directed above.

NUTRIENTS PER 1 SNACK

Calories	80	Protein	4% U.S. RDA
Protein	3g	Vitamin A	<2% U.S. RDA
Carbohydrate	6g	Vitamin C	<2% U.S. RDA
Fat	5g	Thiamine	2% U.S. RDA
Cholesterol	10mg	Riboflavin	2% U.S. RDA
Sodium	160mg	Niacin	2% U.S. RDA
Potassium	50mg	Calcium	<2% U.S. RDA
Dietary Fiber	0g	Iron	2% U.S. RDA

Shrimp Cocktail Crescent Snacks

Puffy Chiles Rellenos

Helen Novak, California
Bake-Off® 29, 1980

2 (3-ounce) cans whole green
chiles
8 ounces Monterey jack or
Cheddar cheese
10-ounce can refrigerated flaky
biscuits

TOPPING
3 eggs, separated
¼ teaspoon salt
8¼-ounce jar chunky taco sauce

Heat oven to 375°F. Grease cookie
sheet. Cut chiles lengthwise to make 10
pieces. Remove seeds and ribs; rinse and
drain. Cut cheese into ten 3 × ½ × ½-
inch pieces. Wrap each piece of cheese
with piece of chile. Separate dough into
10 biscuits. Press or roll out each to
4-inch circle. Place 1 chile-wrapped
cheese piece onto each circle; fold
dough over to cover completely. Firmly
pinch edges to seal. Form each into finger-shaped roll; place seam side up on
greased cookie sheet.*

Bake at 375°F. for 10 to 12 minutes or
until light golden brown. Meanwhile,
prepare topping. In small bowl, beat
egg whites until stiff peaks form. In second small bowl, beat egg yolks and salt.
Gently fold egg yolk mixture into
beaten egg whites until just blended.
Spoon mounds of egg mixture over
each partially baked roll, covering each
completely. Bake an additional 12 to
15 minutes or until golden brown. In
small saucepan, heat taco sauce. Spoon
hot taco sauce over chiles rellenos.
10 servings.

TIP: *To make ahead, rellenos can be
prepared to this point. Cover and refrigerate up to 2 hours. Continue as
directed above.

NUTRIENTS PER 1/10 OF RECIPE

Calories	210	Protein	15% U.S. RDA
Protein	9g	Vitamin A	40% U.S. RDA
Carbohydrate	15g	Vitamin C	10% U.S. RDA
Fat	12g	Thiamine	8% U.S. RDA
Cholesterol	100mg	Riboflavin	10% U.S. RDA
Sodium	800mg	Niacin	4% U.S. RDA
Potassium	130mg	Calcium	20% U.S. RDA
Dietary Fiber	1g	Iron	8% U.S. RDA

Italian Spinach Torta

Larry Elder, North Carolina
Bake-Off® 33, 1988

15-ounce package refrigerated pie
crusts
1 teaspoon flour

FILLING
9-ounce package frozen chopped
spinach in a pouch, thawed,
squeezed to drain
1 cup ricotta cheese
½ cup grated Parmesan cheese
¼ to ½ teaspoon garlic salt
¼ teaspoon pepper
1 egg, separated
1 teaspoon water

Prepare pie crust according to package
directions for *two-crust pie* using 10-
inch tart pan with removable bottom
or 9-inch pie pan. Place 1 prepared
crust in pan; press in bottom and up
sides of pan. Trim edges if necessary.
Place oven rack at lowest position. Heat
oven to 400°F.

In medium bowl, combine spinach,
ricotta cheese, Parmesan cheese, garlic
salt, pepper and egg yolk; blend well.
Spread evenly over pie crust-lined pan.

To make lattice top, cut remaining
crust into ¾-inch wide strips. Arrange
strips in lattice design over spinach
mixture. Trim and seal edges. In small
bowl, combine egg white and water;
beat well. Gently brush over lattice.
Bake at 400°F. on lowest oven rack for
45 to 50 minutes or until dark golden
brown. Cool 10 minutes; remove sides
of pan. Serve warm. **10 to 12 servings.**

TIP: Cover torta with foil during last 5
to 10 minutes of baking if necessary to
prevent excessive browning.

NUTRIENTS PER 1/12 OF RECIPE

Calories	220	Protein	8% U.S. RDA
Protein	6g	Vitamin A	10% U.S. RDA
Carbohydrate	18g	Vitamin C	<2% U.S. RDA
Fat	14g	Thiamine	<2% U.S. RDA
Cholesterol	30mg	Riboflavin	6% U.S. RDA
Sodium	480mg	Niacin	<2% U.S. RDA
Potassium	135mg	Calcium	15% U.S. RDA
Dietary Fiber	1g	Iron	2% U.S. RDA

Italian Spinach Torta

Torta *is an Italian term for
cake or pie. In this recipe, torta
is an impressive appetizer pie.
Serve thin wedges as the first
course at a dinner party.*

Italian Spinach Torta

Italian Biscuit Flat Bread

Italian Biscuit Flat Bread

Edith L. Shulman, Texas
Bake-Off® 32, 1986

⅓ cup mayonnaise or salad
  dressing
⅓ cup grated Parmesan cheese
¼ teaspoon basil leaves
¼ teaspoon oregano leaves
3 green onions, sliced
1 garlic clove, minced, or ⅛
  teaspoon garlic powder
10-ounce can refrigerated flaky
  biscuits

Heat oven to 400°F. In small bowl, combine mayonnaise and Parmesan cheese; stir in basil, oregano, green onions and garlic. Separate dough into 10 biscuits. On ungreased cookie sheets, press or roll out each biscuit to 4-inch circle. Spread about 1 tablespoonful of cheese mixture over each circle to within ¼ inch of edge. Bake at 400°F. for 10 to 13 minutes or until golden brown. Serve warm. **10 servings.**

NUTRIENTS PER 1/10 OF RECIPE

Calories	160	Protein	4% U.S. RDA
Protein	3g	Vitamin A	<2% U.S. RDA
Carbohydrate	12g	Vitamin C	<2% U.S. RDA
Fat	11g	Thiamine	<2% U.S. RDA
Cholesterol	6mg	Riboflavin	4% U.S. RDA
Sodium	390mg	Niacin	4% U.S. RDA
Potassium	35mg	Calcium	6% U.S. RDA
Dietary Fiber	1g	Iron	4% U.S. RDA

Crescent Oriental Egg Rolls

Judith Wilson Merritt, New York
Bake-Off® 32, 1986

PLUM SAUCE
4.75-ounce jar strained plums with
  tapioca baby food*
3 tablespoons brown sugar
2 tablespoons vinegar
¼ teaspoon instant minced onion
⅛ teaspoon garlic powder
⅛ teaspoon ginger

EGG ROLLS
1 cup finely shredded cabbage
½ cup shredded carrots
½ cup finely chopped celery
1 tablespoon oil
½ pound ground beef
1 teaspoon sugar
¼ teaspoon garlic powder
  Dash pepper
2 to 3 tablespoons peanut butter
2 to 4 teaspoons soy sauce
2 (8-ounce) cans refrigerated
  crescent dinner rolls**
1 egg, slightly beaten
1 tablespoon sesame seed

In small saucepan, combine all sauce ingredients; mix well. Bring to a boil, stirring constantly. Remove from heat; cool.

Heat oven to 375°F. Grease large cookie sheet. In large skillet, cook cabbage, carrots and celery in oil until crisp-tender, stirring constantly. Remove vegetables from skillet; set aside. In same skillet, brown ground beef; drain. Stir in sugar, 1/4 teaspoon garlic powder, pepper, peanut butter and soy sauce; cook until peanut butter is melted, stirring frequently. Remove from heat; stir in cooked vegetables.

Separate 1 can dough into 4 rectangles; firmly press perforations to seal. Press or roll out each to 6 × 4-inch rectangle. Cut each rectangle crosswise into three 4 × 2-inch pieces. Spoon 1 tablespoonful of filling on half of each small rectangle to within 1/4 inch of edges. Fold dough in half over filling; pinch edges to seal. Roll slightly to form 3-inch egg roll shape. Place on greased cookie sheet. Repeat with remaining can of dough. Brush beaten egg over rolls; sprinkle with sesame seed. Bake at 375°F. for 12 to 16 minutes or until golden brown. Serve warm with plum sauce. **24 egg rolls.**

TIPS: *One-half cup canned plums can be substituted for baby food. Drain and pit plums; puree in food processor.

**For best results, keep dough refrigerated until ready to use.

To make ahead, prepare, cover and refrigerate up to 2 hours; bake as directed above.

To reheat, wrap loosely in foil; heat at 375°F. for 15 to 18 minutes or until warm.

NUTRIENTS PER 1 EGG ROLL

Calories	120	Protein	6% U.S. RDA
Protein	4g	Vitamin A	10% U.S. RDA
Carbohydrate	11g	Vitamin C	2% U.S. RDA
Fat	7g	Thiamine	4% U.S. RDA
Cholesterol	20mg	Riboflavin	4% U.S. RDA
Sodium	240mg	Niacin	6% U.S. RDA
Potassium	115mg	Calcium	<2% U.S. RDA
Dietary Fiber	<1g	Iron	4% U.S. RDA

Mushroom Phyllo Tarts

❦

Melissa Daston, Maryland
Bake-Off® 33, 1988

3-ounce package cream cheese, softened
1/4 cup dry bread crumbs
1 tablespoon dill weed
1/2 teaspoon salt
3/4 cup dairy sour cream
1 to 2 tablespoons lemon juice
4.5-ounce jar sliced mushrooms, drained
1 garlic clove, minced
1/2 cup butter or margarine
8 (17 × 12-inch) frozen phyllo (fillo) pastry sheets, thawed
4.5-ounce jar whole mushrooms, drained

Heat oven to 350°F. In small bowl, combine cream cheese, bread crumbs, dill weed, salt, sour cream and lemon juice; blend well. Stir in sliced mushrooms. Set aside. In small skillet, over medium heat, cook garlic in butter, about 1 minute. Coat inside of 16 muffin cups with garlic butter; set aside.

Brush large cookie sheet with garlic butter. On work surface, unroll phyllo sheets; cover with plastic wrap or towel. Brush one phyllo sheet lightly with garlic butter; place buttered side up on buttered cookie sheet. Brush second phyllo sheet lightly with garlic butter; place buttered side up on top of first sheet. Repeat with remaining phyllo sheets. With sharp knife, cut through all layers of phyllo sheets to make sixteen 3 × 4 1/4-inch rectangles. Place one rectangle in each buttered muffin cup. Spoon heaping tablespoonful of cream cheese mixture into each cup. Top each with whole mushrooms, pushing stems into cream cheese mixture; drizzle with remaining garlic butter. Bake at 350°F. for 18 to 20 minutes or until light golden brown. **16 appetizers.**

NUTRIENTS PER 1 APPETIZER

Calories	120	Protein	2% U.S. RDA
Protein	2g	Vitamin A	8% U.S. RDA
Carbohydrate	5g	Vitamin C	2% U.S. RDA
Fat	10g	Thiamine	<2% U.S. RDA
Cholesterol	25mg	Riboflavin	4% U.S. RDA
Sodium	230mg	Niacin	2% U.S. RDA
Potassium	60mg	Calcium	2% U.S. RDA
Dietary Fiber	0g	Iron	2% U.S. RDA

Mushroom Phyllo Tarts

❦

Tender, flaky phyllo dough is placed in muffin cups, filled with a well-seasoned cream cheese mixture and topped with whole mushrooms to create this appetizer. These are easy to make and so impressive to serve!

Hungry Boy's Casserole, page 48

Main Dishes and Side Dishes

❧❧❧

During the early years of the Bake-Off® Contest, it was not uncommon for a prizewinning main dish recipe to call for more than fifteen ingredients. Contest rules at that time required that each entry "must be able to be completed in one day."

Today's favorite Bake-Off® recipes have a more streamlined look. Also, vegetables and other fresh ingredients play an increasingly important role in meals. The familiar ingredients of Broccoli Cauliflower Tetrazzini take on a distinctive personality as they are combined in a new way. Easy yet glamorous one-dish meals like Chicken Prosciutto with Mushroom Sauce feature unique combinations of vegetables and other flavorful ingredients.

Yesteryear's favorite main dish staples—ground beef and ham—are flanked by today's choices, chicken and fish. Light 'n Easy Seafood Dinner and Chicken Broccoli Stroganoff demonstrate this trend. At the same time, recipes like Biscuit Stuffin' Atop Chops indicate an enduring love for hearty, down-home main dishes.

Flavor combinations are often reminiscent of old-time regional and foreign classics. Italian Cheese Rustica Pie, Oriental Cornish Chicks and Hearty Mexican Pizza are among the recipes that so deliciously incorporate foreign flavors with familiar American ingredients. But the recipe preparation techniques—with an emphasis on convenience products— are anything but old-time.

In this chapter, you'll find popular Bake-Off® recipes from decades past—often updated to add cooking convenience—as well as the best from recent contests. All are sure to become favorites in your file of special main dishes and side dishes.

Italian-Style Fish and Vegetables

Italian-Style Fish and Vegetables

Louise Bobzin, Florida
Bake-Off® 33, 1988

2 tablespoons olive or vegetable oil
1 medium onion, sliced
2.5-ounce jar sliced mushrooms, drained
½ teaspoon basil leaves
½ teaspoon fennel seed
2 cups frozen mixed vegetables
1½ pounds fresh or frozen catfish, orange roughy or sole fillets, thawed
¼ teaspoon salt
¼ teaspoon pepper
2 medium tomatoes, sliced
⅓ cup grated Parmesan cheese

In large skillet over medium heat, heat oil. Add onion, mushrooms, basil and fennel seed; cook 4 minutes or until onion is tender. Stir in frozen vegetables. Place fish over vegetables; sprinkle with salt and pepper. Arrange tomato slices over fish. Reduce heat to low; cover and cook 12 to 16 minutes or until fish flakes easily with fork. Remove from heat; sprinkle with Parmesan cheese. Cover; let stand about 3 minutes or until Parmesan cheese is melted. **6 servings.**

NUTRIENTS PER 1/6 OF RECIPE
Calories	240	Protein	40% U.S. RDA
Protein	25g	Vitamin A	60% U.S. RDA
Carbohydrate	11g	Vitamin C	10% U.S. RDA
Fat	10g	Thiamine	8% U.S. RDA
Cholesterol	70mg	Riboflavin	6% U.S. RDA
Sodium	400mg	Niacin	15% U.S. RDA
Potassium	590mg	Calcium	10% U.S. RDA
Dietary Fiber	3g	Iron	8% U.S. RDA

Crafty Crescent Lasagne

Betty Taylor, Texas
Bake-Off® 19, 1968

MEAT FILLING
½ pound pork sausage
½ pound ground beef
¾ cup chopped onions
1 tablespoon parsley flakes
½ teaspoon basil leaves
½ teaspoon oregano leaves
1 small garlic clove, minced
Dash pepper
6-ounce can tomato paste

CHEESE FILLING
¼ cup grated Parmesan cheese
1 cup creamed cottage cheese
1 egg

CRUST
2 (8-ounce) cans refrigerated crescent dinner rolls
2 (7 × 4-inch) slices mozzarella cheese
1 tablespoon milk
1 tablespoon sesame seed

In large skillet, brown sausage and ground beef; drain. Stir in remaining meat filling ingredients; simmer uncovered 5 minutes, stirring occasionally.

Heat oven to 375°F. In small bowl, combine all cheese filling ingredients; blend well. Unroll dough into 4 long rectangles. Place on ungreased cookie sheet with long sides overlapping ½ inch; firmly press edges and perforations to seal. Press or roll out to form 15 × 13-inch rectangle. Spoon half of meat filling mixture in 6-inch strip lengthwise down center of dough to within 1 inch of each end. Spoon cheese filling mixture over meat mixture; top with remaining meat mixture. Arrange mozzarella cheese slices over meat mixture. Fold shortest sides of dough 1 inch over filling. Fold long sides of dough tightly over filling, overlapping edges in center ¼ inch; firmly pinch center seam and ends to seal. Brush with milk; sprinkle with sesame seed. Bake at 375°F. for 23 to 27 minutes or until deep golden brown. **6 to 8 servings.**

TIP: To reheat, wrap loosely in foil; heat at 375°F. for 18 to 20 minutes or until warm.

NUTRIENTS PER 1/8 OF RECIPE
Calories	430	Protein	35% U.S. RDA
Protein	22g	Vitamin A	15% U.S. RDA
Carbohydrate	30g	Vitamin C	10% U.S. RDA
Fat	25g	Thiamine	20% U.S. RDA
Cholesterol	80mg	Riboflavin	20% U.S. RDA
Sodium	1070mg	Niacin	20% U.S. RDA
Potassium	520mg	Calcium	20% U.S. RDA
Dietary Fiber	2g	Iron	15% U.S. RDA

Crafty Crescent Lasagne

A crescent dough crust is stuffed with a well-seasoned meat and cheese filling. It's a crafty way to get to a great-tasting lasagne.

Oriental Cornish Chicks

Oriental Cornish Chicks

⊸°⊶

Lentsey M. Carlson, New York
Bake-Off® 31, 1984

10-ounce package frozen long grain rice with peas and mushrooms in a pouch
¼ cup thinly sliced water chestnuts
1 teaspoon finely chopped candied ginger
8-ounce can (4 slices) sliced pineapple, cut into bite-sized pieces, drained, reserving 2 tablespoons liquid
2 (1½-pound) Cornish game hens
3 tablespoons margarine or butter
1½ teaspoons paprika
Parsley, if desired
Fresh fruit, if desired

Heat oven to 450°F. Cook rice as directed on package. In small bowl, combine cooked rice, water chestnuts, ginger and pineapple; toss lightly. Spoon equal portions of rice mixture into body cavity of each hen. Secure openings with toothpicks or wooden skewers. Place hens breast side up on rack in shallow roasting pan. If desired, tie legs together and wings to body with string.

In small saucepan, melt margarine. Stir in paprika and reserved 2 tablespoons pineapple liquid. Brush half of margarine mixture over hens. Place hens in oven; immediately reduce oven temperature to 350°F. Bake 1 to 1¼ hours or until golden brown and tender, basting occasionally with remaining margarine mixture and pan drippings. (Remove string from legs after first 30 minutes of baking.) Let stand 5 minutes before serving. Garnish with parsley and fresh fruit. **2 to 4 servings.**

MICROWAVE DIRECTIONS: Make a small slit in center of rice pouch. Microwave on MEDIUM for 3 to 4 minutes to partially thaw. In small bowl, separate rice and vegetables. Add water chestnuts, ginger and pineapple; toss lightly. Spoon equal portions of rice mixture into body cavity of each hen. Secure openings with toothpicks or wooden skewers. If desired, tie legs together and wings to body with string.

Place margarine in small microwave-safe bowl. Microwave on HIGH for 30 to 45 seconds or until melted. Stir in paprika and reserved 2 tablespoons pineapple liquid. Brush half of margarine mixture over hens. Place hens breast side down in 12 × 8-inch or 8-inch (2 quart) square microwave-safe baking dish. Cover; microwave on HIGH for 18 minutes, rotating dish ½ turn halfway through cooking. Turn hens breast side up; baste with remaining margarine mixture. Microwave on HIGH for 6 minutes or until juices run clear when pierced with fork between thigh and body of hens. If juices are not clear, rotate dish and microwave on HIGH an additional 2 to 6 minutes. Let stand 5 minutes before serving.

TIP: Body cavities of hens vary in size. Any leftover rice mixture can be baked in oven or heated in microwave-safe container in microwave.

NUTRIENTS PER 1/4 OF RECIPE

Calories	460	Protein	50% U.S. RDA
Protein	35g	Vitamin A	25% U.S. RDA
Carbohydrate	37g	Vitamin C	110% U.S. RDA
Fat	19g	Thiamine	30% U.S. RDA
Cholesterol	100mg	Riboflavin	20% U.S. RDA
Sodium	370mg	Niacin	60% U.S. RDA
Potassium	740mg	Calcium	6% U.S. RDA
Dietary Fiber	1g	Iron	20% U.S. RDA

Biscuit-Topped Italian Casserole

Robert Wick, Florida
Bake-Off® 33, 1988

    1 pound ground beef
 ½ cup chopped onion
    1 tablespoon oil, if desired
 ¾ cup water
 ½ teaspoon salt, if desired
 ¼ teaspoon pepper
    8-ounce can tomato sauce
    6-ounce can tomato paste
    8 ounces (2 cups) shredded mozzarella cheese
    9-ounce package frozen mixed vegetables in a pouch, thawed
    2 (10-ounce) cans refrigerated flaky biscuits
    1 tablespoon margarine or butter, melted
 ½ teaspoon oregano leaves, crushed

Heat oven to 375°F. Grease 13 × 9-inch (3-quart) baking dish. In large skillet, brown ground beef and onion in oil; drain. Stir in water, salt, pepper, tomato sauce and tomato paste; simmer 15 minutes, stirring occasionally. Place half of *hot* meat mixture in greased baking dish; sprinkle with ⅔ cup of the cheese. Spoon mixed vegetables evenly over cheese; sprinkle an additional ⅔ cup cheese over vegetables. Spoon remaining *hot* meat mixture evenly over cheese and vegetables; sprinkle with remaining ⅔ cup cheese.

Separate dough into 20 biscuits. Separate each biscuit into 3 layers. Arrange layers over hot meat mixture, overlapping, in 3 rows of 20 layers each. Gently brush biscuits with margarine; sprinkle with oregano. Bake at 375°F. for 22 to 27 minutes or until biscuit topping is golden brown. **8 to 10 servings.**

NUTRIENTS PER 1/10 OF RECIPE

Calories	380	Protein	25% U.S. RDA
Protein	15g	Vitamin A	40% U.S. RDA
Carbohydrate	34g	Vitamin C	15% U.S. RDA
Fat	20g	Thiamine	25% U.S. RDA
Cholesterol	30mg	Riboflavin	20% U.S. RDA
Sodium	1340mg	Niacin	20% U.S. RDA
Potassium	420mg	Calcium	20% U.S. RDA
Dietary Fiber	3g	Iron	15% U.S. RDA

The great skillet hunt—

Pillsbury supplies all of the utensils as well as the ingredients needed by each contestant to bake the contest recipe. Occasionally the search for specialized cooking gear can lead to some exciting moments. On the eve of the 8th Bake-Off®, it was discovered that an iron skillet desired by a finalist had not been manufactured for many years. A task force of Pillsbury managers and advertising executives from the company's agency fanned out across Manhattan to suppliers of cooking utensils. Retailers and wholesalers were telephoned at their homes to lead the search through storage rooms, basements and musty warehouses. It was nearly 2 A.M. when Bake-Off® headquarters received a call that the proper skillet had been located in a warehouse in Brooklyn, putting an end to one of the greatest skillet hunts in history.

Chicken Prosciutto with Mushroom Sauce

Chicken Prosciutto with Mushroom Sauce

❧❧

Prosciutto—Italian thin-sliced smoked ham—is tucked under tender breasts of chicken in this outstanding main dish. The special flavors of the ham and mushroom-wine sauce make this dish perfect for entertaining.

❧❧

Frances Kovar, New York
Bake-Off® 33, 1988

3 whole chicken breasts, skinned, boned, halved
5 tablespoons margarine or butter
1/4 cup chopped onion
1/4 cup all purpose or unbleached flour
2 tablespoons Dijon mustard
1 cup chicken broth
1 cup half-and-half
1/4 cup dry white wine or water
3 (4.5-ounce) jars sliced mushrooms, drained
4 ounces (1 cup) shredded Swiss cheese
16-ounce package frozen cut broccoli
6 slices prosciutto or thinly sliced cooked ham
Paprika

Place 1 chicken breast half between 2 pieces of plastic wrap. Pound chicken with meat mallet or rolling pin until about 1/4 inch thick; remove wrap. Repeat with remaining chicken breasts.

Heat oven to 400°F. In large skillet over medium heat, melt 2 tablespoons of the margarine. Cook chicken in margarine until lightly browned on both sides, about 5 minutes. Remove chicken. In same skillet, melt remaining 3 tablespoons margarine; add onion. Cook until onion is tender, about 2 minutes, stirring frequently. Remove from heat; stir in flour and mustard. Gradually stir in chicken broth, half-and-half and wine. Cook over low heat until mixture thickens and boils, stirring constantly. Add mushrooms and 1/2 cup of the cheese; stir until cheese is melted.

Arrange broccoli in bottom of ungreased 13 × 9-inch (3-quart) baking dish. Spoon half (2 cups) of sauce over broccoli. Alternate ham slices and chicken breasts, slightly overlapping, over sauce and broccoli down center of dish. Tuck ends of ham slices under chicken. Pour remaining sauce over chicken.

Bake at 400°F. for 20 to 30 minutes or until chicken is tender and no longer pink. Remove from oven; sprinkle with remaining 1/2 cup cheese and paprika. Bake an additional 2 minutes or until cheese is melted. **6 servings.**

NUTRIENTS PER 1/6 OF RECIPE

Calories	460	Protein	70% U.S. RDA
Protein	42g	Vitamin A	30% U.S. RDA
Carbohydrate	13g	Vitamin C	70% U.S. RDA
Fat	25g	Thiamine	25% U.S. RDA
Cholesterol	110mg	Riboflavin	30% U.S. RDA
Sodium	1040mg	Niacin	70% U.S. RDA
Potassium	680mg	Calcium	30% U.S. RDA
Dietary Fiber	3g	Iron	15% U.S. RDA

Grand Prize Winner

Chick-n-Broccoli Pot Pies

❧❧

Linda Wood, Indiana
Bake-Off® 28, 1978

10-ounce can refrigerated flaky biscuits
3 ounces (2/3 cup) shredded Cheddar or American cheese
2/3 cup crisp rice cereal
9-ounce package frozen cut broccoli in a pouch, cooked, well drained
1 cup cubed cooked chicken or turkey
10 3/4-ounce can condensed cream of chicken or mushroom soup
1/3 cup slivered or sliced almonds

Heat oven to 375°F. Separate dough into 10 biscuits. Place 1 biscuit in each ungreased muffin cup; firmly press in bottom and up sides forming 1/2-inch rim over edge of muffin cup. Spoon about 1 tablespoonful each of cheese and cereal into each biscuit-lined cup. Press mixture into bottom of each cup. Cut large pieces of broccoli in half. In large bowl, combine broccoli, chicken and soup; mix well. Spoon about 1/3 cup of chicken mixture over cereal. Sprinkle with almonds. Bake at 375°F. for 20 to 25 minutes or until edges of biscuits are deep golden brown. **10 servings.**

NUTRIENTS PER 1/10 OF RECIPE

Calories	210	Protein	15% U.S. RDA
Protein	10g	Vitamin A	15% U.S. RDA
Carbohydrate	18g	Vitamin C	10% U.S. RDA
Fat	11g	Thiamine	10% U.S. RDA
Cholesterol	25mg	Riboflavin	10% U.S. RDA
Sodium	620mg	Niacin	15% U.S. RDA
Potassium	160mg	Calcium	8% U.S. RDA
Dietary Fiber	2g	Iron	8% U.S. RDA

Chicken Prosciutto with Mushroom Sauce

Zucchini Crescent Supper Torte

Zucchini Crescent Supper Torte

Kristy McMath, California
Bake-Off® 33, 1988

8-ounce can refrigerated crescent dinner rolls
4 slices bacon
4 cups thinly sliced zucchini
½ cup finely chopped onion
⅓ cup finely chopped green bell pepper
1 garlic clove, minced
1 cup tomatoes, chopped, seeded, drained
½ teaspoon salt
½ teaspoon Italian seasoning
¼ teaspoon pepper
8 ounces (2 cups) shredded Cheddar cheese

TOPPING
½ cup all purpose or unbleached flour
¼ cup grated Parmesan cheese
1 teaspoon baking powder
½ teaspoon salt
½ cup milk
8-ounce carton (1 cup) plain yogurt
2 eggs

Heat oven to 375°F. Separate dough into 8 triangles. Place in ungreased 9-inch springform pan or 9-inch square pan; press over bottom and ¾ of the way up sides to form crust. Seal perforations.

In large skillet, cook bacon until crisp. Remove bacon from skillet; drain, reserving 1 tablespoon drippings in skillet. Crumble bacon; set aside. Add zucchini, onion, green pepper and garlic to drippings in skillet; cook over medium heat until vegetables are tender.* Stir in cooked bacon, tomatoes, 1/2 teaspoon salt, Italian seasoning and pepper. Spoon into crust-lined pan; sprinkle with Cheddar cheese. Lightly spoon flour into measuring cup; level off. In medium bowl, combine all topping ingredients; beat until smooth. Pour over vegetable mixture.

Bake at 375°F. for 50 to 55 minutes or until top is puffed and deep golden brown around edges. Cool 10 minutes on wire rack. Carefully remove sides of pan. To serve, cut into wedges. Serve immediately. **8 servings.**

TIP: *If zucchini mixture is watery, drain well.

HIGH ALTITUDE—Above 3500 Feet: No change.

NUTRIENTS PER 1/8 OF RECIPE

Calories	340	Protein	25% U.S. RDA
Protein	17g	Vitamin A	15% U.S. RDA
Carbohydrate	24g	Vitamin C	20% U.S. RDA
Fat	20g	Thiamine	15% U.S. RDA
Cholesterol	110mg	Riboflavin	20% U.S. RDA
Sodium	880mg	Niacin	8% U.S. RDA
Potassium	440mg	Calcium	35% U.S. RDA
Dietary Fiber	2g	Iron	10% U.S. RDA

Italian Country Loaf Rustica
☙

Miranda Desantis, New Jersey
Bake-Off® 33, 1988

FILLING
- 1 pound sweet Italian sausage
- 1/2 cup chopped onion
- 2 to 4 garlic cloves, minced
- 8 ounces (2 cups) cubed mozzarella cheese
- 7-ounce jar mild roasted red peppers, drained, chopped*

BREAD
- 1 1/2 cups all purpose or unbleached flour**
- 1/2 cup whole wheat flour
- 1/2 cup yellow cornmeal
- 1 tablespoon sugar
- 1/2 teaspoon salt
- 1 package fast-acting dry yeast
- 1 1/4 cups hot water (120 to 130°F.)
- 2 teaspoons margarine or butter, softened
- 1 egg, beaten
- 2 to 3 teaspoons sesame seed

If sausage comes in casing, remove casing; break up. In large skillet, brown sausage, onion and garlic.*** Drain; set aside.

Lightly spoon flour into measuring cup; level off. In large bowl, combine 1/2 cup all purpose flour, whole wheat flour, cornmeal, sugar, salt and yeast; blend well. Stir in water and margarine; mix well. Stir in remaining 1 cup all purpose flour to form a stiff batter. Cover; let rest 10 minutes.

Grease 9 or 10-inch springform pan. Stir down dough. Spread about 2/3 of dough in bottom and 2 inches up sides of greased pan. Add cheese and peppers to meat mixture; spoon over dough. Gently pull dough on sides over meat mixture. Drop tablespoonfuls of remaining dough over filling. With back of spoon or buttered fingers, carefully spread to cover. (Top will appear rough.) Cover loosely with plastic wrap and cloth towel. Let rise in warm place (80 to 85°F.) until light, 20 to 30 minutes.

Heat oven to 400°F. Brush top of dough with beaten egg; sprinkle with sesame seed. Bake at 400°F. for 25 to 35 minutes or until bread begins to pull away from sides of pan and edges are deep golden brown. Cool 5 minutes. Loosen edges with knife; remove sides of pan. To serve, cut into wedges. Store in refrigerator. **8 servings.**

TIPS: *Two medium (1 1/4 cups) chopped red bell peppers can be substituted for roasted red peppers.

**Self-rising flour is not recommended.

***If using chopped red bell peppers, cook with sausage, onion and garlic. Continue as directed above.

HIGH ALTITUDE—Above 3500 Feet: No change.

NUTRIENTS PER 1/8 OF RECIPE

Calories	350	Protein	30% U.S. RDA
Protein	19g	Vitamin A	30% U.S. RDA
Carbohydrate	35g	Vitamin C	50% U.S. RDA
Fat	15g	Thiamine	30% U.S. RDA
Cholesterol	70mg	Riboflavin	20% U.S. RDA
Sodium	550mg	Niacin	15% U.S. RDA
Potassium	270mg	Calcium	25% U.S. RDA
Dietary Fiber	3g	Iron	15% U.S. RDA

Italian Country Loaf Rustica
☙

Savory Italian sausage, cheese and red peppers are baked inside batter bread to make a hearty, attractive main dish. Surprisingly easy to prepare, it is sliced into wedges to serve.

Zucchini Crescent Supper Torte
☙

An impressive main dish in a crust. Seasoned garden-fresh vegetables are the filling, and a souffle-like topping is the finishing touch. Superb!

Hungry Boy's Casserole
❧

Mira Walilko, Michigan
Bake-Off® 15, 1963

1½ pounds ground beef
1 cup chopped celery
½ cup chopped onion
½ cup chopped green bell pepper
1 garlic clove, minced
6-ounce can tomato paste
¾ cup water
1 teaspoon paprika
½ teaspoon salt
16-ounce can pork and beans, undrained
15-ounce can garbanzo beans or lima beans, drained

BISCUITS
1½ cups all purpose, unbleached or self-rising flour*
2 teaspoons baking powder
½ teaspoon salt
¼ cup margarine or butter
½ to ¾ cup milk
2 tablespoons sliced stuffed green olives
1 tablespoon slivered almonds

In large skillet, combine ground beef, celery, onion, green pepper and garlic. Cook until meat is browned and vegetables are tender; drain. Stir in tomato paste, water, paprika and ½ teaspoon salt. Add pork and beans and garbanzo beans; simmer while preparing biscuits, stirring occasionally.

Heat oven to 425°F. Lightly spoon flour into measuring cup; level off. In large bowl, combine flour, baking powder and ½ teaspoon salt; mix well. Using pastry blender or fork, cut in margarine until mixture resembles coarse crumbs. Gradually stir in enough milk until mixture leaves sides of bowl and forms a soft, moist dough. On floured surface, gently knead dough 8 times. Roll dough to ¼-inch thickness; cut with floured 2½-inch doughnut cutter, saving holes. Reserve ½ cup of hot meat mixture. Pour remaining hot meat mixture into ungreased 13 × 9-inch (3-quart) baking dish. Arrange biscuits without centers over hot meat mixture. Stir olives and almonds into reserved ½ cup meat mixture; spoon into hole of each biscuit. Top each with biscuit holes.

Bake at 425°F. for 15 to 25 minutes or until biscuits are golden brown.
6 to 8 servings.

TIP: *If using self-rising flour, omit baking powder and salt in biscuits.

HIGH ALTITUDE—Above 3500 Feet: No change.

NUTRIENTS PER 1/8 OF RECIPE

Calories	450	Protein	35% U.S. RDA
Protein	24g	Vitamin A	25% U.S. RDA
Carbohydrate	42g	Vitamin C	25% U.S. RDA
Fat	21g	Thiamine	15% U.S. RDA
Cholesterol	60mg	Riboflavin	20% U.S. RDA
Sodium	1010mg	Niacin	30% U.S. RDA
Potassium	740mg	Calcium	15% U.S. RDA
Dietary Fiber	7g	Iron	25% U.S. RDA

Hungry Boy's Casserole
❧

Light, tender biscuits top this beef-and-bean casserole. It is a Grand Prize winner that will satisfy the heartiest appetites.

Potato-Beef Quick Meal
❧

Ruth Emerson, Nebraska
Bake-Off® 25, 1974

2 pounds ground beef
1 cup chopped onions
¼ cup chopped green bell pepper
1 teaspoon brown sugar
Dash cayenne pepper, if desired
1¾ cups water
½ cup chili sauce or ketchup
½ teaspoon Worcestershire sauce
1 package au gratin or cheese scalloped potato mix
16-ounce can tomatoes, undrained, cut up
1 to 2 ounces (¼ to ½ cup) shredded mozzarella cheese

Heat oven to 350°F. In large ovenproof skillet, brown ground beef; drain. Add onions, green pepper, brown sugar, cayenne pepper, water, chili sauce, Worcestershire sauce, potato slices, contents of seasoning mix envelope and tomatoes; mix well. Bring mixture to a boil; stir. Carefully place skillet in oven. Bake at 350°F. for 35 to 45 minutes or until potatoes are tender, stirring occasionally. Sprinkle with cheese. Bake an additional 1 to 2 minutes or until cheese is melted. **8 (1-cup) servings.**

NUTRIENTS PER 1/8 OF RECIPE

Calories	300	Protein	35% U.S. RDA
Protein	22g	Vitamin A	20% U.S. RDA
Carbohydrate	13g	Vitamin C	25% U.S. RDA
Fat	18g	Thiamine	6% U.S. RDA
Cholesterol	70mg	Riboflavin	10% U.S. RDA
Sodium	410mg	Niacin	25% U.S. RDA
Potassium	510mg	Calcium	8% U.S. RDA
Dietary Fiber	3g	Iron	15% U.S. RDA

Potato-Beef Quick Meal

Chicken Picadillo Pie

❧
Nina Reyes, Florida
Bake-Off® 32, 1986

15-ounce package refrigerated pie crusts
1 teaspoon flour

FILLING
1 tablespoon margarine or butter
1 tablespoon cornstarch
1/8 teaspoon ginger
Dash pepper
1 tablespoon prepared mustard
1 tablespoon soy sauce, if desired
1 tablespoon Worcestershire sauce
1 cup orange juice
2 tablespoons margarine or butter
2 large whole chicken breasts, skinned, boned, cut into bite-sized pieces
1 cup finely chopped onions
1/4 cup finely chopped green bell pepper
2 garlic cloves, minced
1/2 cup coconut
1/4 cup slivered almonds
1/4 cup raisins
1/4 to 1/2 cup chopped pimiento-stuffed green olives
2 tablespoons capers, drained, if desired

Prepare pie crust according to package directions for *two-crust pie* using 9-inch pie pan. Heat oven to 400°F.

In small saucepan, melt 1 tablespoon margarine. Blend in cornstarch, ginger, pepper, mustard, soy sauce and Worcestershire sauce. Gradually stir in orange juice. Bring to a boil; cook until mixture thickens, stirring constantly. Set aside.

In large skillet over medium heat, melt 2 tablespoons margarine. Cook chicken, onions, green pepper and garlic in margarine until chicken is completely cooked. Stir in coconut, almonds, raisins, olives, capers and the orange sauce. Reduce heat to low; cook until thoroughly heated, stirring occasionally. Spoon filling mixture into pie crust-lined pan. Top with second crust; seal and flute. Cut slits in several places. Bake at 400°F. for 30 to 40 minutes or until golden brown. Let stand 5 minutes before serving. **8 servings.**

NUTRIENTS PER 1/8 OF RECIPE

Calories	470	Protein	35% U.S. RDA
Protein	21g	Vitamin A	8% U.S. RDA
Carbohydrate	37g	Vitamin C	30% U.S. RDA
Fat	26g	Thiamine	6% U.S. RDA
Cholesterol	60mg	Riboflavin	6% U.S. RDA
Sodium	680mg	Niacin	40% U.S. RDA
Potassium	380mg	Calcium	4% U.S. RDA
Dietary Fiber	3g	Iron	8% U.S. RDA

Italian Cheese Rustica Pie

❧
Gloria Bove, Pennsylvania
Bake-Off® 32, 1986

15-ounce package refrigerated pie crusts
1 tablespoon flour

FILLING
3 eggs
1 cup cubed cooked ham
1 cup ricotta or small curd cottage cheese
4 ounces (1 cup) shredded mozzarella cheese
4 ounces (1 cup) cubed provolone or Swiss cheese
4 tablespoons grated Parmesan cheese
1 tablespoon finely chopped fresh parsley or 1/2 teaspoon flakes
1/4 teaspoon oregano leaves
Dash pepper
Beaten egg, if desired

Prepare pie crust according to package directions for *two-crust pie* using 9-inch pie pan. Place oven rack at lowest position. Heat oven to 375°F.

In large bowl, slightly beat 3 eggs. Add ham, ricotta cheese, mozzarella cheese, provolone cheese, 3 tablespoons of the Parmesan cheese, parsley, oregano and pepper; blend well. Spoon filling mixture into pie crust-lined pan. Top with second crust; seal edges and flute. Cut slits in crust in several places. Brush beaten egg over crust. Sprinkle with remaining 1 tablespoon Parmesan cheese. Bake at 375°F. for 50 to 60 minutes or until golden brown. Let stand 10 minutes before serving. **6 to 8 servings.**

NUTRIENTS PER 1/8 OF RECIPE

Calories	450	Protein	30% U.S. RDA
Protein	20g	Vitamin A	10% U.S. RDA
Carbohydrate	27g	Vitamin C	4% U.S. RDA
Fat	29g	Thiamine	10% U.S. RDA
Cholesterol	180mg	Riboflavin	15% U.S. RDA
Sodium	860mg	Niacin	4% U.S. RDA
Potassium	180mg	Calcium	35% U.S. RDA
Dietary Fiber	1g	Iron	6% U.S. RDA

❧
Ooops!—

Money winners at the contest have their own special dreams for the prize money, but the $10,000 winner at the first contest almost had an abrupt change of plans. She had tucked the check into her purse before a quick shopping trip—and a variety-store pickpocket lifted it. Pillsbury quickly stopped payment on the missing check and issued a duplicate to the dismayed young woman.

Pictured top to bottom: Chicken Picadillo Pie, Italian Cheese Rustica Pie

Pictured left to right: Enchilada-Style Chicken Pie, Country Corn Pudding Pie

Country Corn Pudding Pie

━━━━━━━ ❧❧ ━━━━━━━

Delores Rector, Indiana
Bake-Off® 32, 1986

15-ounce package refrigerated pie
crusts
1 teaspoon flour

FILLING
3 tablespoons margarine or butter
2 tablespoons all purpose or
unbleached flour
2 tablespoons sugar
½ to 1 teaspoon salt, if desired
1 cup milk
3 eggs
⅓ cup chopped green bell pepper
17-ounce can whole kernel corn,
drained
4 slices bacon, crisply cooked,
crumbled

MICROWAVE DIRECTIONS: Prepare pie crust according to package directions for *unfilled one-crust pie* using 9-inch microwave-safe pie pan. (Refrigerate remaining crust for later use.) Flute, if desired. Generously prick crust with fork. Microwave on HIGH for 6 to 8 minutes, rotating pan ½ turn every 2 minutes. Crust is done when surface appears dry and flaky. Cool.

In 1-quart microwave-safe bowl, microwave margarine on HIGH for 30 seconds or until melted. Blend in 2 tablespoons flour, sugar and salt. Stir in milk and eggs; blend well using wire whisk. Stir in green pepper and corn. Microwave on HIGH for 5 minutes, stirring every 1½ minutes until smooth, using wire whisk. Pour filling mixture into cooked pie crust; sprinkle top with bacon. In microwave, elevate pie pan 1 to 2 inches by placing on inverted microwave-safe dish or on shelf provided. Microwave on HIGH for 4 to 6 minutes, rotating pan once halfway through cooking. Pie is done when knife inserted near center comes out clean. Let stand on flat surface for 5 minutes before serving. Garnish with additional green pepper or as desired. **6 to 8 servings.**

Enchilada-Style Chicken Pie

Nancy Jo Mathison, California
Bake-Off® 32, 1986

CRUST
15-ounce package refrigerated pie
  crusts
1 teaspoon flour
1 egg
1 teaspoon Worcestershire sauce

FILLING
1 cup chopped onions
5-ounce can chunk chicken,
  drained, chopped
4-ounce can chopped green
  chiles, well drained
³/₄ cup sliced ripe olives, drained
4 ounces (1 cup) shredded
  Monterey jack or Cheddar
  cheese*
¹/₂ cup milk
3 eggs
¹/₂ teaspoon salt, if desired
¹/₄ teaspoon cumin
¹/₈ teaspoon garlic powder
¹/₈ teaspoon pepper
3 drops hot pepper sauce
  Chile salsa, sour cream, avocado
  slices and parsley, if desired

MICROWAVE DIRECTIONS: Prepare pie crust according to package directions for *unfilled one-crust pie* using 9-inch microwave-safe pie pan or 10-inch microwave-safe tart pan. (Refrigerate remaining crust for later use.) Flute, if desired. Generously prick crust with fork. In medium bowl, combine 1 egg and Worcestershire sauce; blend well. Brush lightly over pie crust. (Reserve any remaining egg mixture for filling.) Microwave on HIGH for 6 to 8 minutes, rotating pan ¹/₂ turn every 2 minutes. Crust is done when surface appears dry and flaky.

Place onions in small microwave-safe bowl. Cover with microwave-safe plastic wrap. Microwave on HIGH for 3 minutes or until crisp-tender. Drain well; set aside. To assemble pie, layer chicken, cooked onions, chiles, olives and cheese in cooked pie crust. To reserved egg mixture, add milk, 3 eggs, salt, cumin, garlic powder, pepper and hot pepper sauce; blend well. Pour mixture slowly over cheese. Microwave on HIGH for 8 to 11 minutes or until knife inserted near center comes out clean, rotating pan once halfway through cooking. Let stand on flat surface 5 minutes before serving. To serve, top each serving with salsa, sour cream, avocado slice and parsley. **6 to 8 servings.**

TIP: *A combination of Monterey jack and Cheddar cheese can be used.

Enchilada-Style Chicken Pie

Contemporary microwave preparation and refrigerated pie crusts are featured in this delicious Mexican-flavored pie.

California Casserole

Grand Prize Winner

California Casserole

Mrs. H. H. Hatheway, California
Bake-Off® 8, 1956

¹/₃ cup all purpose or unbleached flour
1 teaspoon paprika
2 pounds boneless veal, cut into 1-inch pieces*
¹/₄ cup oil
¹/₂ teaspoon salt
¹/₈ teaspoon pepper
1 cup water
10³/₄-ounce can condensed cream of chicken soup
1¹/₂ cups water
16-ounce can (1³/₄ cups) small onions, drained

DUMPLINGS
2 cups all purpose or unbleached flour
4 teaspoons baking powder
1 tablespoon poppy seed, if desired
1 teaspoon onion flakes
1 teaspoon celery seed
1 teaspoon poultry seasoning
¹/₄ teaspoon salt
³/₄ to 1 cup milk
¹/₄ cup oil
¹/₄ cup margarine or butter, melted
1 cup dry bread crumbs

SAUCE
10³/₄-ounce can condensed cream of chicken soup
1 cup dairy sour cream
¹/₄ cup milk

In small bowl or plastic bag, combine ¹/₃ cup flour and paprika. Add veal; coat well with flour mixture. In large skillet, brown veal in ¹/₄ cup oil. Add ¹/₂ teaspoon salt, pepper and 1 cup water. Bring to a boil. Reduce heat; simmer uncovered 30 minutes or until veal is tender. Transfer veal mixture to ungreased 13 × 9-inch (3-quart) baking dish or 3-quart casserole.

In same skillet, combine 1 can cream of chicken soup and 1¹/₂ cups water; bring to a boil, stirring constantly. Pour over veal mixture in baking dish. Add onions; mix well.

Heat oven to 425°F. Lightly spoon flour into measuring cup; level off. In large bowl, combine 2 cups flour, baking powder, poppy seed, onion flakes, celery seed, poultry seasoning and ¹/₄ teaspoon salt; mix well. Add milk and ¹/₄ cup oil; stir until dry ingredients are just moistened. In small bowl, combine margarine and bread crumbs. Drop rounded tablespoons of dough into crumb mixture; roll to coat well. Arrange dumplings over warm veal mixture. Bake at 425°F. for 20 to 25 minutes or until dumplings are deep golden brown.

Meanwhile, in small saucepan combine all sauce ingredients. Bring just to a boil. Reduce heat; simmer 2 to 3 minutes or until thoroughly heated, stirring frequently. Serve sauce with veal casserole and dumplings. **8 to 10 servings.**

TIP: *Boneless pork, cut into 1-inch pieces, can be substituted for veal.

NUTRIENTS PER 1/10 OF RECIPE

Calories	560	Protein	40% U.S. RDA
Protein	26g	Vitamin A	15% U.S. RDA
Carbohydrate	40g	Vitamin C	2% U.S. RDA
Fat	33g	Thiamine	20% U.S. RDA
Cholesterol	100mg	Riboflavin	25% U.S. RDA
Sodium	960mg	Niacin	30% U.S. RDA
Potassium	440mg	Calcium	20% U.S. RDA
Dietary Fiber	2g	Iron	25% U.S. RDA

Quick-Topped Vegetable Chicken Casserole

Bernice Malinowski, Wisconsin
Bake-Off® 31, 1984

10¾-ounce can condensed cream of
    chicken soup
  3-ounce package cream cheese,
    softened
 ½ cup milk
 ½ cup chopped celery
 ½ cup chopped onion
 ¼ cup Parmesan cheese
 ¼ cup chopped green bell pepper
 ¼ cup shredded carrot
 ½ teaspoon salt
  2 to 3 cups cubed cooked chicken
  9-ounce package frozen cut
    broccoli in a pouch, cooked,
    drained

TOPPING
  1 cup complete or buttermilk
    pancake mix
 ¼ cup slivered almonds
  4 ounces (1 cup) shredded
    Cheddar cheese
 ¼ cup milk
  1 tablespoon oil
  1 egg, slightly beaten

Heat oven to 375°F. In large saucepan, combine soup, cream cheese, milk, celery, onion, Parmesan cheese, green pepper, carrot and salt. Cook over medium heat until mixture is hot and cream cheese is melted, stirring frequently. Stir in chicken and broccoli. Pour into ungreased 2-quart casserole or 12 × 8-inch (2-quart) baking dish. In medium bowl, combine all topping ingredients; blend well. Spoon tablespoonfuls of topping over warm chicken mixture. Bake at 375°F. for 20 to 30 minutes or until topping is golden brown and chicken mixture bubbles around edges. **6 servings.**

HIGH ALTITUDE—Above 3500 Feet: No change.

NUTRIENTS PER 1/6 OF RECIPE

Calories	480	Protein	50% U.S. RDA
Protein	34g	Vitamin A	45% U.S. RDA
Carbohydrate	28g	Vitamin C	35% U.S. RDA
Fat	25g	Thiamine	15% U.S. RDA
Cholesterol	140mg	Riboflavin	25% U.S. RDA
Sodium	1310mg	Niacin	45% U.S. RDA
Potassium	500mg	Calcium	40% U.S. RDA
Dietary Fiber	3g	Iron	15% U.S. RDA

Chicken Broccoli Stroganoff

Patricia Kiewiet, Illinois
Bake-Off® 33, 1988

  2 cups frozen cut broccoli
  1 tablespoon margarine or butter
 ¼ cup chopped onion
  3 tablespoons flour
10¾-ounce can condensed chicken
    broth
  2 cups cubed cooked chicken
 2.5-ounce jar sliced mushrooms,
    drained
  8-ounce carton (1 cup) dairy sour
    cream
    Hot cooked noodles
    Chopped fresh parsley

MICROWAVE DIRECTIONS: Cook broccoli in microwave until crisp-tender according to package directions. Drain; set aside. In 2-quart microwave-safe casserole, microwave margarine on HIGH for 20 seconds or until melted. Add onion; toss to coat. Cover with microwave-safe plastic wrap. Microwave on HIGH for 2 minutes or until crisp-tender. Add flour; blend well. Using wire whisk, stir chicken broth into onion mixture; blend well. Microwave on HIGH for 4 to 6 minutes or until mixture thickens and bubbles, stirring once halfway through cooking.* Add chicken, cooked broccoli, mushrooms and sour cream; blend well. Microwave on HIGH for 3 to 5 minutes or until mixture is thoroughly heated and bubbles around edges, stirring once halfway through cooking. Serve over noodles; garnish with parsley.
6 servings.

TIP: *For compact microwave ovens under 600 watts, microwave chicken broth-onion mixture on HIGH for 7 to 8 minutes or until mixture thickens and bubbles, stirring once halfway through cooking. Continue as directed above.

NUTRIENTS PER 1/6 OF RECIPE

Calories	490	Protein	40% U.S. RDA
Protein	26g	Vitamin A	25% U.S. RDA
Carbohydrate	58g	Vitamin C	40% U.S. RDA
Fat	17g	Thiamine	25% U.S. RDA
Cholesterol	120mg	Riboflavin	25% U.S. RDA
Sodium	445mg	Niacin	40% U.S. RDA
Potassium	510mg	Calcium	10% U.S. RDA
Dietary Fiber	3g	Iron	20% U.S. RDA

Quick-Topped Vegetable Chicken Casserole

Colorful vegetables and chicken are hidden under a topping made from pancake mix. So simple to prepare!

Chicken Broccoli Stroganoff

Chicken and broccoli in a light cream sauce create a new version of a popular family main dish. Make it in minutes in your microwave.

Hearty Mexican Pizza

Linda Loda, Illinois
Bake-Off® 33, 1988

CRUST
1 tablespoon cornmeal
1 to 1½ cups self-rising flour*
1 cup whole wheat flour
¾ cup beer, room temperature
¼ cup oil

TOPPING
16-ounce can refried beans
1 pound ground beef
⅓ cup chopped onion
8-ounce can tomato sauce
4-ounce can chopped green
 chiles, undrained
8 ounces (2 cups) shredded
 Cheddar, Monterey jack or
 mozzarella cheese
1 medium red or green bell pepper, cut into strips
3 to 4 pitted ripe olives, sliced, if
 desired
 Dairy sour cream, if desired
 Taco or picante sauce, if desired

Heat oven to 400°F. Grease 14-inch pizza pan or 15 × 10 × 1-inch baking pan; sprinkle with cornmeal. Lightly spoon flour into measuring cup; level off. In large bowl, combine ½ cup self-rising flour, whole wheat flour, beer and oil; mix well. By hand, stir in ¼ to ½ cup self-rising flour to form a stiff dough. On floured surface, knead in remaining ¼ to ½ cup self-rising flour until dough is smooth and elastic, 2 to 3 minutes. On lightly floured surface, roll dough to 14-inch circle. Place over cornmeal in greased pan; press dough to fit pan evenly.

Spread refried beans over dough. In large skillet, brown ground beef; drain well. Add onion, tomato sauce and green chiles; blend well. Spoon meat mixture over refried beans; top with cheese, pepper strips and olives. Bake at 400°F. for 25 to 35 minutes or until crust is light golden brown. Let stand 5 minutes before serving. Garnish with sour cream or taco sauce. **8 servings.**

TIP: *All purpose or unbleached flour can be substituted for self-rising flour; add 2 teaspoons baking powder and ½ teaspoon salt.

HIGH ALTITUDE—Above 3500 Feet: No change.

NUTRIENTS PER 1/8 OF RECIPE

Calories	560	Protein	40% U.S. RDA
Protein	25g	Vitamin A	35% U.S. RDA
Carbohydrate	42g	Vitamin C	80% U.S. RDA
Fat	31g	Thiamine	25% U.S. RDA
Cholesterol	70mg	Riboflavin	20% U.S. RDA
Sodium	1100mg	Niacin	25% U.S. RDA
Potassium	600mg	Calcium	35% U.S. RDA
Dietary Fiber	7g	Iron	25% U.S. RDA

Crab Meat Salad Pie

Evelyn Robinson, Washington
Bake-Off® 11, 1959

When this tempting pie was a finalist the filling was spooned into a tender, flaky, made-from-scratch pie shell. In this updated recipe, the idea remains the same, but it all goes together in a flash using the convenience of refrigerated pie crusts.

CRUST
15-ounce package refrigerated pie
 crusts
1 teaspoon flour

FILLING
¾ cup dry bread crumbs
1 cup chopped celery
1 tablespoon finely chopped onion
1 tablespoon finely chopped green
 bell pepper
¾ to 1 cup mayonnaise or salad
 dressing
1 tablespoon lemon juice
6-ounce can crab meat, drained
2 ounces (½ cup) shredded
 Cheddar cheese

Heat oven to 450°F. Prepare pie crust according to package directions for *unfilled one-crust pie* using 9-inch pie pan. (Refrigerate remaining crust for later use.) Bake at 450°F. for 9 to 11 minutes or until light golden brown. Cool completely.

Reserve 2 tablespoons of the bread crumbs. In large bowl, combine remaining bread crumbs, celery, onion, green pepper, mayonnaise, lemon juice and crab meat; toss lightly. Spoon into cooled baked crust. Sprinkle with reserved 2 tablespoons bread crumbs and cheese. Bake at 450°F. for 8 to 10 minutes or until cheese is melted.

6 servings

NUTRIENTS PER 1/6 OF RECIPE

Calories	550	Protein	15% U.S. RDA
Protein	9g	Vitamin A	8% U.S. RDA
Carbohydrate	27g	Vitamin C	4% U.S. RDA
Fat	45g	Thiamine	4% U.S. RDA
Cholesterol	60mg	Riboflavin	6% U.S. RDA
Sodium	810mg	Niacin	6% U.S. RDA
Potassium	150mg	Calcium	10% U.S. RDA
Dietary Fiber	3g	Iron	6% U.S. RDA

Layered Italian Beef Pie

Ruth Boudreaux, Louisiana
Bake-Off® 32, 1986

15-ounce package refrigerated pie
    crusts
1 teaspoon flour

FILLING
1 pound ground beef
1 cup prepared spaghetti sauce
    with mushrooms and onions
2 eggs
1/4 cup grated Parmesan cheese
9-ounce package frozen chopped
    spinach in a pouch, thawed,
    well drained
8 ounces (2 cups) shredded
    mozzarella cheese
1/2 cup sliced ripe olives

Heat oven to 450°F. Prepare pie crust according to package directions for *unfilled one-crust pie* using 9-inch pie pan. (Refrigerate remaining crust for later use.) Bake at 450°F. for 9 to 11 minutes or until light golden brown; cool. Reduce oven temperature to 350°F.

Meanwhile, in large skillet brown ground beef; drain well. Add spaghetti sauce; simmer 10 minutes or until thoroughly heated. In medium bowl, beat eggs. Add Parmesan cheese and spinach; blend well. Spoon half of meat mixture into cooled baked crust; sprinkle with 1 cup of the mozzarella cheese and 1/4 cup of the olives. Spoon spinach mixture evenly over cheese; top with remaining meat mixture.

Bake at 350°F. for 25 to 35 minutes or until thoroughly heated. Sprinkle with remaining 1 cup mozzarella cheese and 1/4 cup olives. Bake an additional 1 to 2 minutes or until cheese is melted. Let stand 5 minutes before serving.
6 to 8 servings.

TIP: Cover edge of pie crust with strip of foil during last 10 to 15 minutes of baking if necessary to prevent excessive browning.

NUTRIENTS PER 1/8 OF RECIPE

Calories	410	Protein	30% U.S. RDA
Protein	20g	Vitamin A	25% U.S. RDA
Carbohydrate	19g	Vitamin C	4% U.S. RDA
Fat	28g	Thiamine	4% U.S. RDA
Cholesterol	140mg	Riboflavin	15% U.S. RDA
Sodium	720mg	Niacin	15% U.S. RDA
Potassium	410mg	Calcium	25% U.S. RDA
Dietary Fiber	2g	Iron	10% U.S. RDA

Broccoli Brunch Braid

Diane Tucker, Idaho
Bake-Off® 33, 1988

1/2 pound ground pork sausage
2 cups frozen cut broccoli
1 egg, beaten
1 tablespoon flour
1/4 teaspoon baking powder
1/2 cup ricotta cheese
4 ounces (1 cup) shredded
    Cheddar cheese
4.5-ounce jar sliced mushrooms,
    drained
8-ounce can refrigerated crescent
    dinner rolls
1 egg white, beaten
1/4 teaspoon caraway seed

In medium skillet, brown sausage. Drain well; set aside. Cook broccoli as directed on package. Drain; set aside.

Heat oven to 325°F. In large bowl, combine 1 beaten egg, flour and baking powder; beat well. Stir in ricotta cheese, Cheddar cheese, mushrooms, cooked sausage and broccoli. Unroll dough into 2 long rectangles. Place on large ungreased cookie sheet with long sides overlapping 1/2 inch; firmly press edges and perforations to seal. Press or roll out to form 14 × 10-inch rectangle. Spoon sausage mixture in 3 1/2-inch strip lengthwise down center of dough to within 1/4 inch of each end. Form sausage mixture into mounded shape. Make cuts 1 inch apart on longest sides of rectangle just to edge of filling. To give braided appearance, fold strips of dough at an angle halfway across filling, alternating from side to side with edges of strips slightly overlapping. Brush with beaten egg white; sprinkle with caraway seed.

Bake at 325°F. for 25 to 35 minutes or until deep golden brown. Cool 5 minutes; remove from cookie sheet. Cut into slices. **8 servings.**

NUTRIENTS PER 1/8 OF RECIPE

Calories	260	Protein	20% U.S. RDA
Protein	12g	Vitamin A	8% U.S. RDA
Carbohydrate	15g	Vitamin C	20% U.S. RDA
Fat	16g	Thiamine	10% U.S. RDA
Cholesterol	70mg	Riboflavin	15% U.S. RDA
Sodium	660mg	Niacin	8% U.S. RDA
Potassium	220mg	Calcium	20% U.S. RDA
Dietary Fiber	1g	Iron	8% U.S. RDA

"I haven't a thing to wear!"

A contestant, whose luggage was misplaced by the airline and who had nothing to wear but her traveling clothes, was taken on a hurried shopping trip by Sally Pillsbury, the wife of an executive, so she could face the awards presentation in a more suitable outfit.

Light 'n Easy
Seafood Dinner

**Light 'n Easy
Seafood Dinner**

~~~~~

Creamy seafood-vegetable sauce is served over tender crescent pinwheels for a quick dinner idea.

Nancy Signorelli, Florida
Bake-Off® 33, 1988

8-ounce can refrigerated crescent dinner rolls
4¼-ounce can tiny shrimp, drained, reserving liquid
1 pound frozen cod or haddock, thawed, cut into ½-inch cubes
4 green onions or scallions, sliced
⅓ cup all purpose or unbleached flour
1 cup milk
1 tablespoon dried parsley flakes
½ to 1 teaspoon garlic powder
1 cup dairy sour cream
3 tablespoons dry sherry, if desired
9-ounce package frozen sweet peas in a pouch, thawed, drained
8-ounce can sliced water chestnuts, drained
2.5-ounce jar sliced mushrooms, drained

Heat oven to 350°F. Remove dough from can in rolled sections; do not unroll. Cut each section into 6 slices. Place on ungreased cookie sheet; slightly flatten each slice. Bake at 350°F. for 13 to 16 minutes or until golden brown. Set aside.

In large skillet, combine reserved shrimp liquid, cod and green onions. Bring to a boil. Reduce heat; cover and simmer 3 to 5 minutes or until fish flakes easily with fork. Remove from heat; do not drain.

In medium saucepan, using wire whisk, stir flour into milk. Cook over medium heat about 2 minutes or until mixture thickens and boils, stirring constantly. Stir in parsley flakes, garlic powder, sour cream and sherry. Add shrimp, peas, water chestnuts and mushrooms; mix well. Gently blend sour cream mixture into fish mixture in skillet.* Heat over low heat about 5 minutes, stirring occasionally. To serve, place 2 baked crescent pinwheels on plate; spoon about 1 cup of fish mixture over pinwheels. **6 servings.**

TIP: *To make ahead, fish mixture can be prepared to this point. Cover and refrigerate. Just before serving, prepare crescent pinwheels as directed. Heat seafood mixture, covered, over low heat, stirring occasionally. Serve as directed above.

NUTRIENTS PER 1/6 OF RECIPE

Calories	410	Protein	40% U.S. RDA
Protein	25g	Vitamin A	10% U.S. RDA
Carbohydrate	37g	Vitamin C	10% U.S. RDA
Fat	17g	Thiamine	25% U.S. RDA
Cholesterol	90mg	Riboflavin	25% U.S. RDA
Sodium	580mg	Niacin	20% U.S. RDA
Potassium	740mg	Calcium	15% U.S. RDA
Dietary Fiber	2g	Iron	15% U.S. RDA

Biscuit Stuffin'
Atop Chops

Marilyn Ohl, Ohio
Bake-Off® 22, 1971

6 pork chops, ½ inch thick
1 tablespoon oil
10¾-ounce can condensed cream of chicken soup
1 cup chopped celery
1 cup chopped onions
¼ teaspoon pepper
⅛ teaspoon poultry seasoning or sage
1 egg
7.5-ounce can refrigerated biscuits

Heat oven to 350°F. In large skillet, brown pork chops in oil. Place in ungreased 13×9-inch pan. In medium bowl, combine soup, celery, onions, pepper, poultry seasoning and egg; mix well. Separate dough into 10 biscuits; cut each into 8 pieces. Stir biscuit pieces into soup mixture; spoon over pork chops. Bake at 350°F. for 45 to 55 minutes or until biscuit pieces are golden brown. **6 servings.**

NUTRIENTS PER 1/6 OF RECIPE

Calories	340	Protein	35% U.S. RDA
Protein	24g	Vitamin A	6% U.S. RDA
Carbohydrate	23g	Vitamin C	4% U.S. RDA
Fat	17g	Thiamine	50% U.S. RDA
Cholesterol	110mg	Riboflavin	25% U.S. RDA
Sodium	770mg	Niacin	30% U.S. RDA
Potassium	570mg	Calcium	4% U.S. RDA
Dietary Fiber	1g	Iron	10% U.S. RDA

Italian Zucchini Crescent Pie

Italian Zucchini Crescent Pie

❦

Millicent Caplan, Florida
Bake-Off® 29, 1980

- **4 cups thinly sliced zucchini**
- **1 cup chopped onions**
- **2 tablespoons margarine or butter**
- **2 tablespoons parsley flakes**
- **½ teaspoon salt**
- **½ teaspoon pepper**
- **¼ teaspoon garlic powder**
- **¼ teaspoon basil leaves**
- **¼ teaspoon oregano leaves**
- **2 eggs, well beaten**
- **8 ounces (2 cups) shredded Muenster or mozzarella cheese**
- **8-ounce can refrigerated crescent dinner rolls**
- **2 teaspoons prepared mustard**

Heat oven to 375°F. In large skillet, cook zucchini and onions in margarine until tender, about 8 minutes. Stir in parsley flakes, salt, pepper, garlic powder, basil and oregano. In large bowl, combine eggs and cheese; mix well. Stir in cooked vegetable mixture.

Separate dough into 8 triangles.* Place in ungreased 10-inch pie pan, 12 × 8-inch (2-quart) baking dish or 11-inch quiche pan; press over bottom and up sides to form crust. Seal perforations. Spread crust with mustard. Pour egg-vegetable mixture evenly into prepared crust. Bake at 375°F. for 18 to 22 minutes or until knife inserted near center comes out clean.** Let stand 10 minutes before serving. **6 servings.**

TIPS: *If using 12 × 8-inch (2-quart) baking dish, unroll dough into 2 long rectangles; press over bottom and 1 inch up sides to form crust. Seal perforations. Continue as directed above.

**Cover edge of crust with strip of foil during last 10 minutes of baking if necessary to prevent excessive browning.

NUTRIENTS PER 1/6 OF RECIPE

Calories	360	Protein	25% U.S. RDA
Protein	15g	Vitamin A	20% U.S. RDA
Carbohydrate	20g	Vitamin C	10% U.S. RDA
Fat	25g	Thiamine	10% U.S. RDA
Cholesterol	130mg	Riboflavin	15% U.S. RDA
Sodium	820mg	Niacin	6% U.S. RDA
Potassium	440mg	Calcium	30% U.S. RDA
Dietary Fiber	2g	Iron	10% U.S. RDA

Garden Chicken Salad

Garden Chicken Salad

Edith Shulman, Texas
Bake-Off® 33, 1988

SALAD

2 cups frozen cut broccoli
4 cups cubed cooked chicken
1/3 cup chopped red or green bell pepper
3 tablespoons sliced ripe olives
2 tablespoons finely chopped red onion
1 large orange, peeled, chopped

DRESSING

3 tablespoons mango chutney
2/3 cup light mayonnaise or mayonnaise
1 tablespoon dry sherry, if desired
2 1/2 teaspoons garlic-flavored wine vinegar or red wine vinegar
1/4 cup sesame seed, toasted*
1/8 teaspoon pepper

Lettuce leaves

Cook broccoli until crisp-tender as directed on package. Drain; cool. In large bowl, combine cooked broccoli and remaining salad ingredients; blend well.

Place chutney in small bowl. Remove any large pieces and finely chop; return to bowl. Stir in remaining dressing ingredients; blend well. Pour dressing over salad; toss gently. Serve on lettuce leaves or in lettuce-lined bowl. Store in refrigerator. **6 (1 1/4-cup) servings.**

TIP: *To toast sesame seed, spread on cookie sheet; bake at 375°F. for about 5 minutes or until light golden brown, stirring occasionally. Or, spread in medium skillet; stir over medium heat for about 10 minutes or until light golden brown.

NUTRIENTS PER 1/6 OF RECIPE

Calories	340	Protein	45% U.S. RDA
Protein	30g	Vitamin A	20% U.S. RDA
Carbohydrate	14g	Vitamin C	90% U.S. RDA
Fat	18g	Thiamine	10% U.S. RDA
Cholesterol	90mg	Riboflavin	15% U.S. RDA
Sodium	290mg	Niacin	45% U.S. RDA
Potassium	450mg	Calcium	6% U.S. RDA
Dietary Fiber	3g	Iron	10% U.S. RDA

Hurry-Up Hot Potato Salad

Ike D. Fowler, Texas
Bake-Off® 19, 1968

3 cups water
1 package scalloped potato mix
3/4 cup mayonnaise or salad dressing
1/4 cup dairy sour cream
2 tablespoons parsley flakes
2 tablespoons Italian salad dressing
14.5-ounce can cut green beans, drained*
4-ounce jar sliced pimiento, drained
Paprika, if desired

Heat oven to 350°F. In medium saucepan, bring water to a boil; add potato slices. Return to a boil; boil 18 to 20 minutes or until tender. Drain. In ungreased 1 1/2-quart casserole, combine contents of seasoning mix envelope, mayonnaise, sour cream, parsley flakes and Italian dressing; blend well. Stir in cooked potato slices, green beans and pimiento; sprinkle with paprika. Bake at 350°F. for 15 to 20 minutes or until thoroughly heated; stir. Serve warm. **6 to 8 servings.**

TIP: An 8-ounce package frozen cut green beans in a pouch, cooked and drained, can be substituted for canned cut green beans.

NUTRIENTS PER 1/8 OF RECIPE

Calories	270	Protein	4% U.S. RDA
Protein	3g	Vitamin A	20% U.S. RDA
Carbohydrate	15g	Vitamin C	10% U.S. RDA
Fat	22g	Thiamine	2% U.S. RDA
Cholesterol	15mg	Riboflavin	4% U.S. RDA
Sodium	420mg	Niacin	4% U.S. RDA
Potassium	210mg	Calcium	4% U.S. RDA
Dietary Fiber	1g	Iron	6% U.S. RDA

Hurry-Up Hot Potato Salad

Shortly after this wonderful potato salad was a Bake-Off® recipe, an ingredient became obsolete. Today, almost twenty years later, Pillsbury's new scalloped potato mix makes it possible to serve this great-tasting recipe again.

Easy Vegetable Bulgur Salad

Easy Vegetable Bulgur Salad

Annette Erbeck, Ohio
Bake-Off® 33, 1988

1 cup bulgur wheat
2 cups boiling water
16-ounce package frozen broccoli, cauliflower and carrots
½ cup chopped fresh parsley
¼ cup sliced green onions
½ to 1 cup Italian dressing

In medium bowl, combine bulgur and boiling water. Let stand 1 hour. Drain well. To thaw vegetables, place in colander under cold running water for 6 minutes. Drain well.

In large bowl, combine softened bulgur, thawed vegetables, parsley, green onions and Italian dressing; blend well. Cover; refrigerate 1 to 2 hours to blend flavors. Store in refrigerator.

12 (½-cup) servings.

NUTRIENTS PER 1/12 OF RECIPE

Calories	160	Protein	2% U.S. RDA
Protein	2g	Vitamin A	25% U.S. RDA
Carbohydrate	15g	Vitamin C	30% U.S. RDA
Fat	10g	Thiamine	2% U.S. RDA
Cholesterol	0mg	Riboflavin	2% U.S. RDA
Sodium	170mg	Niacin	4% U.S. RDA
Potassium	135mg	Calcium	2% U.S. RDA
Dietary Fiber	3g	Iron	6% U.S. RDA

Santa Fe Corn and Cheese Bake

Alda Menoni, California
Bake-Off® 33, 1988

2 eggs, beaten
1 cup creamed cottage cheese
½ cup dairy sour cream
⅓ cup chopped green chiles, drained
3 tablespoons flour
3 tablespoons milk
2 to 3 teaspoons sugar
1 teaspoon onion salt
¼ to ½ teaspoon pepper
17-ounce can whole kernel corn, drained
3 tablespoons chopped ripe olives
1 ounce (¼ cup) shredded Cheddar cheese

Heat oven to 350°F. In large bowl, combine eggs and cottage cheese; blend well. Stir in sour cream and chiles. In small bowl, combine flour and milk; beat until smooth. Add to cottage cheese mixture. Stir in sugar, onion salt, pepper and corn; blend well. Pour into ungreased 8-inch (2-quart) square baking dish or 2-quart casserole.

Bake at 350°F. for 30 to 40 minutes or until knife inserted near center comes out clean. Sprinkle top with olives and Cheddar cheese. Bake an additional 1 to 2 minutes or until cheese is melted. **6 to 8 servings.**

NUTRIENTS PER 1/8 OF RECIPE

Calories	160	Protein	10% U.S. RDA
Protein	8g	Vitamin A	25% U.S. RDA
Carbohydrate	15g	Vitamin C	8% U.S. RDA
Fat	8g	Thiamine	2% U.S. RDA
Cholesterol	80mg	Riboflavin	10% U.S. RDA
Sodium	580mg	Niacin	2% U.S. RDA
Potassium	180mg	Calcium	8% U.S. RDA
Dietary Fiber	1g	Iron	4% U.S. RDA

Easy Cheesy Potato Bake

❧

Ruth Connelly, California
Bake-Off® 25, 1974

1 tablespoon margarine or butter
3 cups water
1 package au gratin potato mix
¼ teaspoon salt, if desired
1½ cups milk
⅛ teaspoon hot pepper sauce or cayenne pepper
3 eggs
½ cup finely chopped onion
8 ounces (2 cups) shredded Cheddar cheese

Heat oven to 350°F. Grease 10-inch deep-dish pie pan or 9-inch square pan with margarine. In medium saucepan, bring water to a boil; add potato slices. Return to a boil; boil 4 minutes. Drain. Arrange partially cooked potato slices over bottom and up sides of greased pan to form crust.

In medium bowl, combine contents of seasoning mix envelope, salt, milk, hot pepper sauce and eggs; stir until smooth. Stir in onion and cheese; pour into crust. Bake at 350°F. for 28 to 35 minutes or until center is set. Let stand 10 minutes before serving. To serve, cut into wedges or squares. **8 to 9 servings.**

NUTRIENTS PER 1/9 OF RECIPE

Calories	180	Protein	15% U.S. RDA
Protein	10g	Vitamin A	10% U.S. RDA
Carbohydrate	6g	Vitamin C	2% U.S. RDA
Fat	13g	Thiamine	2% U.S. RDA
Cholesterol	120mg	Riboflavin	10% U.S. RDA
Sodium	330mg	Niacin	<2% U.S. RDA
Potassium	150mg	Calcium	25% U.S. RDA
Dietary Fiber	1g	Iron	2% U.S. RDA

Hot 'n Spicy Sauteed Mushrooms

❧

Gladys Randall, Texas
Bake-Off® 33, 1988

½ cup margarine or butter
½ cup chopped green bell pepper
½ cup chopped red bell pepper
¼ cup sliced green onions
2 garlic cloves, minced
3 (6-ounce) jars sliced mushrooms, drained*
¼ cup sherry
½ teaspoon creole or cajun seasoning
¼ teaspoon cayenne pepper
¼ teaspoon pepper

In large skillet, melt margarine. Add peppers, green onions and garlic; cook over medium heat until crisp-tender. Stir in remaining ingredients. Simmer 2 to 3 minutes or until thoroughly heated, stirring occasionally. **6 (½-cup) servings.**

MICROWAVE DIRECTIONS: Place margarine in medium microwave-safe bowl. Microwave on HIGH for 45 to 60 seconds or until melted. Stir in peppers, green onions and garlic. Cover with microwave-safe plastic wrap. Microwave on HIGH for 2 to 3 minutes or until peppers are crisp-tender. Stir in remaining ingredients. Microwave on HIGH for 2 to 3 minutes or until thoroughly heated, stirring once halfway through cooking.

TIP: *Four 4.5-ounce jars sliced mushrooms, drained, can be substituted for three 6-ounce jars.

NUTRIENTS PER 1/6 OF RECIPE

Calories	170	Protein	4% U.S. RDA
Protein	3g	Vitamin A	35% U.S. RDA
Carbohydrate	6g	Vitamin C	50% U.S. RDA
Fat	15g	Thiamine	2% U.S. RDA
Cholesterol	0mg	Riboflavin	10% U.S. RDA
Sodium	455mg	Niacin	6% U.S. RDA
Potassium	190mg	Calcium	<2% U.S. RDA
Dietary Fiber	1g	Iron	6% U.S. RDA

Hot 'n Spicy Sauteed Mushrooms

❧

This spicy mushroom-vegetable side dish will add zest to any meal—try serving it on top of steaks or chops. It's sure to please your family or guests.

Microwave Vegetable Pie Supreme

Winnie Osborne, New York
Bake-Off® 33, 1988

2 tablespoons margarine or butter
1 cup coarsely chopped onions
¼ cup chopped green bell pepper
16-ounce package frozen broccoli, cauliflower and carrots
1 cup dry bread crumbs
2 tablespoons chopped fresh parsley
1 to 3 teaspoons basil leaves
½ teaspoon salt
¼ teaspoon pepper
4 ounces (1 cup) shredded Swiss cheese
¼ cup dairy sour cream
3 eggs, beaten

TOPPING
6 tomato slices
1 ounce (¼ cup) shredded Swiss cheese
Dairy sour cream, if desired

MICROWAVE DIRECTIONS: In 9 or 10-inch microwave-safe pie pan, combine margarine, onions and green pepper. Microwave on HIGH for 3 to 4 minutes or until onions and green pepper are crisp-tender, stirring once halfway through cooking.* Add frozen vegetables; cover with microwave-safe plastic wrap. Microwave on HIGH for 4 to 5 minutes or until frozen vegetables are thawed and separated, stirring once halfway through cooking. (Vegetables will feel cold.)

Meanwhile, reserve 1 tablespoon of the bread crumbs. In large bowl, combine remaining bread crumbs, parsley, basil, salt, pepper and 1 cup Swiss cheese; mix well. Stir in vegetable mixture, ¼ cup sour cream and eggs. Return mixture to pie pan; spread evenly. Arrange tomato slices over top of pie. Sprinkle with ¼ cup Swiss cheese and reserved 1 tablespoon bread crumbs.

Microwave on HIGH for 10 to 12 minutes or until knife inserted in center comes out clean, rotating pan ½ turn once halfway through cooking. Let stand on flat surface 5 minutes before serving. To serve, cut into wedges; top each serving with dollop of sour cream. **6 to 8 servings.**

TIP: *For compact microwave ovens under 600 watts, in 9 or 10-inch microwave-safe pie pan, combine margarine, onions and green pepper. Microwave on HIGH for 4 to 6 minutes or until onions and green pepper are crisp-tender, stirring once halfway through cooking. Add frozen vegetables; cover with microwave-safe plastic wrap. Microwave on HIGH for 5 to 6 minutes or until frozen vegetables are thawed and separated, stirring once halfway through cooking. (Vegetables will feel cold.) Continue ingredient preparation as directed above. Microwave on HIGH for 15 to 20 minutes or until knife inserted in center comes out clean, rotating pan ½ turn once halfway through cooking. Let stand on flat surface 5 minutes before serving.

NUTRIENTS PER 1/8 OF RECIPE

Calories	250	Protein	15% U.S. RDA
Protein	11g	Vitamin A	45% U.S. RDA
Carbohydrate	17g	Vitamin C	45% U.S. RDA
Fat	15g	Thiamine	8% U.S. RDA
Cholesterol	130mg	Riboflavin	15% U.S. RDA
Sodium	370mg	Niacin	4% U.S. RDA
Potassium	320mg	Calcium	25% U.S. RDA
Dietary Fiber	3g	Iron	10% U.S. RDA

Bake-Off® recipes lead food trends!

In 1980, just when many home cooks were beginning to experiment with zucchini, Millicent Caplan of Tamarac, Florida, won $40,000 for her recipe, Italian Zucchini Crescent Pie. Bake-Off® recipes continue to lead consumer food trends.

Broccoli Cauliflower Tetrazzini

Broccoli Cauliflower Tetrazzini

Barbara Van Itallie, New York
Bake-Off® 33, 1988

8 ounces uncooked spaghetti,
  broken into thirds
16-ounce package frozen broccoli,
  cauliflower and carrots
2 tablespoons margarine or butter
3 tablespoons flour
2 cups skim or lowfat milk
½ cup grated Parmesan cheese
  Dash pepper
4.5-ounce jar sliced mushrooms,
  drained
2 tablespoons grated Parmesan
  cheese

Cook spaghetti to desired doneness as directed on package. Drain; rinse with hot water. Keep warm; set aside. Cook vegetables until crisp-tender as directed on package. Drain; set aside.

Heat oven to 400°F. Grease 13 × 9-inch pan. In medium saucepan, melt margarine. Stir in flour until smooth. Gradually add milk; blend well. Cook over medium heat 6 to 10 minutes or until mixture thickens and boils, stirring constantly. Stir in ½ cup Parmesan cheese and pepper. Spoon cooked spaghetti into greased pan. Top with cooked vegetables and mushrooms. Pour milk mixture over mushrooms; sprinkle with 2 tablespoons Parmesan cheese. Bake at 400°F. for 15 to 20 minutes or until mixture is thoroughly heated and bubbles around edges.
8 servings.

NUTRIENTS PER 1/8 OF RECIPE

Calories	220	Protein	15% U.S. RDA
Protein	11g	Vitamin A	35% U.S. RDA
Carbohydrate	31g	Vitamin C	25% U.S. RDA
Fat	6g	Thiamine	20% U.S. RDA
Cholesterol	6mg	Riboflavin	20% U.S. RDA
Sodium	275mg	Niacin	10% U.S. RDA
Potassium	300mg	Calcium	20% U.S. RDA
Dietary Fiber	2g	Iron	8% U.S. RDA

Pictured top to bottom: Whole Wheat Raisin Loaf, page 68; Lemon Raspberry Muffins, page 81

Breads

◦৽৵

Breads of infinite variety have been part of the Bake-Off® repertoire since the beginning of the contest . . . Plump, golden-brown loaves of Whole Wheat Raisin Loaf, so crunchy on the outside, yet moist and tender within. Light and delicate Lemon Raspberry Muffins, fruity sweet and delicious. Dilly Casserole Bread, a Bake-Off® classic that's so easy to prepare.

At the first Bake-Off® Contest, breads were second only to cakes in popularity. The appeal of home-baked breads has continued over the years, with each decade offering its own unique inspirations. Traditional "from-scratch" yeast bread recipes have made way for no-knead varieties like Easy Cheese Batter Bread. Modern-day contestants streamline and simplify hand-me-down family recipes with hot roll mix, quick bread mixes and refrigerated fresh dough products. From the Old World come Italian Cheese Bread Ring and Polish Poppy Swirl Loaf, recipes that have been adapted for quick preparation by busy cooks.

What takes many of these recipes out of the ordinary is their distinctive flavoring, such as sesame seed, cheeses, garlic, and dry mustard. Anise and fennel seed and orange peel are unique seasonings that add a whiff of savory magic to Swedish Whole Wheat Dinner Rolls. And the growing ranks of health-conscious bakers have introduced a host of wholesome ingredients including bran, wheat germ and rolled oats as well as vegetables, like the shredded carrots featured in Golden Party Loaves.

This collection offers a glorious bounty of flavors, textures and shapes from the Bake-Off® bread basket. It's proof positive of America's ongoing love affair with home-baked breads.

Dilly Casserole Bread

Easy preparation and innovative flavor gave this soft-textured bread its winning qualities. For even easier preparation of this Bake-Off® classic recipe, food processor directions are now included.

Whole Wheat Raisin Loaf

Lenora Smith, Louisiana
Bake-Off® 27, 1976

3 to 3³/₄ cups all purpose or unbleached flour*
¹/₂ cup sugar
3 teaspoons salt
1 teaspoon cinnamon
¹/₂ teaspoon nutmeg
2 packages active dry yeast
2 cups milk
³/₄ cup water
¹/₄ cup oil
4 cups whole wheat flour
1 cup rolled oats
1 cup raisins
Oil or melted margarine, if desired
Sugar, if desired

Lightly spoon flour into measuring cup; level off. In large bowl, combine 1¹/₂ cups all purpose flour, ¹/₂ cup sugar, salt, cinnamon, nutmeg and yeast; blend well. In small saucepan, heat milk, water and ¹/₄ cup oil until very warm (120 to 130°F.). Add warm liquid to flour mixture. Blend at low speed until moistened; beat 3 minutes at medium speed. By hand, stir in whole wheat flour, rolled oats, raisins and 1 to 1¹/₂ cups all purpose flour until dough pulls cleanly away from sides of bowl.

On floured surface, knead in remaining ¹/₂ to ³/₄ cup all purpose flour until dough is smooth and elastic, about 5 minutes. Place dough in greased bowl; cover loosely with plastic wrap and cloth towel. Let rise in warm place (80 to 85°F.) until light and doubled in size, 20 to 30 minutes.

Grease two 9×5 or 8×4-inch loaf pans. Punch down dough several times to remove all air bubbles. Divide dough in half. Shape each half into a loaf. Place loaves in greased pans; brush tops with oil or margarine. Cover; let rise in warm place until light and doubled in size, 30 to 45 minutes.

Heat oven to 375°F. Uncover dough. Bake 40 to 50 minutes or until deep golden brown and loaves sound hollow when lightly tapped. If loaves become too brown, cover loosely with foil last 10 minutes of baking time. Remove from pans immediately; cool on wire racks. Brush top of warm loaves with oil or margarine; sprinkle with sugar. **2 (16-slice) loaves.**

TIP: *Bread flour can be substituted for all purpose or unbleached flour. Increase kneading time to 10 minutes and allow dough to rest 15 minutes before shaping.

HIGH ALTITUDE—Above 3500 Feet: No change.

NUTRIENTS PER 1 SLICE

Calories	170	Protein	6% U.S. RDA
Protein	5g	Vitamin A	<2% U.S. RDA
Carbohydrate	32g	Vitamin C	<2% U.S. RDA
Fat	3g	Thiamine	15% U.S. RDA
Cholesterol	0mg	Riboflavin	8% U.S. RDA
Sodium	210mg	Niacin	8% U.S. RDA
Potassium	150mg	Calcium	2% U.S. RDA
Dietary Fiber	3g	Iron	8% U.S. RDA

Dilly Casserole Bread

Leona P. Schnuelle, Nebraska
Bake-Off® 12, 1960

2 to 2²/₃ cups all purpose or unbleached flour
2 tablespoons sugar
2 to 3 teaspoons instant minced onion
2 teaspoons dill seed
1 teaspoon salt
¹/₄ teaspoon baking soda
1 package active dry yeast
¹/₄ cup water
1 tablespoon margarine or butter
8-ounce carton (1 cup) creamed cottage cheese
1 egg
Margarine or butter, melted
Coarse salt, if desired

Lightly spoon flour into measuring cup; level off. In large bowl, combine 1 cup flour, sugar, instant minced onion, dill seed, 1 teaspoon salt, baking soda and yeast; blend well. In small saucepan, heat water, 1 tablespoon margarine and cottage cheese until very warm (120 to 130°F.). Add warm liquid and egg to

Dilly Casserole Bread

flour mixture. Blend at low speed until moistened; beat 3 minutes at medium speed. By hand, stir in remaining 1 to 1²/₃ cups flour to form a stiff batter. Cover loosely with plastic wrap and cloth towel. Let rise in warm place (80 to 85°F.) until light and doubled in size, 45 to 60 minutes.

Generously grease 1¹/₂ or 2-quart casserole. Stir down dough to remove all air bubbles. Turn into greased casserole. Cover; let rise in warm place until light and doubled in size, 30 to 45 minutes.

Heat oven to 350°F. Uncover dough. Bake 30 to 40 minutes or until deep golden brown and loaf sounds hollow when lightly tapped. Remove from casserole immediately; cool on wire rack. Brush warm loaf with melted margarine; sprinkle with coarse salt.
1 (18-slice) loaf.

FOOD PROCESSOR DIRECTIONS: In small bowl, soften yeast in ¹/₄ cup warm water (105 to 115°F.). In food processor bowl with metal blade, combine *2 cups* flour, sugar, instant minced onion, dill seed, 1 teaspoon salt, baking soda and 1 tablespoon margarine. Cover; process 5 seconds. Add cottage cheese and egg. Cover; process about 10 seconds or until blended. With machine running, pour yeast mixture through feed tube. Continue processing until blended, about 20 seconds or until mixture pulls away from sides of bowl and forms a ball, adding additional flour if necessary. Carefully scrape dough from blade and bowl; place in lightly greased bowl. Cover loosely with plastic wrap and cloth towel. Let rise in warm place (80 to 85°F.) until light and doubled in size, 45 to 60 minutes. Continue as directed above.

HIGH ALTITUDE—Above 3500 Feet: Bake at 375°F. for 35 to 40 minutes.

NUTRIENTS PER 1 SLICE

Calories	90	Protein	6% U.S. RDA
Protein	4g	Vitamin A	<2% U.S. RDA
Carbohydrate	15g	Vitamin C	<2% U.S. RDA
Fat	2g	Thiamine	8% U.S. RDA
Cholesterol	15mg	Riboflavin	6% U.S. RDA
Sodium	240mg	Niacin	4% U.S. RDA
Potassium	40mg	Calcium	<2% U.S. RDA
Dietary Fiber	<1g	Iron	4% U.S. RDA

Golden Party Loaves

Golden Party Loaves

Effie Cato, Texas
Bake-Off® 31, 1984

4¹/₂ to 5¹/₂ cups bread flour*
1¹/₂ cups finely shredded carrots
1 teaspoon salt
1 package active dry yeast
³/₄ cup apricot nectar
¹/₂ cup plain yogurt
¹/₄ cup honey
¹/₄ cup margarine or butter
1 egg
Margarine or butter, softened

SPREAD
8-ounce package cream cheese, softened
¹/₂ cup apricot preserves

Lightly spoon flour into measuring cup; level off. In large bowl, combine 2 cups flour, carrots, salt and yeast; blend well. In small saucepan, heat apricot nectar, yogurt, honey and ¹/₄ cup margarine until very warm (120 to 130°F.). Add warm liquid and egg to flour mixture. Blend at low speed until moistened; beat 3 minutes at medium speed. By hand, stir in 2 to 2¹/₂ cups flour to form a stiff dough. On floured surface, knead in remaining ¹/₂ to 1 cup flour until dough is smooth and elastic, about 10 minutes. Place dough in greased bowl; cover loosely with plastic wrap and cloth towel. Let rise in warm place (80 to 85°F.) until light and doubled in size, about 1¹/₄ hours.

Grease and flour two 9×5 or 8×4-inch loaf pans. Punch down dough several times to remove all air bubbles. Divide dough in half. Allow to rest on counter, covered with inverted bowl, for 15 minutes. Work dough with hands to remove large air bubbles. Divide each half into thirds. Shape each third into a small loaf. Spread sides of loaves with softened margarine. Place 3 loaves crosswise in greased and floured pan. Repeat with remaining dough. Cover; let rise in warm place until light and doubled in size, about 1 hour.

Heat oven to 375°F. Uncover dough. Bake 30 to 35 minutes or until deep golden brown and loaves sound hollow when lightly tapped. Remove from pans immediately; cool on wire racks. Brush warm loaves with softened margarine. In small bowl, combine spread ingredients; mix well. Serve with bread. 6 (7-slice) loaves.

TIP: *All purpose or unbleached flour can be substituted for bread flour. Decrease kneading time to 5 minutes, omit resting period and decrease each rise time 15 minutes.

HIGH ALTITUDE—Above 3500 Feet: No change.

NUTRIENTS PER 1 SLICE

Calories	120	Protein	4% U.S. RDA
Protein	3g	Vitamin A	25% U.S. RDA
Carbohydrate	18g	Vitamin C	2% U.S. RDA
Fat	4g	Thiamine	8% U.S. RDA
Cholesterol	10mg	Riboflavin	6% U.S. RDA
Sodium	90mg	Niacin	4% U.S. RDA
Potassium	55mg	Calcium	<2% U.S. RDA
Dietary Fiber	<1g	Iron	4% U.S. RDA

Golden Party Loaves

Six wholesome mini-loaves are baked in two loaf pans and served with a tangy apricot spread.

Onion Lover's Twist

Grand Prize Winner

Onion Lover's Twist

-ᴥ-

Nan Robb, Arizona
Bake-Off® 21, 1970

3¹/₂ to 4¹/₂ cups all purpose or unbleached flour*
¹/₄ cup sugar
1¹/₂ teaspoons salt
1 package active dry yeast
³/₄ cup water
¹/₂ cup milk
¹/₄ cup margarine or butter
1 egg

FILLING
¹/₄ cup margarine or butter
1 cup finely chopped onions or ¹/₄ cup instant minced onion
1 tablespoon grated Parmesan cheese
1 tablespoon sesame or poppy seed
¹/₂ to 1 teaspoon garlic salt
1 teaspoon paprika

Lightly spoon flour into measuring cup; level off. In large bowl, combine 2 cups flour, sugar, salt and yeast; blend well. In small saucepan, heat water, milk and ¹/₄ cup margarine until very warm (120 to 130°F.). Add warm liquid and egg to flour mixture. Blend at low speed until moistened; beat 3 minutes at medium speed. By hand, stir in remaining 1¹/₂ to 2¹/₂ cups flour to form a soft dough. Cover loosely with plastic wrap and cloth towel. Let rise in warm place (80 to 85°F.) until light and doubled in size, 45 to 60 minutes.

In small saucepan, melt ¹/₄ cup margarine; stir in remaining filling ingredients. Set aside.

Grease large cookie sheet. Stir down dough to remove all air bubbles. On floured surface, toss dough until no longer sticky. Roll dough to 18 × 12-inch rectangle; spread with filling mixture. Cut rectangle in half crosswise to make two 9 × 12-inch rectangles. Cut each rectangle lengthwise into three 9 × 4-inch strips. Starting with 9-inch side, roll up each strip; pinch edges and ends to seal. On greased cookie sheet, braid 3 rolls together; pinch ends to seal. Repeat with remaining 3 rolls for second loaf. Cover; let rise in warm

place until light and doubled in size, 25 to 30 minutes.

Heat oven to 350°F. Uncover dough. Bake 27 to 35 minutes or until golden brown and loaves sound hollow when lightly tapped. Remove from cookie sheet immediately; cool on wire racks. **2 (16-slice) loaves.**

TIP: *Bread flour can be substituted for all purpose or unbleached flour. Allow dough to rest 15 minutes before shaping.

HIGH ALTITUDE—Above 3500 Feet: No change.

NUTRIENTS PER 1 SLICE

Calories	100	Protein	4% U.S. RDA
Protein	2g	Vitamin A	2% U.S. RDA
Carbohydrate	16g	Vitamin C	<2% U.S. RDA
Fat	3g	Thiamine	8% U.S. RDA
Cholesterol	8mg	Riboflavin	6% U.S. RDA
Sodium	200mg	Niacin	4% U.S. RDA
Potassium	40mg	Calcium	<2% U.S. RDA
Dietary Fiber	<1g	Iron	4% U.S. RDA

Cheesy Garlic Hot Roll Braid

-ᴥ-

Gloria Bradfield, Kansas
Bake-Off® 20, 1969

1 package hot roll mix
³/₄ cup water heated to 120 to 130°F.
¹/₂ cup dairy sour cream
1 egg, separated, reserving white for topping

FILLING
¹/₃ cup Parmesan cheese
1 tablespoon instant minced onion
¹/₂ to ³/₄ teaspoon garlic powder
¹/₂ teaspoon Italian seasoning
¹/₄ teaspoon paprika
2 tablespoons margarine or butter, softened

TOPPING
Reserved egg white
1 tablespoon water
1 tablespoon sesame seed

Grease large cookie sheet. In large bowl, combine flour mixture with yeast from foil packet; blend well. Stir in ³/₄ cup *hot* water, sour cream and egg yolk until dough pulls cleanly away from sides of bowl. Turn dough out

Cheesy Garlic Hot Roll Braid

onto lightly floured surface. With greased or floured hands, shape dough into a ball. Knead dough for 5 minutes until smooth. Cover with large bowl; let rest 5 minutes. In small bowl, combine all filling ingredients except margarine; mix well. Set aside.

On floured surface, roll dough to 13 × 11-inch rectangle. Spread with margarine; sprinkle evenly with filling mixture. Fold 13-inch sides to center, overlapping 1 inch. Press center seam and edges to seal. Place seam side up on greased cookie sheet. Make cuts 1 inch apart on longest sides of rectangle to within 1 inch of center. (Do not cut through center.) To give braided appearance, fold strips of dough at an angle halfway across filling, alternating from side to side. Pinch ends to seal. In small bowl, beat reserved egg white and 1 tablespoon water. Brush top of loaf

with egg white mixture. Sprinkle with sesame seed. Cover loosely with plastic wrap and cloth towel. Let rise in warm place (80 to 85°F.) until almost doubled in size, 25 to 30 minutes.

Heat oven to 375°F. Uncover dough. Bake 20 to 30 minutes or until deep golden brown. Remove from cookie sheet immediately; cool on wire rack. **1 (18-slice) loaf.**

TIP: Cover braid with foil during last 5 to 10 minutes of baking if necessary to prevent excessive browning.

HIGH ALTITUDE — Above 3500 Feet: No change.

NUTRIENTS PER 1 SLICE

Calories	130	Protein	6% U.S. RDA
Protein	4g	Vitamin A	2% U.S. RDA
Carbohydrate	19g	Vitamin C	<2% U.S. RDA
Fat	4g	Thiamine	10% U.S. RDA
Cholesterol	20mg	Riboflavin	10% U.S. RDA
Sodium	230mg	Niacin	8% U.S. RDA
Potassium	60mg	Calcium	4% U.S. RDA
Dietary Fiber	<1g	Iron	6% U.S. RDA

Swedish Whole Wheat Dinner Rolls

Swedish Whole Wheat Dinner Rolls

‍ ‍ ‍

Patty Entringer, Minnesota
Bake-Off® 32, 1986

1 cup whole wheat flour
¹/₂ cup mashed potato flakes
2 tablespoons brown sugar
2 teaspoons salt
1 teaspoon anise seed, crushed
1 teaspoon fennel seed, crushed
1¹/₂ teaspoons grated orange peel
1 package fast-acting dry yeast
1¹/₃ cups water
¹/₄ cup margarine or butter
1 tablespoon instant coffee granules or crystals
2 tablespoons molasses
1 teaspoon orange extract, if desired
1 egg
2¹/₂ to 3¹/₂ cups bread flour
1 tablespoon margarine or butter, softened
¹/₂ teaspoon grated orange peel, if desired

Grease two 8 or 9-inch round cake pans. Lightly spoon flour into measuring cup; level off. In large bowl, combine whole wheat flour, potato flakes, brown sugar, salt, anise seed, fennel seed, 1¹/₂ teaspoons orange peel and yeast; blend well. In small saucepan, heat water, ¹/₄ cup margarine, instant coffee, molasses and orange extract until very warm (120 to 130°F.). Add warm liquid and egg to flour mixture. Blend at low speed until moistened; beat 3 minutes at medium speed. Stir in 2 to 2¹/₂ cups bread flour until dough pulls cleanly away from sides of bowl.

On floured surface, knead in remaining ¹/₂ to 1 cup bread flour until dough is smooth and elastic, about 10 minutes. Allow to rest on counter covered with inverted bowl for 10 minutes. Divide dough in half. Divide each half into 8 equal pieces; shape into balls. Place 8 balls in each greased pan. Cover loosely with plastic wrap and cloth towel. Let rise in warm place (80 to 85°F.) until light and doubled in size, about 1 hour.

Heat oven to 375°F. Uncover dough. Bake 20 to 25 minutes or until golden brown and rolls sound hollow when lightly tapped. Remove from pans immediately; cool on wire racks. Brush warm rolls with 1 tablespoon margarine; sprinkle with ¹/₂ teaspoon orange peel. **16 rolls.**

HIGH ALTITUDE—Above 3500 Feet: No change.

NUTRIENTS PER 1 ROLL

Calories	190	Protein	8% U.S. RDA
Protein	5g	Vitamin A	2% U.S. RDA
Carbohydrate	33g	Vitamin C	<2% U.S. RDA
Fat	4g	Thiamine	15% U.S. RDA
Cholesterol	15mg	Riboflavin	10% U.S. RDA
Sodium	320mg	Niacin	10% U.S. RDA
Potassium	140mg	Calcium	2% U.S. RDA
Dietary Fiber	2g	Iron	10% U.S. RDA

Easy Cheese Batter Bread

Frances Sisinni, Wisconsin
Bake-Off® 23, 1972

2½ cups all purpose or unbleached flour
2 teaspoons sugar
1½ teaspoons salt
1 package active dry yeast
4 ounces (1 cup) shredded Cheddar cheese
¾ cup milk
½ cup margarine or butter
3 eggs

Lightly spoon flour into measuring cup; level off. In large bowl, combine 1½ cups flour, sugar, salt and yeast; blend well. Stir in cheese. In small saucepan, heat milk and margarine until very warm (120 to 130°F.). Add warm liquid and eggs to flour mixture. Blend at low speed until moistened; beat 3 minutes at medium speed. By hand, stir in remaining 1 cup flour. Cover loosely with plastic wrap and cloth towel. Let rise in warm place (80 to 85°F.) until light and doubled in size, 45 to 60 minutes.

Generously grease 1½ or 2-quart casserole or 9 × 5-inch loaf pan. Stir down dough to remove all air bubbles. Turn into greased casserole. Cover; let rise in warm place until light and doubled in size, 20 to 25 minutes.

Heat oven to 350°F. Uncover dough. Bake 40 to 45 minutes or until deep golden brown. Remove from casserole immediately; cool on wire rack.
1 (18-slice) loaf.

HIGH ALTITUDE—Above 3500 Feet: Bake at 375°F. for 40 to 45 minutes.

NUTRIENTS PER 1 SLICE

Calories	150	Protein	8% U.S. RDA
Protein	5g	Vitamin A	6% U.S. RDA
Carbohydrate	15g	Vitamin C	<2% U.S. RDA
Fat	8g	Thiamine	8% U.S. RDA
Cholesterol	50g	Riboflavin	8% U.S. RDA
Sodium	290mg	Niacin	4% U.S. RDA
Potassium	60mg	Calcium	6% U.S. RDA
Dietary Fiber	<1mg	Iron	6% U.S. RDA

Graham Cracker Brown Bread

Grace M. Kain, Maine
Bake-Off® 10, 1958

2 cups (30 squares) finely crushed graham crackers or graham cracker crumbs
½ cup shortening
1¾ cups buttermilk*
¾ cup molasses
2 eggs, slightly beaten
1¾ cups all purpose or unbleached flour
2 teaspoons baking soda
1 teaspoon salt
¼ to ½ teaspoon nutmeg
1 cup raisins

Heat oven to 375°F. Grease and flour bottoms only of two 8×4-inch loaf pans. In large bowl, beat graham cracker crumbs and shortening until well blended. Add buttermilk, molasses and eggs; blend well. Lightly spoon flour into measuring cup; level off. In small bowl, combine flour, baking soda, salt and nutmeg; mix well. Add to graham cracker mixture; mix at low speed until well blended. Fold in raisins. Pour batter into greased and floured pans. Bake at 375°F. for 35 to 40 minutes or until toothpick inserted in center comes out clean. Cool 5 minutes; remove from pans. Cool on wire racks.
2 (16-slice) loaves.

TIP: *To substitute for buttermilk, use 1 tablespoon plus 2 teaspoons vinegar or lemon juice plus milk to make 1¾ cups.

HIGH ALTITUDE—Above 3500 Feet: Increase flour to 2¼ cups.

NUTRIENTS PER 1 SLICE

Calories	120	Protein	2% U.S. RDA
Protein	2g	Vitamin A	<2% U.S. RDA
Carbohydrate	18g	Vitamin C	<2% U.S. RDA
Fat	4g	Thiamine	4% U.S. RDA
Cholesterol	20mg	Riboflavin	6% U.S. RDA
Sodium	190mg	Niacin	2% U.S. RDA
Potassium	170mg	Calcium	4% U.S. RDA
Dietary Fiber	<1g	Iron	6% U.S. RDA

Easy Cheese Batter Bread

This moist, chewy casserole bread is even better the second day after baking.

Graham Cracker Brown Bread

Moist and flavorful, this quick bread tastes great spread with cream cheese or served with sausage and baked beans.

Easy English Muffins

Easy English Muffins

Julia Hauber, Kansas
Bake-Off® 19, 1968

2 packages active dry yeast
2 cups warm water
5 to 6 cups all purpose or
　unbleached flour
1 tablespoon sugar
3 teaspoons salt
1/2 cup shortening
　Cornmeal
　Margarine or butter

In large bowl, dissolve yeast in warm water (105 to 115°F.). Lightly spoon flour into measuring cup; level off. Add 3 cups flour, sugar, salt and shortening to yeast mixture, stirring by hand until moistened. Stir vigorously by hand until smooth. Gradually add remaining 2 to 3 cups flour to form a stiff dough, beating well after each addition. On floured surface, gently knead dough 5 to 6 times until no longer sticky. Roll dough to 1/4 to 3/8-inch thickness; cut with 3 to 4-inch floured round cutter. Sprinkle cornmeal evenly over 2 ungreased cookie sheets. Place cutout dough on cornmeal; sprinkle with additional cornmeal. Cover loosely with plastic wrap and cloth towel. Let rise in warm place until light, 30 to 45 minutes.

Heat griddle to 350°F. With wide spatula, invert dough rounds onto ungreased griddle. Bake 5 to 6 minutes on each side or until light golden brown; cool. Split, toast and butter. **18 to 26 muffins.**

HIGH ALTITUDE—Above 3500 Feet: No change.

NUTRIENTS PER 1 MUFFIN

Calories	250	Protein	4% U.S. RDA
Protein	3g	Vitamin A	8% U.S. RDA
Carbohydrate	24g	Vitamin C	<2% U.S. RDA
Fat	16g	Thiamine	10% U.S. RDA
Cholesterol	0mg	Riboflavin	8% U.S. RDA
Sodium	380mg	Niacin	8% U.S. RDA
Potassium	45mg	Calcium	<2% U.S. RDA
Dietary Fiber	<1g	Iron	8% U.S. RDA

Potato Chive Rolls

Susan H. Cox, Pennsylvania
Bake-Off® 27, 1976

4 1/2 to 5 cups all purpose or
　unbleached flour
1 cup mashed potato flakes
1 tablespoon sugar
3 to 4 teaspoons fresh chopped
　chives or dried chives
2 teaspoons salt
2 packages active dry yeast
2 cups milk
1/2 cup dairy sour cream
2 eggs

Lightly spoon flour into measuring cup; level off. In large bowl, combine 1 1/2 cups flour, potato flakes, sugar, chives, salt and yeast; blend well. In small saucepan, heat milk and sour cream until very warm (120 to 130°F.). Add warm liquid and eggs to flour mixture. Blend at low speed until moistened; beat 3 minutes at medium speed. By hand, stir in remaining 3 to 3 1/2 cups flour to form a stiff dough. Cover loosely with plastic wrap and cloth towel. Let rise in warm place (80 to 85°F.) until light and doubled in size, 45 to 55 minutes.

Generously grease 13 × 9-inch pan. On well-floured surface, toss dough until no longer sticky. Divide dough into 24 equal pieces; shape into balls. Place in greased pan. Cover; let rise in warm place until light and doubled in size, 30 to 35 minutes.

Heat oven to 375°F. Uncover dough. Bake 25 to 35 minutes or until golden brown. Remove from pan immediately; cool on wire rack. If desired, lightly dust tops of rolls with flour. **24 rolls.**

HIGH ALTITUDE—Above 3500 Feet: No change.

NUTRIENTS PER 1 ROLL

Calories	130	Protein	6% U.S. RDA
Protein	4g	Vitamin A	2% U.S. RDA
Carbohydrate	24g	Vitamin C	<2% U.S. RDA
Fat	2g	Thiamine	10% U.S. RDA
Cholesterol	25mg	Riboflavin	10% U.S. RDA
Sodium	200mg	Niacin	8% U.S. RDA
Potassium	115mg	Calcium	4% U.S. RDA
Dietary Fiber	1g	Iron	8% U.S. RDA

Potato Chive Rolls

Mildly flavored with sour cream and chives, these light and airy pull-apart rolls are an excellent addition to any dinner.

Golden Sesame Loaves

Golden Sesame Loaves

—◦҈◦—

Grayce Berggren, Pennsylvania
Bake-Off® 33, 1988

5 to 6 cups bread flour*
¹⁄₂ cup instant nonfat dry milk
¹⁄₂ cup oat bran
¹⁄₂ cup sesame seed, toasted**
1¹⁄₂ teaspoons salt
1 teaspoon sugar
2 packages active dry yeast
1³⁄₄ cups water
¹⁄₄ cup oil
¹⁄₄ cup honey
1 egg
1 egg white, beaten
1 tablespoon sesame seed

Lightly spoon flour into measuring cup; level off. In large bowl, combine 2 cups flour, instant nonfat dry milk, oat bran, ¹⁄₂ cup toasted sesame seed, salt, sugar and yeast; blend well. In small saucepan, heat water, oil and honey until very warm (120 to 130°F.). Add warm liquid and 1 egg to flour mixture. Blend at low speed until moistened; beat 3 minutes at medium speed. By hand, stir in 2³⁄₄ to 3¹⁄₂ cups flour until dough pulls cleanly away from sides of bowl.

On floured surface, knead in remaining ¹⁄₄ to ¹⁄₂ cup flour until dough is smooth and elastic, about 10 minutes. Place dough in greased bowl; cover loosely with plastic wrap and cloth towel. Let rise in warm place (80 to 85°F.) until light and doubled in size, about 1 hour.

Grease two 9 × 5 or three 7 × 3-inch loaf pans. Punch down dough several times to remove all air bubbles. Divide dough in half; shape into balls. Allow to rest on counter covered with inverted bowl for 15 minutes. Shape into 2 loaves by rolling each half into 12 × 8-inch rectangle. Starting with 8-inch side, roll up; pinch edges firmly to seal. Place seam side down in greased pans. Cover; let rise in warm place until dough fills pans and tops of loaves are about 1 inch above pan edges, about 45 minutes.

Heat oven to 350°F. Uncover dough. Carefully brush tops of loaves with beaten egg white. Sprinkle with 1 tablespoon sesame seed. Bake at 350°F. for 30 to 40 minutes or until loaves sound hollow when lightly tapped. Remove from pans immediately; cool on wire racks. **2 (16-slice) loaves.**

TIPS: *All purpose or unbleached flour can be substituted for bread flour. Self-rising flour is not recommended. Omit resting period and decrease each rise time by 10 to 15 minutes.

**To toast sesame seed, spread on cookie sheet; bake at 375°F. for about 5 minutes or until light golden brown, stirring occasionally. Or, spread in medium skillet; stir over medium heat for about 10 minutes or until light golden brown.

HIGH ALTITUDE—Above 3500 Feet: Decrease each rise time by about 15 minutes. Bake at 350°F. for 25 to 35 minutes.

NUTRIENTS PER 1 SLICE

Calories	140	Protein	6% U.S. RDA
Protein	5g	Vitamin A	<2% U.S. RDA
Carbohydrate	24g	Vitamin C	<2% U.S. RDA
Fat	3g	Thiamine	15% U.S. RDA
Cholesterol	8mg	Riboflavin	10% U.S. RDA
Sodium	115mg	Niacin	8% U.S. RDA
Potassium	80mg	Calcium	2% U.S. RDA
Dietary Fiber	1g	Iron	8% U.S. RDA

Cheese 'n Onion Sandwich Buns

Mariette A. Deutsch, Wisconsin
Bake-Off® 24, 1973

- 1 package hot roll mix
- 2 tablespoons dry onion soup mix
- ½ teaspoon dry mustard
- 4 ounces (1 cup) shredded Cheddar or American cheese
- 1 cup water heated to 120° to 130°F.
- 2 tablespoons margarine or butter, softened
- 1 egg

Grease cookie sheets. In large bowl, combine flour mixture with yeast from foil packet. Add soup mix, dry mustard and cheese; blend well. Stir in *hot* water, margarine and egg until dough pulls cleanly away from sides of bowl. Turn dough out onto lightly floured surface. With greased or floured hands, shape dough into a ball. Knead dough for 5 minutes until smooth. Cover with large bowl; let rest 5 minutes.

Divide dough into 8 equal pieces; shape into balls. Place on greased cookie sheets; flatten each ball slightly. Cover loosely with plastic wrap and cloth towel. Let rise in warm place (80 to 85°F.) until almost doubled in size, about 30 minutes.

Heat oven to 375°F. Uncover dough. Bake 12 to 17 minutes or until golden brown. Remove from cookie sheets immediately; cool on wire racks. **8 rolls.**

HIGH ALTITUDE—Above 3500 Feet: No change.

NUTRIENTS PER 1 ROLL

Calories	300	Protein	15% U.S. RDA
Protein	11g	Vitamin A	6% U.S. RDA
Carbohydrate	43g	Vitamin C	<2% U.S. RDA
Fat	9g	Thiamine	25% U.S. RDA
Cholesterol	50mg	Riboflavin	25% U.S. RDA
Sodium	740mg	Niacin	20% U.S. RDA
Potassium	120mg	Calcium	10% U.S. RDA
Dietary Fiber	1g	Iron	10% U.S. RDA

Golden Sesame Loaves

The sesame seed in the bread creates a delicious nutty flavor. You'll love this bread toasted!

Old Plantation Rolls

❧

First Lady Eleanor Roosevelt launched the Bake-Off® Contest when this recipe won recognition. Forty years later it continues to be a natural for today's busy cooks. The no-knead dough bakes into warm, tender rolls—or, if desired, refrigerate the dough overnight for fresh baked rolls the next day.

Old Plantation Rolls

❧

Lucile Baker, Colorado
Bake-Off® 1, 1949

5 to 6 cups all purpose or
   unbleached flour
¼ cup sugar
1 teaspoon baking powder
1 teaspoon salt
½ teaspoon baking soda
1 package active dry yeast
1 cup water
1 cup milk
½ cup shortening
1 egg

Grease 24 muffin cups. Lightly spoon flour into measuring cup; level off. In large bowl, combine 3 cups flour, sugar, baking powder, salt, baking soda and yeast; blend well. In small saucepan, heat water, milk and shortening until very warm (120 to 130°F.). Add warm liquid and egg to flour mixture. Blend at low speed until moistened; beat 3 minutes at medium speed. By hand, stir in remaining 2 to 3 cups flour to form a stiff dough. Cover loosely with greased plastic wrap and cloth towel. Let rise in warm place (80 to 85°F.) until light and doubled in size, about 1 hour.

Punch down dough several times to remove all air bubbles.* On well-floured surface, toss dough until no longer sticky. Divide dough into 24 equal pieces; shape into balls.** Place 1 ball in each greased muffin cup. With scissors or sharp knife, make X-shaped cut in each ball, forming 4 equal pieces. Cover; let rise in warm place until light and doubled in size, 35 to 45 minutes.

Heat oven to 400°F. Uncover dough. Bake 13 to 15 minutes or until golden brown. Remove from pans immediately. **24 rolls.**

TIPS: *Rolls can be prepared to this point, covered and refrigerated overnight. Increase second rise time to 1¼ hours.

**For a more traditional cloverleaf shape, divide dough into 72 pieces; shape into balls. Place 3 balls in each greased muffin cup. Cover; let rise in warm place until light and doubled in size, 35 to 45 minutes. Bake as directed above.

HIGH ALTITUDE—Above 3500 Feet: No change.

NUTRIENTS PER 1 ROLL

Calories	160	Protein	6% U.S. RDA
Protein	4g	Vitamin A	<2% U.S. RDA
Carbohydrate	25g	Vitamin C	<2% U.S. RDA
Fat	5g	Thiamine	10% U.S. RDA
Cholesterol	10mg	Riboflavin	8% U.S. RDA
Sodium	135mg	Niacin	8% U.S. RDA
Potassium	50mg	Calcium	2% U.S. RDA
Dietary Fiber	<1g	Iron	8% U.S. RDA

The Giant's Corn Muffins

❧

Irene McEwen, Indiana
Bake-Off® 33, 1988

MUFFINS
½ cup all purpose, unbleached or
   self-rising flour*
½ cup whole wheat flour
1 cup cornmeal
1 teaspoon baking powder
1 teaspoon baking soda
½ teaspoon salt
¼ teaspoon nutmeg
1 cup plain yogurt or buttermilk
¼ cup margarine or butter, melted
3 tablespoons honey
1 egg
12-ounce can vacuum packed
   whole kernel corn with sweet
   peppers, drained
1 green onion, sliced

TOPPING
1 tablespoon all purpose,
   unbleached or self-rising flour
1 tablespoon cornmeal
   Dash salt
4 teaspoons margarine or butter

Heat oven to 400°F. Grease bottoms only of six 6-oz. custard cups or 12 muffin cups.** Lightly spoon flour into measuring cup; level off. In large bowl, combine ½ cup all purpose flour, whole wheat flour, 1 cup cornmeal, baking powder, baking soda, ½ teaspoon salt and nutmeg; blend well. In medium bowl, combine yogurt, ¼ cup margarine, honey, egg, corn and green onion; mix well. Add to dry ingredients; stir until dry ingredients are just moistened. Spoon batter evenly into greased custard cups. (Cups will be full.) In small bowl, combine all topping ingredients, mix well. Crumble evenly over batter in each cup. Bake at 400°F. for 20 to 30 minutes or until toothpick inserted in center comes out clean. Cool 1 minute; remove from custard cups. **6 large or 12 regular sized muffins.**

TIPS: *If using self-rising flour, omit baking powder, baking soda and salt.

**For easier handling, place custard cups on cookie sheet.

HIGH ALTITUDE—Above 3500 Feet: No change.

NUTRIENTS PER 1 LARGE MUFFIN

Calories	380	Protein	15% U.S. RDA
Protein	9g	Vitamin A	20% U.S. RDA
Carbohydrate	56g	Vitamin C	6% U.S. RDA
Fat	13g	Thiamine	15% U.S. RDA
Cholesterol	50mg	Riboflavin	15% U.S. RDA
Sodium	760mg	Niacin	10% U.S. RDA
Potassium	320mg	Calcium	10% U.S. RDA
Dietary Fiber	2g	Iron	10% U.S. RDA

Dairyland Date Muffins

Phyllis Saevre, Wisconsin
Bake-Off® 20, 1969

1 cup shreds of whole bran cereal
½ cup milk
2 (3-ounce) packages cream cheese
1 cup dairy sour cream
1 package date bread mix
1 egg

Heat oven to 400°F. Line with paper baking cups or grease bottoms only of 16 medium muffin cups or 12 large muffin cups. In large bowl, combine bran cereal and milk; let stand 10 minutes to soften. Cut each package of cream cheese into 6 to 8 equal cubes; set aside. Add sour cream, bread mix and egg to bran mixture; stir by hand 50 to 75 strokes until dry particles are moistened. Divide batter evenly among paper-lined muffin cups. Press cube of cream cheese into batter in each cup; spread batter to completely cover cream cheese. Bake at 400°F. for 19 to

21 minutes or until golden brown. Cool 1 minute; remove from pan. **12 to 16 muffins.**

HIGH ALTITUDE—Above 3500 Feet: Add 1 tablespoon flour to dry bread mix.

NUTRIENTS PER 1 LARGE MUFFIN

Calories	200	Protein	6% U.S. RDA
Protein	4g	Vitamin A	8% U.S. RDA
Carbohydrate	27g	Vitamin C	2% U.S. RDA
Fat	9g	Thiamine	10% U.S. RDA
Cholesterol	35mg	Riboflavin	10% U.S. RDA
Sodium	190mg	Niacin	6% U.S. RDA
Potassium	140mg	Calcium	4% U.S. RDA
Dietary Fiber	2g	Iron	8% U.S. RDA

Lemon Raspberry Muffins

Stephanie Luetkehans, Illinois
Bake-Off® 33, 1988

2 cups all purpose, unbleached or self-rising flour*
1 cup sugar
3 teaspoons baking powder
½ teaspoon salt
1 cup half-and-half
½ cup oil
1 teaspoon lemon extract
2 eggs
1 cup fresh or frozen raspberries without syrup (do not thaw)

Heat oven to 425°F. Line 12 large or 16 medium muffin cups with paper baking cups. Lightly spoon flour into measuring cup; level off. In large bowl, combine flour, sugar, baking powder and salt; mix well. In small bowl, combine half-and-half, oil, lemon extract and eggs; blend well. Add to dry ingredients; stir until dry ingredients are just moistened. Carefully fold in raspberries. Fill paper-lined muffin cups ¾ full. Bake at 425°F. for 18 to 23 minutes or until golden brown. Cool 5 minutes; remove from pan. **12 to 16 muffins.**

TIP: *If using self-rising flour, omit baking powder and salt.

HIGH ALTITUDE—Above 3500 Feet: Decrease baking powder to 2 teaspoons.

NUTRIENTS PER 1 LARGE MUFFIN

Calories	200	Protein	4% U.S. RDA
Protein	3g	Vitamin A	2% U.S. RDA
Carbohydrate	26g	Vitamin C	2% U.S. RDA
Fat	9g	Thiamine	6% U.S. RDA
Cholesterol	40mg	Riboflavin	6% U.S. RDA
Sodium	140mg	Niacin	4% U.S. RDA
Potassium	55mg	Calcium	6% U.S. RDA
Dietary Fiber	<1g	Iron	4% U.S. RDA

Lemon Raspberry Muffins

"After buying and eating dozens of bakery muffins, I decided to make my own," said the finalist who created these $2,000 prize-winning muffins. So rich, tender and flavorful, these muffins can easily be dessert.

Italian Cheese Bread Ring

Italian Cheese Bread Ring

Kayleen L. Sloboden, Washington
Bake-Off® 31, 1984

2 tablespoons sesame seed
4½ to 5¼ cups all purpose,
   unbleached or bread flour*
¼ cup sugar
1½ teaspoons salt
2 packages active dry yeast
1 cup milk
1 cup water
½ cup margarine or butter
2 eggs

FILLING
4 ounces (1 cup) shredded
   mozzarella cheese
½ teaspoon Italian seasoning
¼ teaspoon garlic powder
¼ cup margarine or butter,
   softened

Generously grease 12-cup fluted tube or 10-inch tube pan; sprinkle with sesame seed. Lightly spoon flour into measuring cup; level off. In large bowl, combine 2½ cups flour, sugar, salt and yeast; blend well. In small saucepan, heat milk, water and ½ cup margarine until very warm (120 to 130°F.). Add warm liquid and eggs to flour mixture. Blend at low speed until moistened; beat 3 minutes at medium speed. By hand, stir in remaining 2 to 2¾ cups flour to form a stiff batter.

In small bowl, combine all filling ingredients; mix well. Spoon half of batter over sesame seed in greased pan; spoon filling mixture evenly over batter to within ½ inch of sides of pan. Spoon remaining batter over filling. Cover loosely with plastic wrap and cloth towel. Let rise in warm place (80 to 85°F.) until light and doubled in size, about 30 minutes.

Heat oven to 350°F. Uncover dough. Bake 30 to 40 minutes or until golden brown and loaf sounds hollow when lightly tapped. Remove from pan immediately; cool on wire racks. Serve warm or cool. **1 (24-slice) loaf.**

HIGH ALTITUDE—Above 3500 Feet: No change.

NUTRIENTS PER 1 SLICE

Calories	190	Protein	8% U.S. RDA
Protein	5g	Vitamin A	6% U.S. RDA
Carbohydrate	24g	Vitamin C	<2% U.S. RDA
Fat	8g	Thiamine	15% U.S. RDA
Cholesterol	25mg	Riboflavin	10% U.S. RDA
Sodium	240mg	Niacin	8% U.S. RDA
Potassium	70mg	Calcium	6% U.S. RDA
Dietary Fiber	<1g	Iron	8% U.S. RDA

Banana-Wheat Quick Bread

Barbara Goldstein, California
Bake-Off® 24, 1973

1¼ cups all purpose or unbleached
   flour
½ cup whole wheat flour
1 cup sugar
1 teaspoon baking soda
1 teaspoon salt
1½ cups (3 medium) mashed
   bananas
¼ cup margarine or butter,
   softened
2 tablespoons orange juice
¼ teaspoon lemon juice, if desired
1 egg
¼ to ½ cup raisins

Heat oven to 350°F. Grease and flour bottom only of 9 × 5 or 8 × 4-inch loaf pan. Lightly spoon flour into measuring cup; level off. In large bowl, combine all purpose flour, whole wheat flour and remaining ingredients except raisins; beat 3 minutes at medium speed. Fold in raisins. Pour batter into greased and floured pan. Bake at 350°F. for 55 to 65 minutes or until toothpick inserted in center comes out clean. Cool 10 minutes; remove from pan. Cool on wire rack. **1 (16-slice) loaf.**

HIGH ALTITUDE—Above 3500 Feet: Increase all purpose flour to 1½ cups.

NUTRIENTS PER 1 SLICE

Calories	170	Protein	2% U.S. RDA
Protein	2g	Vitamin A	2% U.S. RDA
Carbohydrate	31g	Vitamin C	2% U.S. RDA
Fat	4g	Thiamine	6% U.S. RDA
Cholesterol	15mg	Riboflavin	4% U.S. RDA
Sodium	240mg	Niacin	4% U.S. RDA
Potassium	150mg	Calcium	<2% U.S. RDA
Dietary Fiber	1g	Iron	4% U.S. RDA

Each event is unique—

Elegant hotels and celebrity spokespeople are as much a part of the Bake-Off® as new recipes. The Duchess of Windsor, Ronald Reagan, Arthur Godfrey, Mamie Eisenhower, Pat Boone, Art Linkletter and Bob Barker have all lent it their names and personal appearances. Eleanor Roosevelt presented prizes at the first event and later wrote in her syndicated column, ''This is a healthy contest and a highly American one. It may sell Pillsbury flour but it also reaches far down into the lives of the housewives of America.'' She hastened to add that three men had qualified for the trip to New York. One of their entries was called ''Quick Man-Prepared Dinner.'' Since its birth in New York, the contest has been transported to different cities nationwide. Honolulu in 1971 drew a surge of entries.

Half-Time Spoon Rolls

Half-Time Spoon Rolls

❧

Virginia Walker, Wisconsin
Bake-Off® 2, 1950

3 to 3½ cups all purpose or unbleached flour
¼ cup sugar
1 teaspoon salt
1 package active dry yeast
¾ cup milk
¾ cup water
⅓ cup margarine or butter
1 egg

Lightly spoon flour into measuring cup; level off. In large bowl, combine 1½ cups flour, sugar, salt and yeast; blend well. In small saucepan, heat milk, water and margarine until very warm (120 to 130°F.). Add warm liquid and egg to flour mixture. Blend at low speed until moistened; beat 3 minutes at medium speed. By hand, stir in remaining 1½ to 2 cups flour to form a stiff batter. Cover loosely with plastic wrap and cloth towel. Let rise in warm place (80 to 85°F.) until light and doubled in size, 45 to 50 minutes.

Grease 18 muffin cups. Stir down dough to remove all air bubbles. Spoon into greased muffin cups, filling about ⅔ full. Cover loosely with greased plastic wrap and cloth towel; let rise in warm place until light and doubled in size, 25 to 35 minutes.

Heat oven to 400°F. Uncover dough. Bake 15 to 20 minutes or until golden brown. Remove from pans immediately; cool on wire racks. **18 rolls.**

HIGH ALTITUDE—Above 3500 Feet: No change.

NUTRIENTS PER 1 ROLL

Calories	140	Protein	4% U.S. RDA
Protein	3g	Vitamin A	2% U.S. RDA
Carbohydrate	22g	Vitamin C	<2% U.S. RDA
Fat	4g	Thiamine	10% U.S. RDA
Cholesterol	15mg	Riboflavin	8% U.S. RDA
Sodium	170mg	Niacin	6% U.S. RDA
Potassium	50mg	Calcium	<2% U.S. RDA
Dietary Fiber	<1g	Iron	6% U.S. RDA

Polish Poppy Swirl Loaf

❧

Gene Swiderski, Minnesota
Bake-Off® 29, 1980

FILLING
¾ cup poppy seed, ground*
½ cup sugar
¾ cup milk
½ teaspoon vanilla
½ teaspoon almond extract
1 egg, separated, reserving yolk for bread

BREAD
1 package hot roll mix
2 tablespoons sugar
¾ cup water heated to 120 to 130°F.
2 tablespoons margarine or butter, softened
½ teaspoon vanilla
½ teaspoon almond extract
2 eggs
Reserved egg yolk

FROSTING
½ cup powdered sugar
1 tablespoon margarine or butter, softened
1 teaspoon water
½ teaspoon vanilla
½ teaspoon almond extract
1 tablespoon slivered almonds

In medium saucepan, combine poppy seed, ½ cup sugar and milk. Cook over medium heat until thick and milk is absorbed, about 15 minutes. Cool slightly; add ½ teaspoon vanilla, ½ teaspoon almond extract and egg white. Cool.

Grease 9×5-inch loaf pan. In large bowl, combine flour mixture with yeast from foil packet and 2 tablespoons sugar; blend well. Stir in *hot* water, 2 tablespoons margarine, ½ teaspoon vanilla, ½ teaspoon almond extract, 2 eggs and reserved egg yolk until dough pulls cleanly away from sides of bowl.

Polish Poppy Swirl Loaf

Turn dough out onto lightly floured surface. With greased or floured hands, shape dough into a ball. Knead dough for 5 minutes until smooth. Cover with large bowl; let rest 5 minutes.

On lightly floured surface, roll dough to 18 × 12-inch rectangle. Spread with cooled filling mixture. Starting with 18-inch side, roll up tightly; pinch edges and ends to seal. Fold roll in half, seam side down. Place seam side down in greased pan. Cover loosely with plastic wrap and cloth towel. Let rise in warm place (80 to 85°F.) until almost doubled in size, about 30 minutes.

Heat oven to 350°F. Uncover dough. Bake 30 to 45 minutes or until deep golden brown and loaf sounds hollow when lightly tapped. Remove from pan immediately; cool on wire rack. In small bowl, blend all frosting ingredients except almonds until smooth. Frost warm loaf; sprinkle with almonds. **1 (18-slice) loaf.**

TIP: *Poppy seed can be ground in blender at medium speed for 1 minute, scraping sides once.

HIGH ALTITUDE—Above 3500 Feet: No change.

NUTRIENTS PER 1 SLICE

Calories	190	Protein	8% U.S. RDA
Protein	5g	Vitamin A	2% U.S. RDA
Carbohydrate	30g	Vitamin C	<2% U.S. RDA
Fat	6g	Thiamine	15% U.S. RDA
Cholesterol	45mg	Riboflavin	10% U.S. RDA
Sodium	210mg	Niacin	8% U.S. RDA
Potassium	105mg	Calcium	10% U.S. RDA
Dietary Fiber	1g	Iron	8% U.S. RDA

Pictured top to bottom: No-Knead Water-Rising Twists, page 93; Magic Marshmallow Crescent Puffs,
page 91; Country Apple Coffee Cake, page 103

Sweet Rolls and Coffee Cakes

No category of Bake-Off® recipes demonstrates greater creativity than this one. From ever-so-tender Country Apple Coffee Cake and Chocolate Almond Crescent Braid to old-fashioned Whole Wheat Caramel Rolls, so gooey and good—these are the tastes that make breakfast worth waking up for.

The sweet rolls and coffee cakes category was off to a spectacular start at the very first Bake-Off® Contest. Grand Prize honors went to No-Knead Water-Rising Twists, a sweet roll recipe featuring an unusual rising method and remarkably delicious results.

Classic from-scratch recipes, such as the Grand Prize-winning Ring-a-Lings, remain the choice of many baking enthusiasts. Others prefer the quick and easy methods used by Bake-Off® finalists to create the Grand Prize winners, Magic Marshmallow Crescent Puffs and Easy Crescent Danish Rolls. But whatever the method, the tantalizing treats in this collection look as though they belong in a showcase at the finest bakery.

Many of these recipes start simply with refrigerated dough or hot roll mix. Luscious fruit or nut fillings, crunchy toppings and flavorings, plus clever shapings turn these convenience products into mouth-watering delicacies.

Many Bake-Off® finalists draw on their own food heritage for recipe inspiration. Recipes like Quick Praline Rolls represent old family favorites that have become easy, any-day breakfast fare. Crescent Dutch Letter Pastries, Hot Roll Moravian Sugar Cake and Danish Almond Crescent Ring are recipes reminiscent of European bakery specialties—adapted for preparation by novice bakers. In short, the goodness of yesterday merges with the convenience of today, thanks to the creativity of Bake-Off® finalists.

Whole Wheat Caramel Rolls

Lorraine Edie, New York
Bake-Off® 9, 1957

1 to 2 cups all purpose or
    unbleached flour
1 cup whole wheat flour
3 tablespoons sugar
1 teaspoon salt
1 package active dry yeast
¾ cup milk
¼ cup water
2 tablespoons shortening
1 cup firmly packed brown sugar
⅓ cup margarine or butter, melted
½ cup chopped nuts

Lightly spoon flour into measuring cup; level off. In large bowl, combine ½ cup all purpose flour, whole wheat flour, sugar, salt and yeast; blend well. In small saucepan, heat milk, water and shortening until very warm (120 to 130°F.). Add warm liquid to flour mixture. By hand, stir until dry ingredients are moistened. Stir in ¼ to ¾ cup all purpose flour to form a stiff dough. On floured surface, knead in remaining ¼ to ¾ cup all purpose flour until dough is smooth and elastic, about 5 minutes. Place dough in greased bowl; cover loosely with plastic wrap and cloth towel. Let rise in warm place (80 to 85°F.) until light and doubled in size, about 1¼ hours.

Grease 9-inch square pan. Punch down dough several times to remove all air bubbles. On lightly floured surface, roll out dough to 16 × 12-inch rectangle. In small bowl, combine brown sugar and margarine; blend well. Spread evenly over dough; sprinkle with nuts. Starting with 16-inch side, roll up tightly; pinch edges to seal. Cut into 16 slices; place cut side down in greased pan. Cover; let rise in warm place until light and doubled in size, 45 to 60 minutes.

Heat oven to 350°F. Uncover dough. Bake 25 to 30 minutes or until golden brown. Cool 2 minutes; invert onto serving plate. **16 rolls.**

HIGH ALTITUDE—Above 3500 Feet: Bake at 375°F. for 25 to 30 minutes.

NUTRIENTS PER 1 ROLL

Calories	210	Protein	4% U.S. RDA
Protein	3g	Vitamin A	4% U.S. RDA
Carbohydrate	31g	Vitamin C	<2% U.S. RDA
Fat	8g	Thiamine	10% U.S. RDA
Cholesterol	0mg	Riboflavin	6% U.S. RDA
Sodium	190mg	Niacin	6% U.S. RDA
Potassium	135mg	Calcium	2% U.S. RDA
Dietary Fiber	2g	Iron	8% U.S. RDA

Twist-of-Honey Orange Rolls

Roxanne Frisbie, Oregon
Bake-Off® 33, 1988

1 tablespoon finely chopped nuts
1 tablespoon grated orange peel
3 tablespoons margarine or butter,
    softened
1 tablespoon honey
10-ounce can refrigerated flaky
    biscuits
½ cup sugar
¼ cup orange juice
1 teaspoon vanilla

Heat oven to 400°F. In small bowl, combine nuts, orange peel, margarine and honey; mix well. Separate dough into 10 biscuits. Separate each biscuit into 2 layers. Spread top of 10 layers with teaspoonful of honey-orange mixture. Top each with remaining layers; press together to form 10 filled biscuits. Gently pull and twist each filled biscuit 4 or 5 times to form 3½-inch twisted roll. Place rolls in ungreased 8 or 9-inch square pan.

In small saucepan, combine sugar, orange juice and vanilla. Cook over medium-high heat until sugar is melted and mixture begins to boil, stirring constantly. Spoon over rolls. (Mixture will glaze rolls while baking.) Bake at 400°F. for 16 to 22 minutes or until golden brown. Cool 2 minutes; invert onto serving plate. Serve warm. **10 rolls.**

NUTRIENTS PER 1 ROLL

Calories	180	Protein	2% U.S. RDA
Protein	2g	Vitamin A	2% U.S. RDA
Carbohydrate	25g	Vitamin C	4% U.S. RDA
Fat	8g	Thiamine	6% U.S. RDA
Cholesterol	0mg	Riboflavin	4% U.S. RDA
Sodium	330mg	Niacin	4% U.S. RDA
Potassium	35mg	Calcium	<2% U.S. RDA
Dietary Fiber	<1g	Iron	4% U.S. RDA

Whole Wheat Caramel Rolls

Bohemian Raisin Biscuit Kolachy

Bohemian Raisin Biscuit Kolachy

—◦◦◦◦—

Margaret Kramer, Wisconsin
Bake-Off® 30, 1982

1 cup raisins or currants
¼ cup firmly packed brown sugar
¼ cup water
1 to 2 teaspoons lemon juice
½ cup sugar
½ teaspoon cinnamon
10-ounce can refrigerated flaky
  biscuits
¼ cup margarine or butter, melted

GLAZE
½ cup powdered sugar
½ teaspoon vanilla
2 to 4 teaspoons milk

Heat oven to 375°F. In small saucepan, combine raisins, brown sugar, water and lemon juice. Cook over medium heat about 7 minutes or until mixture thickens, stirring occasionally. Cool. In small bowl, combine sugar and cinnamon; set aside.

Separate dough into 10 biscuits. Dip both sides of each biscuit in margarine, then in sugar mixture. Place coated biscuits, sides touching, in ungreased 15 × 10 × 1-inch baking pan or 13 × 9-inch pan. With thumb, make wide imprint in center of each biscuit; fill with rounded tablespoonful of raisin mixture. Bake at 375°F. for 15 to 20 minutes or until golden brown. In small bowl, blend powdered sugar, vanilla and enough milk for desired drizzling consistency. Drizzle over warm rolls. **10 rolls.**

NUTRIENTS PER 1 ROLL

Calories	250	Protein	2% U.S. RDA
Protein	2g	Vitamin A	4% U.S. RDA
Carbohydrate	44g	Vitamin C	<2% U.S. RDA
Fat	8g	Thiamine	8% U.S. RDA
Cholesterol	0mg	Riboflavin	4% U.S. RDA
Sodium	350mg	Niacin	4% U.S. RDA
Potassium	150mg	Calcium	2% U.S. RDA
Dietary Fiber	1g	Iron	6% U.S. RDA

Grand Prize Winner

Magic Marshmallow Crescent Puffs

—◦◦◦◦—

Edna (Holmgren) Walker, Minnesota
Bake-Off® 20, 1969

¼ cup sugar
2 tablespoons flour
1 teaspoon cinnamon
2 (8-ounce) cans refrigerated
  crescent dinner rolls
16 large marshmallows
¼ cup margarine or butter, melted

GLAZE
½ cup powdered sugar
½ teaspoon vanilla
2 to 3 teaspoons milk
¼ cup chopped nuts, if desired

Heat oven to 375°F. In small bowl, combine sugar, flour and cinnamon. Separate dough into 16 triangles. Dip 1 marshmallow in margarine; roll in sugar mixture. Place marshmallow on wide end of triangle. Roll up, starting at wide end of triangle and rolling to opposite point. Completely cover marshmallow with dough; firmly pinch edges to seal. Dip one end in remaining margarine; place margarine side down in ungreased large muffin cup or 6-ounce custard cup. Repeat with remaining marshmallows. Bake at 375°F. for 12 to 15 minutes or until golden brown. (Place foil or cookie sheet on rack below muffin cups during baking to catch any spillage.) Remove from muffin cups immediately; cool on wire racks. In small bowl, blend powdered sugar, vanilla and enough milk for desired drizzling consistency. Drizzle over warm rolls. Sprinkle with nuts. **16 rolls.**

NUTRIENTS PER 1 ROLL

Calories	190	Protein	2% U.S. RDA
Protein	2g	Vitamin A	2% U.S. RDA
Carbohydrate	23g	Vitamin C	<2% U.S. RDA
Fat	10g	Thiamine	6% U.S. RDA
Cholesterol	2mg	Riboflavin	4% U.S. RDA
Sodium	270mg	Niacin	4% U.S. RDA
Potassium	80mg	Calcium	<2% U.S. RDA
Dietary Fiber	<1g	Iron	4% U.S. RDA

Bohemian Raisin Biscuit Kolachy

—◦◦◦◦—

This recipe has simplified the preparation of kolachy, a traditional Old World pastry, by using refrigerated flaky biscuits for the dough.

Magic Marshmallow Crescent Puffs

—◦◦◦◦—

"Such a simple way to get great taste," people exclaim when they try this Bake-Off® classic recipe. It is created by wrapping refrigerated crescent roll dough around cinnamon-sugar-coated marshmallows. The marshmallows melt during baking, forming a sweet, hollow puff.

Lemon Nut Rolls

Lemon Nut Rolls

Betty May, Maryland
Bake-Off® 10, 1958

DOUGH
 2¹/₂ to 3¹/₂ cups all purpose or
  unbleached flour
 ¹/₃ cup mashed potato flakes
 ¹/₃ cup sugar
 1 teaspoon salt
 ¹/₂ teaspoon grated lemon peel
 1 package active dry yeast
 ³/₄ cup water
 ¹/₂ cup milk
 ¹/₃ cup margarine or butter
 1 tablespoon lemon juice
 1 egg

FILLING
 2 tablespoons margarine or butter,
  softened
 ³/₄ cup sugar
 ¹/₂ cup chopped pecans
 1 teaspoon grated lemon peel

GLAZE
 ¹/₂ cup powdered sugar
 ¹/₂ teaspoon grated lemon peel
 ¹/₂ teaspoon lemon juice
 2 to 3 teaspoons half-and-half or
  milk

Lightly spoon flour into measuring cup; level off. In large bowl, combine 1 cup flour, potato flakes, ¹/₃ cup sugar, salt, ¹/₂ teaspoon lemon peel and yeast; blend well. In small saucepan, heat water, milk and ¹/₃ cup margarine until very warm (120 to 130°F.). Add warm liquid, 1 tablespoon lemon juice and egg to flour mixture. Blend at low speed until moistened; beat 2 minutes at medium speed. By hand, stir in remaining 1¹/₂ to 2¹/₂ cups flour to form a stiff dough. Cover loosely with plastic wrap and cloth towel. Let rise in warm place (80 to 85°F.) until light and doubled in size, about 1 hour.

Grease two 8 or 9-inch round cake pans. On well-floured surface, toss dough until no longer sticky. Roll out dough to 16 × 12-inch rectangle. Spread with 2 tablespoons margarine. In small bowl, combine remaining filling ingredients; sprinkle evenly over buttered dough. Starting with 16-inch side, roll up tightly; pinch edges to seal. Cut into 16 slices; place cut side down in greased pans. Cover; let rise in warm place (80 to 85°F.) until light and doubled in size, 30 to 40 minutes.

Heat oven to 375°F. Uncover dough. Bake 20 to 30 minutes or until light golden brown. Remove from pans immediately; cool on wire racks. In small bowl, blend all glaze ingredients until smooth and of desired drizzling consistency. Drizzle over warm rolls. **16 rolls.**

HIGH ALTITUDE — Above 3500 Feet: No change.

NUTRIENTS PER 1 ROLL

Calories	250	Protein	6% U.S. RDA
Protein	4g	Vitamin A	4% U.S. RDA
Carbohydrate	40g	Vitamin C	2% U.S. RDA
Fat	9g	Thiamine	15% U.S. RDA
Cholesterol	20mg	Riboflavin	8% U.S. RDA
Sodium	210mg	Niacin	8% U.S. RDA
Potassium	85mg	Calcium	6% U.S. RDA
Dietary Fiber	1g	Iron	8% U.S. RDA

Grand Prize Winner

No-Knead Water-Rising Twists

—⋲∘⋺—

Theodora Smafield, Michigan
Bake-Off® 1, 1949

2¹/₂ to 3¹/₂ cups all purpose or
   unbleached flour
¹/₂ cup sugar
 1 teaspoon salt
 1 package active dry yeast
³/₄ cup milk
¹/₂ cup margarine or butter
 1 teaspoon vanilla
 2 eggs
¹/₂ cup chopped nuts
¹/₂ cup sugar
 1 teaspoon cinnamon

Lightly spoon flour into measuring cup; level off. In large bowl, combine 1 cup flour, ¹/₂ cup sugar, salt and yeast; blend well. In small saucepan, heat milk and margarine until very warm (120 to 130°F.). Add warm liquid, vanilla and eggs to flour mixture. Blend at low speed until moistened; beat 2 minutes at medium speed. By hand, stir in remaining 1¹/₂ to 2¹/₂ cups flour to form a soft dough. Cover loosely with plastic wrap and cloth towel. Let rise in warm place (80 to 85°F.) until light and doubled in size, 30 to 40 minutes. *Dough will be sticky.*

Grease 2 large cookie sheets. In small bowl, combine nuts, ¹/₂ cup sugar and cinnamon; blend well. Drop about ¹/₄ cup of dough into nut-sugar mixture; thoroughly coat. Stretch dough to about 8 inches in length; twist into desired shape. Place on greased cookie sheets. Repeat with remaining dough. Cover; let rise in warm place, 15 minutes.

Heat oven to 375°F. Uncover dough. Bake 8 to 16 minutes or until light golden brown. Remove from cookie sheet immediately; cool on wire racks. Serve warm. **12 rolls.**

HIGH ALTITUDE — Above 3500 Feet: No change.

NUTRIENTS PER 1 ROLL

Calories	320	Protein	8% U.S. RDA
Protein	6g	Vitamin A	8% U.S. RDA
Carbohydrate	47g	Vitamin C	<2% U.S. RDA
Fat	12g	Thiamine	20% U.S. RDA
Cholesterol	45mg	Riboflavin	10% U.S. RDA
Sodium	290mg	Niacin	10% U.S. RDA
Potassium	125mg	Calcium	10% U.S. RDA
Dietary Fiber	1g	Iron	10% U.S. RDA

No-Knead Water-Rising Twists

—⋲∘⋺—

When first a finalist, this recipe had a unique rising method. In that procedure, the dough was wrapped in a tea towel and submerged in warm water to rise. In this updated recipe, we have streamlined the preparation of the dough and the rising method. Use your creativity and twist the cinnamon-sugar-coated dough into any pleasing shape when making these sweet rolls.

Lemon Nut Rolls

—⋲∘⋺—

Soft, tender lemon rolls get extra lightness from potato flakes in the dough. A first-prize winner in the "bride category," these rolls are well worth the time it takes to make them from scratch.

Beehive Buns

Beehive Buns

Janis Chudleigh, Connecticut
Bake-Off® 32, 1986

2 cups whole wheat flour
2 packages active dry yeast
1 teaspoon salt
1 cup raisins
1 cup very hot water
1 cup milk
$\frac{1}{3}$ cup honey
$\frac{1}{3}$ cup margarine or butter
2 eggs
2 to 3$\frac{1}{4}$ cups all purpose or
   unbleached flour

GLAZE

3 tablespoons honey
3 tablespoons margarine or butter
1$\frac{1}{4}$ cups powdered sugar
1 teaspoon vanilla

Lightly spoon flour into measuring cup; level off. In large bowl, combine whole wheat flour, yeast and salt; blend well. Cover raisins with water. Let stand for 1 minute; drain. In small saucepan, heat milk, $\frac{1}{3}$ cup honey and $\frac{1}{3}$ cup margarine until very warm (120 to 130°F.); stir into flour mixture. Beat in eggs, 1 at a time, beating well after each addition. By hand, stir in raisins. Stir in 1$\frac{1}{2}$ to 2 cups all purpose flour until dough pulls cleanly away from sides of bowl.

On floured surface, knead in remaining $\frac{1}{2}$ to 1$\frac{1}{4}$ cups all purpose flour until dough is smooth and elastic, about 5 minutes. Place dough in greased bowl; cover loosely with plastic wrap and cloth towel. Let rise in warm place (80 to 85°F.) until light and doubled in size, 45 to 60 minutes.

Grease 24 muffin cups. Punch down dough several times to remove all air bubbles. Divide dough into 24 equal pieces. (Cover pieces with large bowl to prevent dough from drying out.) Using 1 piece of dough at a time, roll to form 10 to 12-inch rope. To form beehive shape, coil rope in greased muffin cup, tucking end into top center. Repeat with remaining pieces. Cover; let rise in warm place until light and doubled in size, 30 to 45 minutes.

Heat oven to 350°F. Uncover dough. Bake 15 to 20 minutes or until golden brown. Remove from pans immediately; cool on wire racks. In small saucepan, heat 3 tablespoons honey and 3 tablespoons margarine. Stir in powdered sugar and vanilla until smooth. Drizzle over warm rolls. **24 rolls.**

HIGH ALTITUDE—Above 3500 Feet: No change.

NUTRIENTS PER 1 ROLL

Calories	210	Protein	6% U.S. RDA
Protein	4g	Vitamin A	4% U.S. RDA
Carbohydrate	37g	Vitamin C	<2% U.S. RDA
Fat	5g	Thiamine	15% U.S. RDA
Cholesterol	25mg	Riboflavin	8% U.S. RDA
Sodium	150mg	Niacin	8% U.S. RDA
Potassium	140mg	Calcium	6% U.S. RDA
Dietary Fiber	2g	Iron	8% U.S. RDA

Quick Praline Rolls
❧
Alic Houghtaling, California
Bake-Off® 14, 1962

FILLING
- ¾ cup firmly packed brown sugar
- ⅓ cup margarine or butter, softened
- ½ cup chopped walnuts

DOUGH
- 1¾ to 2¾ cups all purpose or unbleached flour
- 2 tablespoons sugar
- 1 teaspoon baking powder
- ½ teaspoon salt
- 1 package active dry yeast
- ⅓ cup milk
- ⅓ cup margarine or butter
- ¼ cup water
- 1 egg
- ¼ cup chopped walnuts

Grease cookie sheets. In small bowl, beat brown sugar and ⅓ cup margarine until light and fluffy. Stir in ½ cup walnuts; set aside.

Lightly spoon flour into measuring cup; level off. In large bowl, combine 1 cup flour, sugar, baking powder, salt and yeast; blend well. In small saucepan, heat milk, ⅓ cup margarine and water until very warm (120 to 130°F.). Add warm liquid and egg to flour mixture. Blend at low speed until moistened; beat 3 minutes at medium speed. Stir in remaining ¾ to 1¾ cups flour to form a soft dough.

On well-floured surface, toss dough until no longer sticky. Roll dough to 15 × 10-inch rectangle. Spread with half of filling mixture. Starting with 15-inch side, roll up tightly; pinch edges to seal. Cut into 15 slices. Place cut side down on greased cookie sheets; flatten each slice to ½-inch thickness. Spread tops of slices with remaining filling; sprinkle with ¼ cup walnuts. Cover loosely with greased plastic wrap and cloth towel. Let rise in warm place (80 to 85°F.) until light, about 45 minutes.

Heat oven to 400°F. Uncover dough. Bake 10 to 12 minutes or until light golden brown. Remove from cookie sheets immediately; cool on wire racks. Serve warm. **15 rolls.**

HIGH ALTITUDE—Above 3500 Feet: No change.

NUTRIENTS PER 1 ROLL

Calories	260	Protein	6% U.S. RDA
Protein	4g	Vitamin A	6% U.S. RDA
Carbohydrate	32g	Vitamin C	<2% U.S. RDA
Fat	13g	Thiamine	10% U.S. RDA
Cholesterol	20mg	Riboflavin	6% U.S. RDA
Sodium	200mg	Niacin	8% U.S. RDA
Potassium	125mg	Calcium	8% U.S. RDA
Dietary Fiber	1g	Iron	8% U.S. RDA

Beehive Buns
❧
Shaped like miniature beehives, these honey-flavored raisin buns are perfect for breakfast. Serve warm with butter.

Quick Praline Rolls
❧
The combined leavening action of yeast and baking powder gives these rolls a biscuit-like texture. After mixing and shaping, the dough rises only once before baking.

Ring-a-Lings

༻•❀•༺

Bertha Jorgensen, Oregon
Bake-Off® 7, 1955

4 to 4½ cups all purpose or
    unbleached flour
⅓ cup sugar
2 teaspoons salt
2 teaspoons grated orange peel
2 packages active dry yeast
1 cup milk
⅓ cup margarine or butter
2 eggs

FILLING

1 cup powdered sugar
⅓ cup margarine or butter,
    softened
1 gup filberts, pecans or walnuts,
    ground

GLAZE

3 tablespoons sugar
¼ cup orange juice

Ring-a-Lings

༻•❀•༺

*This no-knead sweet roll of the
'50s has such a simple way to
fill, twist and curl the dough.
This innovative method and its
refreshing orange flavor are the
attributes that have earned this
recipe a place on the list of
Bake-Off® classics.*

Lightly spoon flour into measuring cup; level off. In large bowl, combine 2 cups flour, ⅓ cup sugar, salt, orange peel and yeast; blend well. In small saucepan, heat milk and ⅓ cup margarine until very warm (120 to 130°F.). Add warm liquid and eggs to flour mixture. Blend at low speed until moistened; beat 3 minutes at medium speed. By hand, stir in remaining 2 to 2½ cups flour to form a stiff dough. Place dough in greased bowl; cover loosely with plastic wrap and cloth towel. Let rise in warm place (80 to 85°F.) until light and doubled in size, 35 to 50 minutes.

In small bowl, blend powdered sugar and ⅓ cup margarine until smooth. Stir in filberts; set aside. In second small bowl, blend glaze ingredients; set aside.

Grease 2 large cookie sheets. Stir down dough to remove all air bubbles. On floured surface, toss dough until no longer sticky. Roll dough to 22 × 12-inch rectangle. Spread filling mixture lengthwise over half of dough. Fold dough over filling. Cut crosswise into 1-inch strips; twist each strip 4 to 5 times. To shape rolls, hold folded end of strip down on greased cookie sheet to form center; coil strip around center. Tuck loose end under. Repeat with remaining twisted strips. Cover; let rise

in warm place until light and doubled in size, 30 to 45 minutes.

Heat oven to 375°F. Uncover dough. Bake 9 to 12 minutes or until light golden brown. Brush tops of rolls with glaze. Bake an addtional 3 to 5 minutes or until golden brown. Remove from cookie sheets immediately; cool on wire racks. **20 to 22 rolls.**

HIGH ALTITUDE—Above 3500 Feet: No change.

NUTRIENTS PER 1 ROLL

Calories	230	Protein	6% U.S. RDA
Protein	5g	Vitamin A	6% U.S. RDA
Carbohydrate	32g	Vitamin C	2% U.S. RDA
Fat	10g	Thiamine	10% U.S. RDA
Cholesterol	25mg	Riboflavin	10% U.S. RDA
Sodium	300mg	Niacin	8% U.S. RDA
Potassium	90mg	Calcium	2% U.S. RDA
Dietary Fiber	1g	Iron	6% U.S. RDA

Orange Date Crescent Claws

༻•❀•༺

Barbara Rhea, Ohio
Bake-Off® 33, 1988

½ cup chopped walnuts or pecans
¼ cup sugar
1 teaspoon grated orange peel
½ cup chopped dates
8-ounce can refrigerated crescent
    dinner rolls
2 tablespoons margarine or butter,
    melted

Heat oven to 375°F. In small bowl, combine walnuts, sugar and orange peel; mix well. Reserve ¼ cup of sugar-nut mixture for topping. Stir dates into remaining mixture; set aside.

Separate dough into 4 rectangles; firmly press perforations to seal. Cut each rectangle in half crosswise; press or roll out each to make eight 4-inch squares. Brush each with margarine. Spoon about 2 tablespoonfuls of date mixture in 1-inch strip across center of each square to within ¼ inch of each end. Fold dough over filling, overlapping in center; pinch center seam and ends to seal. Place seam side down on ungreased cookie sheet. Using scissors or sharp knife, make three ½-inch deep cuts in one folded side of each roll. To form claw shape, separate cut sections by gently curving each roll into crescent shape. Brush top of each claw with margarine; sprinkle with reserved

¼ cup sugar-nut mixture. Bake at 375°F. for 8 to 12 minutes or until golden brown. **8 rolls.**

NUTRIENTS PER 1 ROLL

Calories	240	Protein	4% U.S. RDA
Protein	3g	Vitamin A	2% U.S. RDA
Carbohydrate	27g	Vitamin C	<2% U.S. RDA
Fat	13g	Thiamine	8% U.S. RDA
Cholesterol	2mg	Riboflavin	4% U.S. RDA
Sodium	260mg	Niacin	4% U.S. RDA
Potassium	170mg	Calcium	<2% U.S. RDA
Dietary Fiber	2g	Iron	4% U.S. RDA

Grand Prize Winner

Easy Crescent Danish Rolls

Barbara S. Gibson, Indiana
Bake-Off® 26, 1975

2 (3-ounce) packages cream cheese, softened
⅓ cup sugar
2 teaspoons lemon juice
2 (8-ounce) cans refrigerated crescent dinner rolls
4 teaspoons preserves

GLAZE
½ cup powdered sugar
1 teaspoon vanilla
2 to 3 teaspoons milk

Heat oven to 350°F. In small bowl, blend cream cheese, sugar and lemon juice until smooth. Separate dough into 8 rectangles; firmly press perforations to seal. Spread about 2 tablespoonfuls of cream cheese mixture on each rectangle to within ¼ inch of edges. Starting with longest side, roll up; firmly pinch edges to seal. Gently stretch each roll to about 10 inches in length. Coil loosely, seam side down, on ungreased cookie sheet. Seal ends. With thumb, make deep imprint in center of each roll; fill with ½ teaspoonful preserves.

Bake at 350°F. for 18 to 22 minutes or until golden brown. Remove from cookie sheet; cool on wire racks. In small bowl, blend powdered sugar, vanilla and enough milk for desired drizzling consistency. Drizzle over warm rolls. **8 rolls.**

NUTRIENTS PER 1 ROLL

Calories	350	Protein	8% U.S. RDA
Protein	5g	Vitamin A	6% U.S. RDA
Carbohydrate	39g	Vitamin C	<2% U.S. RDA
Fat	19g	Thiamine	10% U.S. RDA
Cholesterol	30mg	Riboflavin	10% U.S. RDA
Sodium	530mg	Niacin	8% U.S. RDA
Potassium	160mg	Calcium	2% U.S. RDA
Dietary Fiber	<1g	Iron	8% U.S. RDA

Crescent Dutch Letter Pastries

Juddie Word, Alabama
Bake-Off® 32, 1986

1 cup (6 to 7 cookies) crushed crisp coconut macaroon cookies
¾ cup ground almonds
1 tablespoon margarine or butter, softened
3-ounce package cream cheese, softened
8-ounce can refrigerated crescent dinner rolls
1 egg yolk
1 tablespoon water

GLAZE
¾ to 1 cup powdered sugar
1 to 2 tablespoons milk

Heat oven to 375°F. Lightly grease large cookie sheet. In medium bowl, blend cookie crumbs, almonds, margarine and cream cheese until crumbly. Divide mixture into 8 equal portions; shape each into 8-inch rope.

Separate dough into 4 rectangles; firmly press perforations to seal. Press or roll out each to 8 × 4-inch rectangle; cut in half lengthwise to make eight 8 × 2-inch rectangles. Place 1 filling rope on each rectangle. Fold dough over filling, overlapping in center; pinch center seam and ends to seal. Shape into S shape on greased cookie sheet. In small bowl, blend egg yolk and water; brush over rolls.

Bake at 375°F. for 15 to 18 minutes or until golden brown. Remove from cookie sheet; cool on wire racks. In small bowl, blend enough powdered sugar and milk for desired drizzling consistency. Drizzle over warm rolls. **8 rolls.**

NUTRIENTS PER 1 ROLL

Calories	370	Protein	10% U.S. RDA
Protein	6g	Vitamin A	4% U.S. RDA
Carbohydrate	37g	Vitamin C	<2% U.S. RDA
Fat	22g	Thiamine	8% U.S. RDA
Cholesterol	70mg	Riboflavin	10% U.S. RDA
Sodium	290mg	Niacin	6% U.S. RDA
Potassium	250mg	Calcium	6% U.S. RDA
Dietary Fiber	2g	Iron	8% U.S. RDA

Crescent Dutch Letter Pastries

These traditional pastries, made easy with refrigerated crescent roll dough, have an almond-macaroon filling and are shaped into a letter of the alphabet.

Apple Coffee Cake Supreme

Apple Coffee Cake Supreme

Nicole Plaut, Wisconsin
Bake-Off® 32, 1986

1/2 cup sugar
2 eggs
1/2 cup plain yogurt
3 tablespoons margarine or butter, melted
1 to 2 teaspoons grated lemon peel
1 1/3 cups self-rising flour*
3 to 4 cups thinly sliced peeled apples
2 tablespoons sugar
1/2 to 1 cup sliced almonds

GLAZE
1/3 cup sugar
1/3 cup margarine or butter, melted
1 egg, beaten

Heat oven to 375°F. Grease 10-inch tart pan with removable bottom or 8-inch square pan. In small bowl, beat 1/2 cup sugar and 2 eggs until well blended; stir in yogurt, 3 tablespoons margarine and lemon peel. Lightly spoon flour into measuring cup; level off. Add flour to egg mixture; blend well. Pour batter into greased pan.

Arrange apple slices on top of batter, overlapping slightly. Sprinkle with 2 tablespoons sugar and almonds. Bake at 375°F. for 35 to 45 minutes or until golden brown and toothpick inserted in center comes out clean.**

As soon as coffee cake is removed from oven, increase oven temperature to *broil* and prepare glaze. In small bowl, combine all glaze ingredients; blend well. Slowly pour over hot cake; allow mixture to soak into cake. Broil 5 to 6 inches from heat for 1 to 2 minutes or until bubbly. Serve warm. Store in refrigerator. **6 to 8 servings.**

TIPS: *All purpose or unbleached flour can be substituted for self-rising flour; add 2 teaspoons baking powder and 1/2 teaspoon salt.

**If using 8-inch square pan, increase baking time 5 minutes.

HIGH ALTITUDE—Above 3500 Feet: No change.

NUTRIENTS PER 1/8 OF RECIPE

Calories	420	Protein	10% U.S. RDA
Protein	8g	Vitamin A	10% U.S. RDA
Carbohydrate	51g	Vitamin C	<2% U.S. RDA
Fat	21g	Thiamine	10% U.S. RDA
Cholesterol	100mg	Riboflavin	15% U.S. RDA
Sodium	400mg	Niacin	8% U.S. RDA
Potassium	220mg	Calcium	10% U.S. RDA
Dietary Fiber	2g	Iron	10% U.S. RDA

Maple Cream Coffee Treat

Reta Ebbink, California
Bake-Off® 28, 1978

1 cup firmly packed brown sugar
½ cup chopped nuts
⅓ cup maple-flavored syrup or dark corn syrup
¼ cup margarine or butter, melted
8-ounce package cream cheese, softened
¼ cup powdered sugar
2 tablespoons margarine or butter, softened
½ cup coconut
2 (10-ounce) cans refrigerated flaky biscuits

Heat oven to 350°F. In ungreased 13 × 9-inch pan, combine brown sugar, nuts, syrup and ¼ cup margarine; spread evenly in bottom of pan. In small bowl, blend cream cheese, powdered sugar and 2 tablespoons margarine until smooth; stir in coconut. Separate dough into 20 biscuits. Press or roll out each to 4-inch circle. Spoon tablespoonful of cream cheese mixture down center of each circle to within ¼ inch of edge. Overlap sides of dough over filling, forming finger-shaped rolls. Arrange rolls seam side down in 2 rows of 10 rolls each over brown sugar mixture in pan. Bake at 350°F. for 25 to 30 minutes or until deep golden brown. Cool 3 to 5 minutes; invert onto foil or waxed paper. **20 rolls.**

NUTRIENTS PER 1 ROLL

Calories	250	Protein	4% U.S. RDA
Protein	3g	Vitamin A	6% U.S. RDA
Carbohydrate	29g	Vitamin C	<2% U.S. RDA
Fat	14g	Thiamine	6% U.S. RDA
Cholesterol	10mg	Riboflavin	6% U.S. RDA
Sodium	370mg	Niacin	4% U.S. RDA
Potassium	90mg	Calcium	2% U.S. RDA
Dietary Fiber	<1g	Iron	6% U.S. RDA

Cinnamon-Crusted Zucchini Coffee Cake

Vickie L. Storey, Pennsylvania
Bake-Off® 32, 1986

1 tablespoon sugar
½ teaspoon cinnamon
1¾ cups whole wheat flour
1 cup sugar
½ cup chopped nuts, if desired
1 teaspoon baking soda
1 teaspoon cinnamon
2 cups shredded zucchini
½ cup buttermilk*
¼ cup pineapple-orange or orange juice
¼ cup oil
1 teaspoon vanilla
1 egg

MICROWAVE DIRECTIONS: Grease 12-cup microwave-safe fluted tube pan or 6-cup microwave-safe ring pan. In small bowl, blend 1 tablespoon sugar and ½ teaspoon cinnamon; coat inside of pan with mixture. Lightly spoon flour into measuring cup; level off. In large bowl, combine flour and all remaining ingredients. Blend at low speed until moistened; beat 2 minutes at medium speed. Pour into greased and sugared pan.

Microwave on HIGH for 10 to 14 minutes, rotating pan ¼ turn every 4 minutes. Coffee cake is done when toothpick inserted in center comes out clean. Cool in pan on flat surface 2 minutes. Invert onto serving plate. Drizzle with powdered sugar glaze, if desired.** Store in refrigerator. **6 to 8 servings.**

TIPS: *To substitute for buttermilk, use 1½ teaspoons vinegar or lemon juice plus milk to make ½ cup.

****Powdered Sugar Glaze:** In small bowl, blend ½ cup powdered sugar and 2 to 3 teaspoons water until smooth and of desired glaze consistency.

HIGH ALTITUDE—Above 3500 Feet: No change.

NUTRIENTS PER 1/8 OF RECIPE

Calories	340	Protein	8% U.S. RDA
Protein	6g	Vitamin A	2% U.S. RDA
Carbohydrate	49g	Vitamin C	4% U.S. RDA
Fat	13g	Thiamine	10% U.S. RDA
Cholesterol	35mg	Riboflavin	4% U.S. RDA
Sodium	170mg	Niacin	6% U.S. RDA
Potassium	230mg	Calcium	4% U.S. RDA
Dietary Fiber	4g	Iron	8% U.S. RDA

Maple Cream Coffee Treat

Friends and family will praise the baker who serves these cream-filled, caramel-topped sweet rolls. The judges were also impressed and awarded the recipe first prize in its category.

Chocolate Almond Crescent Braid

Susie P. Dempsey, Illinois
Bake-Off® 29, 1980

2 ounces (2 squares) semi-sweet
   baking chocolate, melted,
   cooled
⅓ cup sugar
¼ cup dairy sour cream
2 tablespoons chopped toasted
   almonds*
8-ounce can refrigerated crescent
   dinner rolls

GLAZE

½ cup powdered sugar
¼ teaspoon almond extract
3 to 4 teaspoons milk
2 tablespoons chopped toasted
   almonds*

Heat oven to 350°F. In small bowl, combine chocolate, sugar and sour cream; mix until smooth. Stir in 2 tablespoons almonds. Unroll dough into 2 long rectangles. Place on ungreased cookie sheet with long sides overlapping ½ inch; roll out to 14 × 7-inch rectangle. Firmly press edges and perforations to seal. Spread chocolate mixture in 2-inch strip lengthwise down center of dough to within ¼ inch of each end. Make cuts 2 inches apart on long sides of rectangle to within ½ inch of filling. To give braided appearance, fold strips of dough at an angle halfway across filling, alternating from side to side. Fold ends of braid under to seal.

Bake at 350°F. for 18 to 23 minutes or until golden brown. Cool 5 minutes; remove from cookie sheet. Cool on wire rack. In small bowl, blend powdered sugar, almond extract and enough milk for desired drizzling consistency. Drizzle over warm braid. Sprinkle with 2 tablespoons almonds. Cut into slices. **8 servings.**

TIP: *To toast almonds, spread on cookie sheet; bake at 375°F. for 3 to 5 minutes or until light golden brown, stirring occasionally. Or, spread in thin layer in microwave-safe pie pan; microwave on HIGH for 2 to 4 minutes or until light golden brown, stirring frequently.

NUTRIENTS PER 1/8 OF RECIPE

Calories	240	Protein	4% U.S. RDA
Protein	3g	Vitamin A	<2% U.S. RDA
Carbohydrate	31g	Vitamin C	<2% U.S. RDA
Fat	12g	Thiamine	6% U.S. RDA
Cholesterol	6mg	Riboflavin	6% U.S. RDA
Sodium	240mg	Niacin	4% U.S. RDA
Potassium	125mg	Calcium	2% U.S. RDA
Dietary Fiber	1g	Iron	4% U.S. RDA

Honeycomb Coffee Cake

This scrumptious coffee cake will melt in your mouth as you encounter warm pockets of honey throughout a moist and flaky bread.

Honeycomb Coffee Cake

Beverly A. Sebastian, Texas
Bake-Off® 30, 1982

¼ cup firmly packed brown sugar
1 teaspoon cinnamon
¼ teaspoon ground mace or
   nutmeg
¼ cup margarine or butter, melted
1 tablespoon lemon juice
10-ounce can refrigerated flaky
   biscuits
¼ to ⅓ cup (4 squares) finely
   crushed graham crackers or
   graham cracker crumbs
¼ cup finely chopped nuts, if
   desired
2 to 4 tablespoons honey

Heat oven to 400°F. Grease 9 or 8-inch round cake pan. In small bowl, combine brown sugar, cinnamon and mace; mix well. In second small bowl, blend margarine and lemon juice.

Separate dough into 10 biscuits; cut each into 4 pieces. Place biscuit pieces and graham cracker crumbs in bag; toss gently to coat. Arrange coated pieces evenly in greased pan. With small wooden spoon handle, poke a deep hole in each biscuit piece. Sprinkle brown sugar mixture over pieces; drizzle with margarine mixture. Sprinkle with nuts. Bake at 400°F. for 12 to 18 minutes or until golden brown. Turn onto wire rack; invert onto serving plate. Fill holes with honey. Serve warm. **10 servings.**

NUTRIENTS PER 1/10 OF RECIPE

Calories	210	Protein	2% U.S. RDA
Protein	2g	Vitamin A	4% U.S. RDA
Carbohydrate	27g	Vitamin C	<2% U.S. RDA
Fat	10g	Thiamine	6% U.S. RDA
Cholesterol	0mg	Riboflavin	4% U.S. RDA
Sodium	370mg	Niacin	4% U.S. RDA
Potassium	70mg	Calcium	<2% U.S. RDA
Dietary Fiber	<1g	Iron	6% U.S. RDA

Honeycomb Coffee Cake

Lemon Almond Breakfast Pastry

Lemon Almond Breakfast Pastry

Sharon Richardson, Texas
Bake-Off® 33, 1988

FILLING
- ½ cup butter or margarine, softened
- 7-ounce tube almond paste, broken into small pieces
- 2 eggs
- 5 teaspoons flour
- 1 to 2 teaspoons grated lemon peel

CRUST
- 15-ounce package refrigerated pie crusts
- 1 teaspoon flour
- 1 egg, beaten
- 1 tablespoon milk
- 2 tablespoons sugar

In small bowl or food processor bowl with metal blade, combine butter and almond paste; beat or process until smooth. Add 2 eggs; mix well. By hand, stir in 5 teaspoons flour and lemon peel until just blended. Cover; place in freezer for 20 to 30 minutes or until mixture is thick.

Allow both crust pouches to stand at room temperature for 15 to 20 minutes. Heat oven to 400°F. Remove 1 crust from pouch. Unfold; remove top plastic sheet. Press out fold lines; sprinkle with 1 teaspoon flour. Place floured side down on ungreased 12-inch pizza pan or cookie sheet; remove remaining plastic sheet. Spread cold filling over crust to within 2 inches of edge. Brush edge with beaten egg. Refrigerate while preparing top crust.

Remove remaining crust from pouch. Unfold; remove both plastic sheets. Press out fold lines; cut 1-inch circle from center of crust. Using very sharp knife and curving motions, decoratively score crust in pinwheel design. (Do not cut through crust or filling will leak out.) Carefully place over filled bottom crust. Press edges to seal; flute. In small bowl, combine remaining beaten egg and milk. Brush over crust; sprinkle with sugar. Bake at 400°F. for 22 to 27 minutes or until golden brown. Serve warm. **12 to 16 servings.**

NUTRIENTS PER 1/16 OF RECIPE

Calories	250	Protein	4% U.S. RDA
Protein	3g	Vitamin A	4% U.S. RDA
Carbohydrate	20g	Vitamin C	<2% U.S. RDA
Fat	18g	Thiamine	2% U.S. RDA
Cholesterol	70mg	Riboflavin	8% U.S. RDA
Sodium	240mg	Niacin	2% U.S. RDA
Potassium	110mg	Calcium	4% U.S. RDA
Dietary Fiber	1g	Iron	2% U.S. RDA

One-Step Tropical Coffee Cake

Sharon Schubert, Ohio
Bake-Off® 24, 1973

CAKE
1½ cups all purpose or unbleached flour
1 cup sugar
2 teaspoons baking powder
½ teaspoon salt
½ cup oil
8-ounce carton pineapple or plain yogurt
2 eggs

TOPPING
1 cup coconut
⅓ cup sugar
1 teaspoon cinnamon

Heat oven to 350°F. Grease 9-inch square or 11×7-inch pan. Lightly spoon flour into measuring cup; level off. In large bowl, combine flour and all remaining cake ingredients; stir 70 to 80 strokes until well blended. Pour batter into greased pan. In small bowl, combine all topping ingredients; mix well. Sprinkle evenly over batter. Bake at 350°F. for 35 to 40 minutes or until toothpick inserted in center comes out clean. **9 servings.**

HIGH ALTITUDE—Above 3500 Feet: Decrease sugar to 1 cup minus 2 tablespoons. Decrease baking powder to 1½ teaspoons. Bake as directed above.

NUTRIENTS PER 1/9 OF RECIPE

Calories	390	Protein	6% U.S. RDA
Protein	5g	Vitamin A	<2% U.S. RDA
Carbohydrate	54g	Vitamin C	<2% U.S. RDA
Fat	17g	Thiamine	10% U.S. RDA
Cholesterol	60mg	Riboflavin	8% U.S. RDA
Sodium	220mg	Niacin	6% U.S. RDA
Potassium	125mg	Calcium	15% U.S. RDA
Dietary Fiber	1g	Iron	8% U.S. RDA

Grand Prize Winner

Country Apple Coffee Cake

Sue Porubcan, Wisconsin
Bake-Off® 31, 1984

2 tablespoons margarine or butter, softened
1½ cups chopped peeled apples
10-ounce can refrigerated flaky biscuits
⅓ cup firmly packed brown sugar
¼ teaspoon cinnamon
⅓ cup light corn syrup
1½ teaspoons whiskey, if desired
1 egg
½ cup pecan halves or pieces

GLAZE
⅓ cup powdered sugar
¼ teaspoon vanilla
1 to 2 teaspoons milk

Heat oven to 350°F. Using 1 tablespoon of the margarine, generously grease 9-inch round cake pan or 8-inch square pan. Spread 1 cup of the apples in greased pan. Separate dough into 10 biscuits; cut each into 4 pieces. Arrange biscuit pieces point side up over apples. Top with remaining ½ cup apples. In small bowl, combine remaining 1 tablespoon margarine, brown sugar, cinnamon, corn syrup, whiskey and egg; beat 2 to 3 minutes until sugar is partially dissolved. Stir in pecans; spoon over biscuit pieces and apples.

Bake at 350°F. for 35 to 45 minutes or until *deep* golden brown. Cool 5 minutes. In small bowl, blend powdered sugar, vanilla and enough milk for desired drizzling consistency. Drizzle over warm coffee cake. Store in refrigerator. **6 to 8 servings.**

TIP: If desired, serve as dessert with cream.

NUTRIENTS PER 1/8 OF RECIPE

Calories	300	Protein	4% U.S. RDA
Protein	3g	Vitamin A	2% U.S. RDA
Carbohydrate	43g	Vitamin C	<2% U.S. RDA
Fat	13g	Thiamine	10% U.S. RDA
Cholesterol	35mg	Riboflavin	6% U.S. RDA
Sodium	420mg	Niacin	6% U.S. RDA
Potassium	120mg	Calcium	2% U.S. RDA
Dietary Fiber	1g	Iron	10% U.S. RDA

Lemon Almond Breakfast Pastry

Filled with a light, lemon-flavored almond paste, this large round pastry is similar to pastries found in France and Switzerland. Cut in thin wedges to serve.

Hot Roll Moravian Sugar Cake

ᴥ

Mary Simpson, South Carolina
Bake-Off® 29, 1980

1 package hot roll mix
⅓ cup sugar
⅓ cup instant nonfat dry milk
⅓ cup mashed potato flakes
1 cup water heated to 120 to
    130°F.
⅓ cup margarine or butter, melted
2 eggs

TOPPING
⅔ cup firmly packed light brown
    sugar
1 teaspoon cinnamon
½ cup margarine or butter, melted
½ cup chopped nuts

Grease 13 × 9-inch pan. In large bowl, combine flour mixture with yeast from foil packet, sugar, instant nonfat dry milk and potato flakes; blend well. Stir in *hot* water, ⅓ cup margarine and eggs until well blended and dough forms. (Dough will be sticky.) Cover; let rest 5 minutes.

Press dough evenly in greased pan. Cover loosely with greased plastic wrap and cloth towel. Let rise in warm place (80 to 85°F.) until almost double in size, about 45 minutes.

Heat oven to 375°F. In small bowl, combine brown sugar and cinnamon; set aside. Make small pockets in dough by pressing lightly with floured fingertip. Sprinkle brown sugar mixture over dough. Drizzle with ½ cup margarine; sprinkle with nuts. Bake at 375°F. for 15 to 20 minutes or until golden brown. **15 servings.**

HIGH ALTITUDE—Above 3500 Feet: No change.

NUTRIENTS PER 1/15 OF RECIPE

Calories	300	Protein	8% U.S. RDA
Protein	6g	Vitamin A	10% U.S. RDA
Carbohydrate	39g	Vitamin C	<2% U.S. RDA
Fat	14g	Thiamine	15% U.S. RDA
Cholesterol	35mg	Riboflavin	15% U.S. RDA
Sodium	350mg	Niacin	10% U.S. RDA
Potassium	170mg	Calcium	6% U.S. RDA
Dietary Fiber	1g	Iron	8% U.S. RDA

ᴥ

What next?

In 1949, *Life* magazine wanted a group photograph of the 100 final dishes in the first Grand National Baking and Cooking Contest. The magazine succeeded—almost. Someone couldn't resist and ate one of the desserts. The 99 others made the picture.

Quick Cheese Coffee Cake

ᴥ

Joanna Yoakum, California
Bake-Off® 30, 1982

8-ounce package cream cheese,
    softened
½ cup sugar
1 tablespoon flour
1 egg
10-ounce can refrigerated flaky
    biscuits
1½ teaspoons sugar
¼ teaspoon cinnamon

Heat oven to 350°F. In small bowl, beat cream cheese, ½ cup sugar, flour and egg until smooth. Separate dough into 10 biscuits. Place in ungreased 8 or 9-inch round cake pan; press over bottom and 1 inch up sides to form crust. Pour cream cheese mixture into crust-lined pan. In second small bowl, blend 1½ teaspoons sugar and cinnamon; sprinkle over cream cheese mixture. Bake at 350°F. for 24 to 30 minutes or until filling is set and edges of crust are deep golden brown. Cool 20 minutes. Serve warm or cool. Store in refrigerator. **6 to 8 servings.**

NUTRIENTS PER 1/8 OF RECIPE

Calories	270	Protein	8% U.S. RDA
Protein	5g	Vitamin A	8% U.S. RDA
Carbohydrate	30g	Vitamin C	<2% U.S. RDA
Fat	15g	Thiamine	8% U.S. RDA
Cholesterol	70mg	Riboflavin	8% U.S. RDA
Sodium	460mg	Niacin	6% U.S. RDA
Potassium	65mg	Calcium	2% U.S. RDA
Dietary Fiber	<1g	Iron	8% U.S. RDA

Quick Cheese Coffee Cake

Raspberry Ripple Crescent Coffee Cake

Raspberry Ripple Crescent Coffee Cake

Priscilla Yee, California
Bake-Off® 32, 1986

¾ cup sugar
¼ cup margarine, softened
2 eggs
¾ cup ground almonds
¼ cup all purpose or unbleached flour
1 teaspoon grated lemon peel
8-ounce can refrigerated crescent dinner rolls
8 teaspoons raspberry preserves
¼ cup sliced almonds

GLAZE
⅓ cup powdered sugar
1 to 2 teaspoons milk

Heat oven to 375°F. Grease 9-inch round cake pan or 9-inch pie pan. In small bowl, beat sugar, margarine and eggs until smooth. Stir in ground almonds, flour and lemon peel; set aside. Separate dough into 8 triangles.

Spread teaspoonful of the preserves on each triangle. Roll up, starting at shortest side of triangle and rolling to opposite point. Place rolls in greased pan in 2 circles, arranging 5 rolls around outside edge and 3 in center. Pour and carefully spread almond mixture evenly over rolls; sprinkle with almonds.

Bake at 375°F. for 25 to 35 minutes or until deep golden brown and knife inserted in center comes out clean. In small bowl, blend powdered sugar and enough milk for desired drizzling consistency. Drizzle over warm coffee cake. Serve warm. **8 servings.**

TIP: Cover coffee cake with foil during last 5 to 10 minutes of baking if necessary to prevent excessive browning.

NUTRIENTS PER 1/8 OF RECIPE

Calories	360	Protein	8% U.S. RDA
Protein	6g	Vitamin A	6% U.S. RDA
Carbohydrate	44g	Vitamin C	<2% U.S. RDA
Fat	18g	Thiamine	8% U.S. RDA
Cholesterol	70mg	Riboflavin	10% U.S. RDA
Sodium	320mg	Niacin	6% U.S. RDA
Potassium	170mg	Calcium	4% U.S. RDA
Dietary Fiber	2g	Iron	8% U.S. RDA

Quick Apple Pancake

Eileen Thorston, Minnesota
Bake-Off® 31, 1984

¼ cup margarine or butter
1½ cups thinly sliced peeled apples
½ cup sugar
½ teaspoon cinnamon
¼ teaspoon nutmeg

BATTER
1 cup complete or buttermilk complete pancake mix
½ teaspoon cinnamon
¼ teaspoon nutmeg
¾ cup water
1 teaspoon vanilla

TOPPING
1 tablespoon sugar
¼ teaspoon cinnamon

Heat oven to 350°F. In 9-inch pie pan or round cake pan, melt margarine in oven. Stir in apples, ½ cup sugar, ½ teaspoon cinnamon and ¼ teaspoon nutmeg. Bake at 350°F. for 10 minutes. In medium bowl, combine all batter ingredients; blend well. Pour evenly over cooked apples. In small bowl, blend topping ingredients; sprinkle over batter. Bake an additional 15 to 20 minutes or until toothpick inserted in center comes out clean. Let stand 2 minutes. Invert onto serving plate. To serve, cut into wedges. If desired, top with cheese slice or ice cream. **6 servings.**

MICROWAVE DIRECTIONS: In 9-inch microwave-safe pie pan or round cake pan, microwave margarine on HIGH for 30 to 45 seconds or until margarine is melted. Stir in apples, ½ cup sugar, ½ teaspoon cinnamon and ¼ teaspoon nutmeg. Cover; microwave on HIGH for 3 to 4 minutes or until apples are tender. In medium bowl, combine all batter ingredients; blend well. Pour evenly over cooked apples. In small bowl, blend topping ingredients; sprinkle over batter. Microwave on HIGH for 3 to 5 minutes or until toothpick inserted 1½ to 2 inches from edge comes out clean. Let stand 5 minutes on flat surface. Invert onto serving plate. Continue as directed above.

HIGH ALTITUDE—Above 3500 Feet: No change.

NUTRIENTS PER 1/6 OF RECIPE

Calories	240	Protein	2% U.S. RDA
Protein	2g	Vitamin A	6% U.S. RDA
Carbohydrate	39g	Vitamin C	2% U.S. RDA
Fat	9g	Thiamine	8% U.S. RDA
Cholesterol	0mg	Riboflavin	4% U.S. RDA
Sodium	390mg	Niacin	4% U.S. RDA
Potassium	55mg	Calcium	6% U.S. RDA
Dietary Fiber	1g	Iron	6% U.S. RDA

Danish Almond Crescent Ring

Lynette Theodore, Wisconsin
Bake-Off® 33, 1988

¼ cup sugar
3 tablespoons margarine or butter, softened
3½-ounce tube almond paste, broken into small pieces
8-ounce can refrigerated crescent dinner rolls
1 egg, beaten
2 teaspoons sugar
¼ cup sliced almonds

Heat oven to 375°F. Lightly grease cookie sheet. In small bowl using fork, combine ¼ cup sugar, margarine and almond paste; mix well. Set aside.

Unroll dough into 2 long rectangles. Overlap long sides ½ inch; firmly press edges and perforations to seal. Press or roll out to form 16 × 8-inch rectangle; cut lengthwise into 3 equal strips. Place 3 tablespoonfuls of filling mixture evenly down center of each strip. Gently press filling to form 1-inch wide strip. Fold dough over filling, overlapping in center; firmly pinch center seam and ends to seal. On greased cookie sheet, loosely braid 3 filled strips. Form braid into ring; pinch ends of strips together to seal. Brush braid with beaten egg; sprinkle with 2 teaspoons sugar and almonds. Bake at 375°F. for 15 to 22 minutes or until golden brown. Cool 5 minutes; remove from cookie sheet. Serve warm. **8 servings.**

NUTRIENTS PER 1/8 OF RECIPE

Calories	250	Protein	6% U.S. RDA
Protein	5g	Vitamin A	4% U.S. RDA
Carbohydrate	24g	Vitamin C	<2% U.S. RDA
Fat	15g	Thiamine	8% U.S. RDA
Cholesterol	35mg	Riboflavin	10% U.S. RDA
Sodium	290mg	Niacin	6% U.S. RDA
Potassium	180mg	Calcium	4% U.S. RDA
Dietary Fiber	1g	Iron	6% U.S. RDA

Quick Apple Pancake

This recipe, a microwave winner, can also be prepared in a conventional oven. It makes a great dessert when topped with ice cream.

Danish Almond Crescent Ring

The contestant who created this recipe says, "I like this recipe because it's easy to make and uses only a few ingredients, yet it resembles pastries that are more time-consuming to prepare." Refrigerated crescent dinner roll dough is the easy-to-use pastry in this European-style coffee cake.

Pictured top to bottom: Cherry Winks, page 111; Salted Peanut Chews, page 123; Peanut Blossoms, page 124

Cookies and Bars

Delectable cookies and bars of all shapes, sizes and flavors have filled the Bake-Off® cookie jar to overflowing. Recipes have ranged from indulgent, dessert-type sweets featuring chocolate and marshmallows to healthful snacks accented with the wholesome goodness of raisins, granola or oatmeal.

In the early days, recipe preparation was often time-consuming and complicated. Here's how one recipe from the 1950s was described: "Butter-rich coconut rounds topped with a chocolate layer, coated with coconut and crushed cereal and then easily shaped into a five-pointed star." By the 1970s, bar coookies outnumbered all other types of cookies. The 13 × 9-inch baking pan became standard equipment in all kitchens. And even with multiple layers and frostings or toppings, convenient mixes and refrigerated dough products made quick work of preparation.

While creative cooks have turned to inventive new ways of preparing cookies and bars, they still cherish the old favorite recipes from the early years of the Bake-Off® Contest. Several have become classics, although many people who treasure these recipes and use them often are unaware of their origin. Among these heritage recipes are Cherry Winks, Snappy Turtle Cookies, Peanut Blossoms and Oatmeal Carmelitas.

Flavors that were popular in cookies of those early Bake-Off® years are still favorites today—lemon, banana, peanut butter, coconut, cherry, and caramel. And at the top of the list is chocolate. At the first competition there were chocolate kisses, bits, shot, and mint wafers plus unsweetened baking chocolate and cocoa. Today the list has grown to include all of these and even more types of chocolate candies as well as white baking chocolate, as featured in the recipe for premium-style White Chocolate Chunk Cookies.

Within this chapter are ingenious recipes combining both familiar and unusual flavors. Some tuck special surprises inside. Others feature a creative blend of sweet and wholesome ingredients for marvelous new taste treats. And all are tantalizing additions to any family's cookie jar.

White Chocolate Chunk Cookies

White Chocolate Chunk Cookies

꼬ꏿꋖ

Dottie Due, Kentucky
Bake-Off® 33, 1988

 1 cup shortening
³/₄ cup sugar
³/₄ cup firmly packed brown sugar
 3 eggs
 1 teaspoon vanilla
2¹/₂ cups all purpose, unbleached or
  self-rising flour*
 1 teaspoon baking powder
 1 teaspoon baking soda
¹/₂ teaspoon salt
 1 cup flaked coconut
¹/₂ cup rolled oats
¹/₂ cup chopped walnuts
 2 (6-ounce) packages white
  baking bars, cut into
  ¹/₄ to ¹/₂-inch chunks**

Heat oven to 350°F. In large bowl, beat shortening, sugar and brown sugar until light and fluffy. Add eggs, 1 at a time, beating well after each addition. Add vanilla; blend well. Lightly spoon flour into measuring cup; level off. In small bowl, combine flour, baking powder, baking soda and salt; mix well. Add to sugar mixture; mix at low speed until well blended. By hand, stir in remaining ingredients. Drop by rounded table-spoonfuls 2 inches apart onto un-greased cookie sheets. Bake at 350°F. for 10 to 15 minutes or until light golden brown. Cool 1 minute; remove from cookie sheets. **5 dozen cookies.**

TIPS: *If using self-rising flour, omit baking powder, baking soda and salt.

**One 10-ounce package white baking pieces or 12-ounce package vanilla milk chips can be substituted for two 6-ounce packages white baking bars. Do not substitute almond bark or va-nilla-flavored candy coating.

HIGH ALTITUDE—Above 3500 Feet: Decrease baking powder to ¹/₂ tea-spoon. Decrease baking soda to ¹/₂ tea-spoon. Bake at 375°F. for 8 to 12 minutes.

NUTRIENTS PER 1 COOKIE

Calories	120	Protein	2% U.S. RDA
Protein	1g	Vitamin A	<2% U.S. RDA
Carbohydrate	14g	Vitamin C	<2% U.S. RDA
Fat	6g	Thiamine	2% U.S. RDA
Cholesterol	15mg	Riboflavin	2% U.S. RDA
Sodium	60mg	Niacin	2% U.S. RDA
Potassium	45mg	Calcium	2% U.S. RDA
Dietary Fiber	<1g	Iron	2% U.S. RDA

Maple Oat Chewies

Kitty Cahill, Minnesota
Bake-Off® 32, 1986

1 cup sugar
1 cup firmly packed brown sugar
1 cup margarine or butter, softened
1 tablespoon molasses
2 teaspoons maple extract
2 eggs
1¾ cups all purpose or unbleached flour
2 teaspoons baking powder
1 teaspoon cinnamon
½ teaspoon salt
2 cups rolled oats
2 cups crisp rice cereal

Heat oven to 350°F. Grease cookie sheets. In large bowl, beat sugar, brown sugar and margarine until light and fluffy. Add molasses, maple extract and eggs; blend well. Lightly spoon flour into measuring cup; level off. Add flour, baking powder, cinnamon and salt; mix at medium speed until well blended. By hand, stir in rolled oats and cereal.* Drop by heaping teaspoonfuls 2 inches apart onto greased cookie sheets. Bake at 350°F. for 8 to 12 minutes or until light golden brown. Cool 2 minutes; remove from cookie sheets. **5 dozen cookies.**

TIP: *One cup butterscotch chips can be added with rolled oats and cereal, if desired.

HIGH ALTITUDE—Above 3500 Feet: No change.

NUTRIENTS PER 1 COOKIE

Calories	80	Protein	<2% U.S. RDA
Protein	1g	Vitamin A	2% U.S. RDA
Carbohydrate	13g	Vitamin C	<2% U.S. RDA
Fat	3g	Thiamine	4% U.S. RDA
Cholesterol	8mg	Riboflavin	2% U.S. RDA
Sodium	80mg	Niacin	<2% U.S. RDA
Potassium	35mg	Calcium	<2% U.S. RDA
Dietary Fiber	<1g	Iron	2% U.S. RDA

Cherry Winks

Ruth Derousseau, Wisconsin
Bake-Off® 2, 1950

1 cup sugar
¾ cup shortening
2 tablespoons milk
1 teaspoon vanilla
2 eggs
2¼ cups all purpose or unbleached flour
1 teaspoon baking powder
½ teaspoon baking soda
½ teaspoon salt
1 cup chopped pecans
1 cup chopped dates
⅓ cup chopped maraschino cherries, well drained
1½ cups coarsely crushed cornflakes cereal
15 maraschino cherries, quartered, drained

Heat oven to 375°F. Grease cookie sheets. In large bowl, combine sugar, shortening, milk, vanilla and eggs at medium speed until well mixed. Lightly spoon flour into measuring cup; level off. In small bowl, combine flour, baking powder, baking soda and salt; mix well. Add to sugar mixture; mix at low speed until well blended. By hand, stir in pecans, dates and ⅓ cup chopped cherries.* Drop by rounded teaspoonfuls into cereal; thoroughly coat. Shape into balls; place 2 inches apart on greased cookie sheets. Gently press maraschino cherry piece into top of each ball. Bake at 375°F. for 10 to 15 minutes or until light golden brown. **5 dozen cookies.**

TIP: *If desired, cover and refrigerate dough for easier handling.

HIGH ALTITUDE—Above 3500 Feet: No change.

NUTRIENTS PER 1 COOKIE

Calories	90	Protein	<2% U.S. RDA
Protein	1g	Vitamin A	2% U.S. RDA
Carbohydrate	12g	Vitamin C	<2% U.S. RDA
Fat	4g	Thiamine	4% U.S. RDA
Cholesterol	8mg	Riboflavin	2% U.S. RDA
Sodium	60mg	Niacin	2% U.S. RDA
Potassium	40mg	Calcium	<2% U.S. RDA
Dietary Fiber	<1g	Iron	2% U.S. RDA

Cherry Winks

The cherry pressed in the top of each cookie gives these ever popular cookies their name. Their crunchy texture—from cornflakes cereal on the outside, and pecans, dates and cherries hidden inside—appeals to both young and old alike.

Choco-Peanut Toppers

Mary C. Berbano, New Jersey
Bake-Off® 12, 1960

COOKIES
 ½ cup sugar
 1 cup margarine or butter, softened
 1¾ cups all purpose or unbleached flour
 2 teaspoons vanilla

TOPPING
 ⅓ cup firmly packed brown sugar
 ⅓ cup peanut butter
 ¼ cup margarine or butter, softened

GLAZE
 ⅓ cup semi-sweet chocolate chips
 ⅓ cup powdered sugar
 3 to 4 tablespoons milk

Heat oven to 325°F. In large bowl, beat sugar and 1 cup margarine until light and fluffy. Lightly spoon flour into measuring cup; level off. Stir in flour and vanilla; mix well. Drop by teaspoonfuls 2 inches apart onto ungreased cookie sheets. Flatten to ¼-inch thickness with bottom of glass dipped in sugar. Bake at 325°F. for 10 to 15 minutes or until edges are light golden brown. Remove from cookie sheets.

In small bowl, beat brown sugar, peanut butter and ¼ cup margarine until light and fluffy. Spread over *warm* cookies.

In small saucepan over low heat, melt chocolate chips, stirring until smooth. Stir in powdered sugar and enough milk for desired drizzling consistency. Drizzle over cookies. Allow glaze to set before storing cookies.
3 dozen cookies.

HIGH ALTITUDE—Above 3500 Feet: No change.

NUTRIENTS PER 1 COOKIE

Calories	120	Protein	2% U.S. RDA
Protein	1g	Vitamin A	4% U.S. RDA
Carbohydrate	12g	Vitamin C	<2% U.S. RDA
Fat	8g	Thiamine	2% U.S. RDA
Cholesterol	0mg	Riboflavin	<2% U.S. RDA
Sodium	85mg	Niacin	2% U.S. RDA
Potassium	40mg	Calcium	<2% U.S. RDA
Dietary Fiber	<1g	Iron	2% U.S. RDA

Texan-Sized Almond Crunch Cookies

Barbara Hodgson, Indiana
Bake-Off® 30, 1982

 1 cup sugar
 1 cup powdered sugar
 1 cup margarine or butter, softened
 1 cup oil
 1 teaspoon almond extract
 2 eggs
 3½ cups all purpose or unbleached flour
 1 cup whole wheat flour
 1 teaspoon baking soda
 1 teaspoon cream of tartar
 1 teaspoon salt
 2 cups coarsely chopped almonds
 6-ounce package almond brickle baking chips
 Sugar

Heat oven to 350°F. In large bowl, blend sugar, powdered sugar, margarine and oil until well mixed. Add almond extract and eggs; mix well. Lightly spoon flour into measuring cup; level off. In second large bowl, combine all purpose flour, whole wheat flour, baking soda, cream of tartar and salt; mix well. Add to sugar mixture; mix at low speed until well blended. By hand, stir in almonds and brickle chips.* Using large tablespoonfuls of dough, shape into balls. Roll in sugar. Place 5 inches apart on ungreased cookie sheets. With fork dipped in sugar, flatten in crisscross pattern. Bake at 350°F. for 12 to 18 minutes or until light golden brown around edges. Cool 1 minute; remove from cookie sheets.
3½ dozen (4-inch) cookies.

TIP: *For easier handling, refrigerate dough about 30 minutes.

HIGH ALTITUDE—Above 3500 feet: No change.

NUTRIENTS PER 1 COOKIE

Calories	230	Protein	4% U.S. RDA
Protein	3g	Vitamin A	4% U.S. RDA
Carbohydrate	22g	Vitamin C	<2% U.S. RDA
Fat	15g	Thiamine	6% U.S. RDA
Cholesterol	10mg	Riboflavin	6% U.S. RDA
Sodium	135mg	Niacin	4% U.S. RDA
Potassium	70mg	Calcium	2% U.S. RDA
Dietary Fiber	1g	Iron	4% U.S. RDA

Peekaberry Boos

Peekaberry Boos

—❧❧—

Margaret Gregg, Washington
Bake-Off® 10, 1958

1 cup firmly packed brown sugar
³/₄ cup sugar
1 cup margarine or butter, softened
¹/₂ cup water
1 teaspoon almond extract
2 eggs
3 cups all purpose or unbleached flour
2 cups quick-cooking rolled oats
1 teaspoon baking soda
¹/₂ teaspoon salt
¹/₂ teaspoon cinnamon
²/₃ cup raspberry preserves

Heat oven to 400°F. In large bowl, beat brown sugar, sugar and margarine until light and fluffy. Add water, almond extract and eggs; blend well. (Mixture will look curdled.) Lightly spoon flour into measuring cup; level off. In medium bowl, combine flour, rolled oats, baking soda, salt and cinnamon; mix well. Add to sugar mixture; mix at low speed until well blended. Drop by rounded teaspoonfuls 2 inches apart onto ungreased cookie sheets. With back of spoon, make depression in center of each cookie. Fill each depression with ¹/₂ teaspoonful of the preserves. Drop scant teaspoonful of dough over preserves on each cookie. Bake at 400°F. for 6 to 9 minutes or until light golden brown. Remove from cookie sheets immediately.

4¹/₂ to 5 dozen cookies.

HIGH ALTITUDE—Above 3500 Feet: Decrease sugar to ¹/₂ cup. Bake as directed above.

NUTRIENTS PER 1 COOKIE

Calories	100	Protein	2% U.S. RDA
Protein	1g	Vitamin A	2% U.S. RDA
Carbohydrate	15g	Vitamin C	<2% U.S. RDA
Fat	3g	Thiamine	4% U.S. RDA
Cholesterol	8mg	Riboflavin	2% U.S. RDA
Sodium	75mg	Niacin	<2% U.S. RDA
Potassium	35mg	Calcium	<2% U.S. RDA
Dietary Fiber	<1g	Iron	2% U.S. RDA

Sachertorte Cookies

Sachertorte Cookies

Phyllis Wolf, Oregon
Bake-Off® 30, 1982

1 cup margarine or butter,
  softened
4¹/₂-ounce package instant chocolate
  pudding and pie filling mix
1 egg
2 cups all purpose or unbleached
  flour
3 tablespoons sugar
¹/₂ cup apricot or cherry preserves
¹/₂ cup semi-sweet chocolate chips
3 tablespoons margarine or butter,
  melted

Heat oven to 325°F. In large bowl, beat margarine and pudding mix until light and fluffy; beat in egg. Lightly spoon flour into measuring cup; level off. Gradually blend in flour at low speed until dough forms. Shape into 1-inch balls; roll in sugar. Place 2 inches apart on ungreased cookie sheets. With thumb, make depression in center of each cookie.

Bake at 325°F. for 15 to 18 minutes or until firm to touch. Remove from cookie sheets immediately; cool on wire racks. Fill each depression with ¹/₂ teaspoonful of the preserves. In small saucepan over low heat, melt chocolate chips and margarine, stirring until smooth. Drizzle ¹/₂ teaspoonful over each cookie. **4 dozen cookies.**

HIGH ALTITUDE—Above 3500 Feet: Bake at 350°F. for 12 to 15 minutes.

NUTRIENTS PER 1 COOKIE

Calories	90	Protein	<2% U.S. RDA
Protein	1g	Vitamin A	4% U.S. RDA
Carbohydrate	11g	Vitamin C	<2% U.S. RDA
Fat	5g	Thiamine	2% U.S. RDA
Cholesterol	6mg	Riboflavin	<2% U.S. RDA
Sodium	65mg	Niacin	<2% U.S. RDA
Potassium	20mg	Calcium	2% U.S. RDA
Dietary Fiber	<1g	Iron	2% U.S. RDA

Lemon Kiss Cookies

Sandi Lamberton, California
Bake-Off® 33, 1988

1¹/₂ cups butter or margarine,
  softened
³/₄ cup sugar
1 tablespoon lemon extract
2³/₄ cups all purpose or unbleached
  flour
1¹/₂ cups finely chopped almonds
14-ounce package milk chocolate
  candy kisses
Powdered sugar
¹/₂ cup semi-sweet chocolate chips
1 tablespoon shortening

In large bowl, beat butter, sugar and lemon extract until light and fluffy. Lightly spoon flour into measuring cup; level off. Gradually blend in flour and almonds at low speed until well mixed. Cover; refrigerate at least 1 hour for easier handling.

Heat oven to 375°F. Using scant tablespoonful of dough, press around each candy kiss, covering completely. Roll in hands to form ball. Place on ungreased cookie sheets. Bake at 375°F. for 8 to 12 minutes or until set and bottom edges are light golden brown. Cool 1 minute; remove from cookie sheets. Cool completely.

Lightly sprinkle cooled cookies with powdered sugar. In small saucepan over low heat, melt chocolate chips and shortening, stirring until smooth. Drizzle over each cookie.

About 6 dozen cookies.

HIGH ALTITUDE—Above 3500 Feet: Decrease butter to 1¹/₄ cups. Bake as directed above.

NUTRIENTS PER 1 COOKIE

Calories	120	Protein	2% U.S. RDA
Protein	2g	Vitamin A	2% U.S. RDA
Carbohydrate	10g	Vitamin C	<2% U.S. RDA
Fat	8g	Thiamine	2% U.S. RDA
Cholesterol	10mg	Riboflavin	2% U.S. RDA
Sodium	45mg	Niacin	<2% U.S. RDA
Potassium	50mg	Calcium	2% U.S. RDA
Dietary Fiber	<1g	Iron	2% U.S. RDA

Lemon Kiss Cookies

Delicate lemon-flavored cookie dough wraps up a chocolate kiss to make these cookies. They are special enough for entertaining.

Chocolate Almond Bonbons

Mrs. J. Rosoff, California
Bake-Off® 4, 1952

4-ounce bar sweet cooking chocolate
2 tablespoons milk
1/4 cup sugar
3/4 cup margarine or butter, softened
2 teaspoons vanilla
2 cups all purpose or unbleached flour
1/4 teaspoon salt
3 1/2-ounce tube almond paste
Sugar

Heat oven to 350°F. In small saucepan over low heat, melt chocolate in milk, stirring until smooth. In large bowl, beat 1/4 cup sugar and margarine until light and fluffy. Blend in chocolate mixture and vanilla. Lightly spoon flour into measuring cup; level off. Stir in flour and salt; mix well. Using rounded teaspoonfuls of dough, shape into balls. Place 2 inches apart on ungreased cookie sheets. Make a depression in center of each ball. Fill each with scant 1/4 teaspoonful of the almond paste; press dough around filling, covering completely. Bake at 350°F. for 9 to 11 minutes or until set. Remove from cookie sheets; roll in sugar.

4 dozen cookies.

HIGH ALTITUDE—Above 3500 Feet: No change.

NUTRIENTS PER 1 COOKIE

Calories	70	Protein	<2% U.S. RDA
Protein	1g	Vitamin A	2% U.S. RDA
Carbohydrate	8g	Vitamin C	<2% U.S. RDA
Fat	4g	Thiamine	2% U.S. RDA
Cholesterol	0mg	Riboflavin	2% U.S. RDA
Sodium	45mg	Niacin	<2% U.S. RDA
Potassium	25mg	Calcium	<2% U.S. RDA
Dietary Fiber	<1g	Iron	<2% U.S. RDA

Sweet success—

Sweet treats have always counted strongly among Bake-Off® entries. Since 1949, finalist recipes have included a total of 1,903 sweets: 597 cakes, 283 pies, 340 desserts and 683 cookies and bars.

Swedish Heirloom Cookies

Bernice Wheaton, Minnesota
Bake-Off® 3, 1951

2 cups all purpose or unbleached flour
1 cup powdered sugar
1/4 teaspoon salt
1 cup butter or margarine
1 cup finely chopped almonds
1 tablespoon vanilla
Powdered sugar

Heat oven to 325°F. Lightly spoon flour into measuring cup; level off. In large bowl, combine flour, 1 cup powdered sugar and salt; mix well. Using pastry blender or fork, cut in butter until mixture resembles coarse crumbs. Add almonds and vanilla; knead by hand to form a smooth dough. Using rounded teaspoonfuls of dough, shape into balls or crescents. Place 1 inch apart on ungreased cookie sheets. Bake at 325°F. for 12 to 15 minutes or until set. *Do not brown.* Remove from cookie sheets; roll in powdered sugar.

4 to 5 dozen cookies.

HIGH ALTITUDE—Above 3500 Feet: No change.

NUTRIENTS PER 1 COOKIE

Calories	60	Protein	<2% U.S. RDA
Protein	1g	Vitamin A	2% U.S. RDA
Carbohydrate	5g	Vitamin C	<2% U.S. RDA
Fat	4g	Thiamine	2% U.S. RDA
Cholesterol	8mg	Riboflavin	2% U.S. RDA
Sodium	40mg	Niacin	<2% U.S. RDA
Potassium	20mg	Calcium	<2% U.S. RDA
Dietary Fiber	<1g	Iron	<2% U.S. RDA

Pictured left to right: Chocolate Almond Bonbons, Swedish Heirloom Cookies

Pictured top to bottom: Orange and Oats Chewies, page 119; Chewy Microwave Granola Bars, page 132

Orange and Oats Chewies

Maryann Goschka, Michigan
Bake-Off® 31, 1984

2 cups firmly packed brown sugar
1 cup shortening
1 tablespoon grated orange peel
3 tablespoons frozen orange juice concentrate, thawed
2 eggs
2 cups all purpose, unbleached or self-rising flour*
1 teaspoon baking soda
3/4 teaspoon salt
2 cups rolled oats
1 cup chopped nuts
1/3 cup coconut

Heat oven to 350°F. Grease cookie sheets. In large bowl, combine brown sugar, shortening, orange peel, orange juice concentrate and eggs at medium speed until well mixed. Lightly spoon flour into measuring cup; level off. In small bowl, combine flour, baking soda and salt; mix well. Add to sugar mixture; mix at low speed until well blended. By hand, stir in rolled oats, nuts and coconut. Drop by rounded teaspoonfuls 2 inches apart onto greased cookie sheets. Bake at 350°F. for 10 to 12 minutes or until light golden brown. Cool 1 minute; remove from cookie sheets. **5 dozen cookies.**

TIP: *If using self-rising flour, omit baking soda and salt.

HIGH ALTITUDE—Above 3500 Feet: Increase flour to 2 1/2 cups. Bake at 375°F. for 9 to 12 minutes.

NUTRIENTS PER 1 COOKIE

Calories	100	Protein	2% U.S. RDA
Protein	1g	Vitamin A	2% U.S. RDA
Carbohydrate	13g	Vitamin C	<2% U.S. RDA
Fat	5g	Thiamine	6% U.S. RDA
Cholesterol	8mg	Riboflavin	2% U.S. RDA
Sodium	75mg	Niacin	4% U.S. RDA
Potassium	60mg	Calcium	2% U.S. RDA
Dietary Fiber	<1g	Iron	6% U.S. RDA

Marshmallow Cookie Tarts

Susan McCray, Nebraska
Bake-Off® 13, 1961

TARTS
20-ounce package refrigerated sliceable sugar cookie dough
3/4 cup coconut
1 to 1 1/2 cups marshmallow creme

TOPPINGS
Chocolate chips
Chocolate mint candy wafers
Chopped nuts
Peanut butter
Preserves
Toasted Coconut

Heat oven to 325°F. Generously grease 36 muffin cups. Slice cookie dough into 1/4-inch slices. Place one slice in bottom of each greased muffin cup. Sprinkle each with 1 teaspoon of the coconut. Bake at 325°F. for 12 to 15 minutes or until edges are golden brown. Cool 5 minutes; remove from pans. Cool completely. Fill each tart with 1 to 2 teaspoonfuls of the marshmallow creme. Top each with desired toppings. **3 dozen tarts.**

NUTRIENTS PER 1 TART (NO TOPPING)

Calories	90	Protein	<2% U.S. RDA
Protein	1g	Vitamin A	<2% U.S. RDA
Carbohydrate	14g	Vitamin C	<2% U.S. RDA
Fat	3g	Thiamine	2% U.S. RDA
Cholesterol	0mg	Riboflavin	2% U.S. RDA
Sodium	65mg	Niacin	<2% U.S. RDA
Potassium	30mg	Calcium	<2% U.S. RDA
Dietary Fiber	<1g	Iron	<2% U.S. RDA

Marshmallow Cookie Tarts

Marshmallow creme and a choice of toppings fill these delightful cookie tarts. This updated version uses refrigerated sugar cookie dough for the crust, making this favorite from 1961 even quicker to prepare today.

Candy Bar Cookies
—∂₀∂—

Alice Reese, Minnesota
Bake-Off® 13, 1961

BASE
2 cups all purpose or unbleached flour

¾ cup powdered sugar

¾ cup margarine or butter, softened

2 tablespoons whipping cream

1 teaspoon vanilla

FILLING
28 caramels

¼ cup whipping cream

¼ cup margarine or butter

1 cup powdered sugar

1 cup chopped pecans

GLAZE
½ cup semi-sweet chocolate chips

2 tablespoons whipping cream

1 tablespoon margarine or butter

¼ cup powdered sugar

1 teaspoon vanilla

Pecan halves, if desired

Heat oven to 325°F. Lightly spoon flour into measuring cup; level off. In large bowl, blend flour and all remaining base ingredients at low speed until crumbly. Press crumb mixture into ungreased 15 × 10 × 1-inch baking pan. Bake at 325°F. for 15 to 20 minutes or until light golden brown.

In small saucepan over low heat, melt caramels with ¼ cup whipping cream and ¼ cup margarine, stirring until smooth. Remove from heat; stir in 1 cup powdered sugar and pecans. (Add additional cream if necessary for spreading consistency.) Spread filling mixture over base.

In small saucepan over low heat, melt chocolate chips with 2 tablespoons whipping cream and 1 tablespoon margarine, stirring until smooth. Remove from heat; stir in ¼ cup powdered sugar and vanilla. Drizzle glaze over filling. Cut into bars. Decorate each bar with pecan half. **48 cookies.**

Candy Bar Cookies
—∂₀∂—

To make this champion cookie more convenient, we replaced rolling and cutting out the cookie dough with a tender, buttery, press-in-the-pan crust. The baked crust is topped, as in the original recipe, with a turtle-like mixture of caramel, chocolate and pecans.

Split Seconds
—∂₀∂—

Jelly-filled strips of dough are baked and cut to form an attractive shortbread cookie. Use your favorite flavor of jelly or preserves.

HIGH ALTITUDE—Above 3500 Feet: No change.

NUTRIENTS PER 1 COOKIE

Calories	140	Protein	<2% U.S. RDA
Protein	1g	Vitamin A	4% U.S. RDA
Carbohydrate	14g	Vitamin C	<2% U.S. RDA
Fat	9g	Thiamine	4% U.S. RDA
Cholesterol	2mg	Riboflavin	2% U.S. RDA
Sodium	60mg	Niacin	<2% U.S. RDA
Potassium	40mg	Calcium	<2% U.S. RDA
Dietary Fiber	<1g	Iron	2% U.S. RDA

Split Seconds
—∂₀∂—

Karin Fellows, Maryland
Bake-Off® 6, 1954

⅔ cup sugar

¾ cup margarine or butter, softened

2 teaspoons vanilla

1 egg

2 cups all purpose or unbleached flour

½ teaspoon baking powder

½ cup red jelly or preserves

Heat oven to 350°F. In large bowl, beat sugar and margarine until light and fluffy. Blend in vanilla and egg. Lightly spoon flour into measuring cup; level off. Stir in flour and baking powder; mix well. Divide dough into 4 equal parts. On lightly floured surface, shape each part into 12 × ¾-inch roll; place on ungreased cookie sheets. Using handle of wooden spoon or finger, make a depression about ½ inch wide and ¼ inch deep, lengthwise down center of each roll. Fill each with 2 tablespoonfuls of the jelly. Bake at 350°F. for 15 to 20 minutes or until light golden brown. Cool slightly; cut diagonally into bars. Cool on wire racks. **4 dozen cookies.**

HIGH ALTITUDE—Above 3500 Feet: No change.

NUTRIENTS PER 1 COOKIE

Calories	70	Protein	<2% U.S. RDA
Protein	1g	Vitamin A	2% U.S. RDA
Carbohydrate	9g	Vitamin C	<2% U.S. RDA
Fat	3g	Thiamine	2% U.S. RDA
Cholesterol	6mg	Riboflavin	<2% U.S. RDA
Sodium	40mg	Niacin	<2% U.S. RDA
Potassium	10mg	Calcium	<2% U.S. RDA
Dietary Fiber	<1g	Iron	<2% U.S. RDA

Split Seconds

Snappy Turtle Cookies

Beatrice Harlib, Illinois
Bake-Off® 4, 1952

Snappy Turtle Cookies

These rich brown sugar cookies resemble the well-known turtle-shaped candies. This is another recipe that has earned the rank of Bake-Off® classic.

Starlight Mint Surprise Cookies

The idea for this cookie came to the originator when she was given a package of mint-flavored chocolate candies. Brown sugar cookie dough is pressed around each candy so each cookie has a surprise chocolate mint in the center.

COOKIES
¹/₂ cup firmly packed brown sugar
¹/₂ cup margarine or butter, softened
¹/₄ teaspoon vanilla
¹/₈ teaspoon maple flavoring, if desired
1 egg
1 egg, separated
1¹/₂ cups all purpose or unbleached flour
¹/₄ teaspoon baking soda
¹/₄ teaspoon salt
1¹/₂ to 2 cups split pecan halves

FROSTING
¹/₃ cup semi-sweet chocolate chips
3 tablespoons milk
1 tablespoon margarine or butter
1 cup powdered sugar

In large bowl, beat brown sugar and ¹/₂ cup margarine until light and fluffy. Blend in vanilla, maple flavoring, 1 whole egg and 1 egg yolk. Lightly spoon flour into measuring cup; level off. Add flour, baking soda and salt; mix at low speed until well blended. Cover; refrigerate for easier handling.

Heat oven to 350°F. Grease cookie sheets. Arrange pecan pieces in groups of 5 on greased cookie sheets to resemble head and legs of turtle. In small bowl, beat 1 egg white. Using rounded teaspoonfuls of dough, shape into balls. Dip bottoms into beaten egg white; gently press onto pecans. (Tips of pecans should show.) Bake at 350°F. for 10 to 12 minutes or until light golden brown around edges. *Do not overbake.* Remove from cookie sheets immediately. Cool on wire racks.

In small saucepan over low heat, melt chocolate chips with milk and 1 tablespoon margarine, stirring until smooth. Remove from heat; stir in powdered sugar. Add additional powdered sugar if necessary for desired spreading consistency. Frost cookies. **42 cookies.**

HIGH ALTITUDE—Above 3500 Feet: No change.

NUTRIENTS PER 1 COOKIE.

Calories	110	Protein	<2% U.S. RDA
Protein	1g	Vitamin A	2% U.S. RDA
Carbohydrate	10g	Vitamin C	<2% U.S. RDA
Fat	7g	Thiamine	4% U.S. RDA
Cholesterol	10mg	Riboflavin	<2% U.S. RDA
Sodium	50mg	Niacin	<2% U.S. RDA
Potassium	45mg	Calcium	<2% U.S. RDA
Dietary Fiber	<1g	Iron	2% U.S. RDA

Starlight Mint Surprise Cookies

Laura Rott, Illinois
Bake-Off® 1, 1949

1 cup sugar
¹/₂ cup firmly packed brown sugar
³/₄ cup margarine or butter, softened
2 tablespoons water
1 teaspoon vanilla
2 eggs
3 cups all purpose or unbleached flour
1 teaspoon baking soda
¹/₂ teaspoon salt
2 (6-ounce) packages solid chocolate mint candy wafers, unwrapped
60 walnut halves

In large bowl, blend sugar, brown sugar, margarine, water, vanilla and eggs until well mixed. Lightly spoon flour into measuring cup; level off. In medium bowl, combine flour, baking soda and salt; mix well. Add to sugar mixture; mix at low speed until well blended. Cover; refrigerate at least 2 hours for easier handling.

Heat oven to 375°F. Using about 1 tablespoonful of dough, press around each candy water to cover completely. Place 2 inches apart on ungreased cookie sheets. Top each with walnut half. Bake at 375°F. for 7 to 9 minutes or until light golden brown.
5 dozen cookies.

HIGH ALTITUDE—Above 3500 Feet: No change.

NUTRIENTS PER 1 COOKIE

Calories	100	Protein	<2% U.S. RDA
Protein	1g	Vitamin A	2% U.S. RDA
Carbohydrate	13g	Vitamin C	<2% U.S. RDA
Fat	5g	Thiamine	2% U.S. RDA
Cholesterol	8mg	Riboflavin	<2% U.S. RDA
Sodium	65mg	Niacin	<2% U.S. RDA
Potassium	40mg	Calcium	<2% U.S. RDA
Dietary Fiber	<1g	Iron	2% U.S. RDA

Salted Peanut Chews

Gertrude Schweitzerhof, California
Bake-Off® 29, 1980

CRUST
1½ cups all purpose or unbleached
flour
⅔ cup firmly packed brown sugar
½ teaspoon baking powder
½ teaspoon salt
¼ teaspoon baking soda
½ cup margarine or butter,
softened
1 teaspoon vanilla
2 egg yolks
3 cups miniature marshmallows

TOPPING
⅔ cup corn syrup
¼ cup margarine or butter
2 tablespoons vanilla
12-ounce package (2 cups) peanut
butter chips
2 cups crisp rice cereal
2 cups salted peanuts

Heat oven to 350°F. Lightly spoon flour into measuring cup; level off. In large bowl, combine flour and remaining crust ingredients except marshmallows on low speed until crumbly. Press firmly in bottom of ungreased 13 × 9-inch pan. Bake at 350°F. for 12 to 15 minutes or until light golden brown. Immediately sprinkle marshmallows over top. Bake an additional 1 to 2 minutes or until marshmallows just begin to puff. Cool while preparing topping.

In large saucepan over low heat, heat corn syrup, ¼ cup margarine, 2 teaspoons vanilla and peanut butter chips just until chips are melted and mixture is smooth, stirring constantly. Remove from heat. Stir in cereal and peanuts. Immediately spoon warm topping over marshmallows; spread to cover. Refrigerate until firm. Cut into bars. **36 bars.**

MICROWAVE DIRECTIONS Combine all crust ingredients as directed above. Press in bottom of ungreased 13 × 9-inch (3-quart) microwave-safe baking dish. Microwave on HIGH for 4 to 5½ minutes, rotating pan ½ turn halfway through cooking. Immediately sprinkle with marshmallows. Microwave on HIGH for 1 to 1½ minutes or until marshmallows begin to puff.

In 2-quart microwave-safe casserole, combine corn syrup, ¼ cup margarine, 2 teaspoons vanilla and peanut butter chips. Microwave on HIGH for 2 to 2½ minutes or until chips are melted, stirring once. Stir in cereal and peanuts. Immediately spoon warm topping over marshmallows; spread to cover. Refrigerate until firm. Cut into bars.

HIGH ALTITUDE—Above 3500 Feet: No change.

NUTRIENTS PER 1 BAR

Calories	210	Protein	6% U.S. RDA
Protein	5g	Vitamin A	4% U.S. RDA
Carbohydrate	23g	Vitamin C	<2% U.S. RDA
Fat	11g	Thiamine	6% U.S. RDA
Cholesterol	15mg	Riboflavin	4% U.S. RDA
Sodium	200mg	Niacin	10% U.S. RDA
Potassium	125mg	Calcium	2% U.S. RDA
Dietary Fiber	<1g	Iron	6% U.S. RDA

Lemon-Go-Lightly Cookies

Margaret Conway, California
Bake-Off® 27, 1976

2 cups all purpose or unbleached
flour
2 cups mashed potato flakes
1 cup sugar
1 cup firmly packed brown sugar
½ to ¾ cup finely chopped nuts
1 teaspoon baking soda
¾ cup margarine or butter, melted
1 teaspoon grated lemon peel
2 eggs
¼ cup sugar

Heat oven to 350°F. Lightly spoon flour into measuring cup; level off. In large bowl, blend flour and remaining ingredients except ¼ cup sugar until well mixed. (Mixture will be crumbly.) Firmly press mixture into 1-inch balls; roll in ¼ cup sugar. Place 2 inches apart on ungreased cookie sheets. Bake at 350°F. for 9 to 12 minutes or until golden brown. Cool 1 minute; remove from cookie sheets.
6 dozen cookies.

HIGH ALTITUDE—Above 3500 Feet: No change.

NUTRIENTS PER 1 COOKIE

Calories	70	Protein	<2% U.S. RDA
Protein	1g	Vitamin A	<2% U.S. RDA
Carbohydrate	11g	Vitamin C	<2% U.S. RDA
Fat	3g	Thiamine	2% U.S. RDA
Cholesterol	8mg	Riboflavin	<2% U.S. RDA
Sodium	45mg	Niacin	<2% U.S. RDA
Potassium	45mg	Calcium	<2% U.S. RDA
Dietary Fiber	<1g	Iron	<2% U.S. RDA

Salted Peanut Chews

This frequently made bar cookie, reminiscent of a popular candy bar, is equally successful when baked in microwave or conventional oven.

Lemon-Go-Lightly Cookies

Potato flakes are the secret ingredient in these soft, chewy, delicately flavored cookies.

Peanut Blossoms

Freda Smith, Ohio
Bake-Off® 9, 1957

1³/₄ **cups all purpose or unbleached flour**
¹/₂ **cup sugar**
¹/₂ **cup firmly packed brown sugar**
1 **teaspoon baking soda**
¹/₂ **teaspoon salt**
¹/₂ **cup shortening**
¹/₂ **cup peanut butter**
2 **tablespoons milk**
1 **teaspoon vanilla**
1 **egg**
  Sugar
  About 48 milk chocolate candy kisses

Heat oven to 375°F. Lightly spoon flour into measuring cup; level off. In large bowl, blend flour, ¹/₂ cup sugar, brown sugar, baking soda, salt, shortening, peanut butter, milk, vanilla and egg at low speed until stiff dough forms. Shape into 1-inch balls; roll in sugar. Place 2 inches apart on ungreased cookie sheets. Bake at 375°F. for 10 to 12 minutes or until golden brown. Immediately top each cookie with a candy kiss, pressing down firmly so cookie cracks around edge; remove from cookie sheets. **About 4 dozen cookies.**

HIGH ALTITUDE—Above 3500 Feet: No change.

NUTRIENTS PER 1 COOKIE

Calories	100	Protein	2% U.S. RDA
Protein	2g	Vitamin A	<2% U.S. RDA
Carbohydrate	12g	Vitamin C	<2% U.S. RDA
Fat	5g	Thiamine	2% U.S. RDA
Cholesterol	6mg	Riboflavin	2% U.S. RDA
Sodium	65mg	Niacin	2% U.S. RDA
Potassium	55mg	Calcium	<2% U.S. RDA
Dietary Fiber	<1g	Iron	2% U.S. RDA

Peanut Blossoms

Have you ever wondered where old-fashioned cookie favorites such as these originated? This cookie made its first appearance as a prizewinner in a Bake-Off® Contest.

Easy Lemon Sours

Irene E. Souza, California
Bake-Off® 30, 1982

BASE
1 **package pudding-included yellow cake mix**
2 **cups crushed cornflakes cereal**
¹/₂ **cup firmly packed brown sugar**
¹/₃ **cup chopped nuts**
¹/₂ **cup margarine or butter, softened**

FILLING
  3-ounce package lemon pudding and pie filling mix (not instant)
  14-ounce can sweetened condensed milk (not evaporated)
³/₄ **teaspoon lemon extract**

GLAZE
1 **cup powdered sugar, sifted**
¹/₄ **teaspoon lemon extract**
3 **to 5 teaspoons water**

Heat oven to 350°F. Generously grease 15×10×1-inch baking pan. In large bowl, combine all base ingredients at low speed until crumbly. Reserve 1¹/₂ cups of crumb mixture for topping. Press remaining mixture in bottom of greased pan. In small bowl, combine all filling ingredients; mix well. Pour filling mixture evenly over base; gently spread. Sprinkle with reserved 1¹/₂ cups crumb mixture.

Bake at 350°F. for 20 to 30 minutes or until golden brown. Loosen edges. In small bowl, blend powdered sugar, ¹/₄ teaspoon lemon extract and enough water for desired drizzling consistency. Drizzle over warm bars. Cool completely. Cut into bars. **48 bars.**

HIGH ALTITUDE—Above 3500 Feet: No change.

NUTRIENTS PER 1 BAR

Calories	140	Protein	2% U.S. RDA
Protein	2g	Vitamin A	4% U.S. RDA
Carbohydrate	23g	Vitamin C	2% U.S. RDA
Fat	5g	Thiamine	6% U.S. RDA
Cholesterol	4mg	Riboflavin	6% U.S. RDA
Sodium	150mg	Niacin	4% U.S. RDA
Potassium	65mg	Calcium	4% U.S. RDA
Dietary Fiber	<1g	Iron	2% U.S. RDA

Easy Lemon Sours

Oatmeal Carmelitas

Erlyce Larson, Minnesota
Bake-Off® 18, 1967

Oatmeal Carmelitas

o%do

This layered oatmeal bar cookie with its indulgent chocolate-caramel filling is a time-tested favorite.

CRUST

2 cups all purpose or unbleached flour
2 cups quick-cooking rolled oats
1½ cups firmly packed brown sugar
1 teaspoon baking soda
½ teaspoon salt
1¼ cups margarine or butter, softened

FILLING

6-ounce package (1 cup) semi-sweet chocolate chips
½ cup chopped nuts
12-ounce jar (1 cup) caramel ice cream topping
3 tablespoons flour

Heat oven to 350°F. Grease 13 × 9-inch pan. Lightly spoon flour into measuring cup; level off. In large bowl, blend flour and all remaining crust ingredients at low speed until crumbly. Press half (about 3 cups) of crumb mixture in bottom of greased pan. Reserve remaining crumb mixture for topping. Bake at 350°F. for 10 minutes.

Sprinkle warm crust with chocolate chips and nuts. In small bowl, combine caramel topping and 3 tablespoons flour; drizzle evenly over chocolate chips and nuts. Sprinkle with reserved crumb mixture. Bake an additional 18 to 22 minutes or until golden brown. Cool completely. Refrigerate 1 to 2 hours or until filling is set. Cut into bars. **36 bars.**

HIGH ALTITUDE—Above 3500 Feet: No change.

NUTRIENTS PER 1 BAR

Calories	200	Protein	4% U.S. RDA
Protein	2g	Vitamin A	10% U.S. RDA
Carbohydrate	26g	Vitamin C	<2% U.S. RDA
Fat	9g	Thiamine	8% U.S. RDA
Cholesterol	0mg	Riboflavin	4% U.S. RDA
Sodium	200mg	Niacin	6% U.S. RDA
Potassium	80mg	Calcium	4% U.S. RDA
Dietary Fiber	1g	Iron	10% U.S. RDA

Apricot Almond Squares

o%do

Sandy Munson, Colorado
Bake-Off® 32, 1986

BASE

1 package pudding-included yellow or white cake mix
½ cup margarine or butter, melted
½ cup finely chopped almonds
1 cup apricot preserves

FILLING

8-ounce package cream cheese, softened
¼ cup sugar
2 tablespoons flour
⅛ teaspoon salt
1 teaspoon vanilla
1 egg
⅓ cup apricot preserves
½ cup coconut

Heat oven to 350°F. Generously grease 13 × 9-inch pan. In large bowl, combine cake mix and margarine at low speed until crumbly. Stir in almonds. Reserve 1 cup of crumb mixture for filling. Press remaining mixture in bottom of greased pan. Carefully spread 1 cup preserves over base.*

In same bowl, beat cream cheese, sugar, flour, salt, vanilla and egg until well blended. Stir in ⅓ cup preserves at low speed. Carefully spread filling mixture over base. In small bowl, combine reserved 1 cup crumb mixture and coconut; mix well. Sprinkle over filling. Bake at 350°F. for 30 to 40 minutes or until golden brown and center is set. Cool completely. Store in refrigerator. **36 bars.**

TIP: *For ease in spreading, preserves can be warmed slightly.

HIGH ALTITUDE—Above 3500 Feet: No change.

NUTRIENTS PER 1 BAR

Calories	170	Protein	2% U.S. RDA
Protein	2g	Vitamin A	4% U.S. RDA
Carbohydrate	22g	Vitamin C	<2% U.S. RDA
Fat	8g	Thiamine	2% U.S. RDA
Cholesterol	15mg	Riboflavin	2% U.S. RDA
Sodium	150mg	Niacin	2% U.S. RDA
Potassium	45mg	Calcium	2% U.S. RDA
Dietary Fiber	<1g	Iron	2% U.S. RDA

White Chocolate Almond Brownies

Sally Vog, Oregon
Bake-Off® 33, 1988

BARS

 2 (5-ounce) Alpine White® candy bars with chopped almonds
 ¼ cup margarine or butter
 ½ cup sugar
 ⅛ teaspoon salt
 2 eggs
 1 teaspoon vanilla
 ¼ teaspoon almond extract
 1 cup all purpose or unbleached flour
 ¼ teaspoon baking powder

GLAZE

 1 teaspoon shortening
 1 ounce (1 square) semi-sweet chocolate, cut into pieces

Heat oven to 350°F. Grease 8 or 9-inch square pan. Cut 1 of the candy bars into ⅜-inch pieces; set aside. In small saucepan over low heat, melt second candy bar and margarine, stirring until smooth. In large bowl, combine sugar, salt and eggs; beat at high speed until light in color, about 4 minutes. Add melted candy bar mixture, vanilla and almond extract; mix at medium speed until well blended. Lightly spoon flour into measuring cup; level off. By hand, stir in flour and baking powder until just combined. Fold in candy bar pieces. Pour into greased pan. Bake at 350°F. for 25 to 30 minutes or until center is set and top is light golden brown. Cool completely.

In small saucepan over low heat, melt shortening and semi-sweet chocolate, stirring until smooth. Drizzle over cooled bars. Allow glaze to set before cutting into bars. Cut into bars.
24 to 36 bars.

HIGH ALTITUDE—Above 3500 Feet: No change.

NUTRIENTS PER 1 BAR

Calories	90	Protein	2% U.S. RDA
Protein	1g	Vitamin A	<2% U.S. RDA
Carbohydrate	11g	Vitamin C	<2% U.S. RDA
Fat	5g	Thiamine	<2% U.S. RDA
Cholesterol	15mg	Riboflavin	2% U.S. RDA
Sodium	35mg	Niacin	<2% U.S. RDA
Potassium	40mg	Calcium	2% U.S. RDA
Dietary Fiber	<1g	Iron	<2% U.S. RDA

Chewy Microwave Granola Bars

Ann Scates, Illinois
Bake-Off® 31, 1984

 1 cup firmly packed brown sugar
 ¼ cup sugar
 ½ cup margarine or butter, softened
 2 tablespoons honey
 ½ teaspoon vanilla
 1 egg
 1 cup all purpose or unbleached flour
 1 teaspoon cinnamon
 ½ teaspoon baking powder
 ¼ teaspoon salt
 1½ cups rolled oats
 1¼ cups crisp rice cereal
 1 cup chopped almonds
 1 cup semi-sweet chocolate chips
 ½ cup wheat germ

MICROWAVE DIRECTIONS: Grease 12 × 8-inch (2-quart) or 13 × 9-inch (3-quart) microwave-safe dish. In large bowl, beat brown sugar, sugar and margarine until light and fluffy. Blend in honey, vanilla and egg. Lightly spoon flour into measuring cup; level off. Gradually blend in flour, cinnamon, baking powder and salt at low speed until well mixed. By hand, stir in remaining ingredients. Press firmly in bottom of greased dish. Microwave on MEDIUM for 7 to 9 minutes or until set, rotating dish ½ turn every 3 minutes during cooking. (Bars will firm up as they stand.) Cool completely. **24 bars.**

CONVENTIONAL DIRECTIONS: Heat oven to 350°F. Grease 13 × 9-inch pan. In large bowl, combine ingredients as directed above. Press firmly in bottom of greased pan. Bake at 350°F. for 20 to 25 minutes or until edges are light golden brown and center appears set. Cool completely. Cut into bars.

HIGH ALTITUDE—Above 3500 Feet: No change.

NUTRIENTS PER 1 BAR

Calories	210	Protein	4% U.S. RDA
Protein	3g	Vitamin A	10% U.S. RDA
Carbohydrate	27g	Vitamin C	<2% U.S. RDA
Fat	10g	Thiamine	10% U.S. RDA
Cholesterol	10mg	Riboflavin	8% U.S. RDA
Sodium	160mg	Niacin	8% U.S. RDA
Potassium	135mg	Calcium	6% U.S. RDA
Dietary Fiber	1g	Iron	10% U.S. RDA

Persistence pays off!

Food editors, reporters and cameras all contribute to the hubbub of the contest area. One flustered contestant, trying politely to answer a reporter's questions, omitted an important ingredient in his cake and didn't discover the error until it came out of the oven. His next try was completed just seconds before the contest time officially ended. But persistence paid off—he was a $2,000-prize winner.

Peanut Butter 'n Fudge Brownies

Peanut Butter 'n Fudge Brownies

Jeannie Hobel, California
Bake-Off® 31, 1984

BROWNIES
- 2 cups sugar
- 1 cup margarine or butter, softened
- 4 eggs
- 2 teaspoons vanilla
- 1½ cups all purpose or unbleached flour
- ¾ cup unsweetened cocoa
- 1 teaspoon baking powder
- ½ teaspoon salt
- 1 cup peanut butter chips
- ¾ peanut butter
- ⅓ cup margarine or butter, softened
- ⅓ cup sugar
- 2 tablespoons flour
- ¾ teaspoon vanilla
- 2 eggs

FROSTING
- 3 tablespoons margarine or butter
- 3-ounces (3 squares) unsweetened chocolate
- 2⅔ cups powdered sugar
- ¼ teaspoon salt
- ¾ teaspoon vanilla
- 4 to 5 tablespoons water

Heat oven to 350°F. Grease 13 × 9-inch pan. In large bowl, beat 2 cups sugar and 1 cup margarine until light and fluffy. Add 4 eggs, 1 at a time, beating well after each addition. Add 2 teaspoons vanilla; mix well. Lightly spoon flour into measuring cup; level off. In small bowl, combine 1½ cups flour, cocoa, baking powder and ½ teaspoon salt; mix well. Add to sugar mixture; mix at low speed until well blended. By hand, stir in peanut butter chips.

In small bowl, beat peanut butter and ⅓ cup margarine until smooth. Add ⅓ cup sugar and 2 tablespoons flour; mix well. Add ¾ teaspoon vanilla and 2 eggs; beat until smooth. Spread half of chocolate mixture in greased pan. Spread peanut butter mixture evenly over chocolate mixture. Spread remaining chocolate mixture evenly over peanut butter mixture. To marble, pull knife through layers in wide curves. Bake at 350°F. for 40 to 50 minutes or until top springs back when touched lightly in center and brownies begin to pull away from sides of pan. Cool completely.

In medium saucepan over low heat, melt 3 tablespoons margarine and chocolate, stirring until smooth. Remove from heat. Blend in powdered sugar, 1/4 teaspoon salt, 3/4 teaspoon vanilla and enough water for desired spreading consistency. Frost cooled brownies. Cut into bars. **36 bars.**

HIGH ALTITUDE — Above 3500 Feet: No change.

NUTRIENTS PER 1 BAR

Calories	260	Protein	6% U.S. RDA
Protein	5g	Vitamin A	6% U.S. RDA
Carbohydrate	29g	Vitamin C	<2% U.S. RDA
Fat	14g	Thiamine	4% U.S. RDA
Cholesterol	45mg	Riboflavin	4% U.S. RDA
Sodium	200mg	Niacin	8% U.S. RDA
Potassium	115mg	Calcium	2% U.S. RDA
Dietary Fiber	1g	Iron	4% U.S. RDA

Chocolate Mint Parfait Bars

Cheryl Wolf, Oregon
Bake-Off® 30, 1982

BASE
1 package pudding-included devil's food cake mix
1/3 cup margarine or butter, softened
1 egg

FILLING
1 envelope unflavored gelatin
1/4 cup boiling water
4 cups powdered sugar
1/2 cup margarine or butter, softened
1/2 cup shortening
1/4 teaspoon peppermint extract
2 to 3 drops green food coloring

FROSTING
3 tablespoons margarine or butter
6-ounce package (1 cup) semi-sweet chocolate chips

Heat oven to 350°F. Grease 15 × 10 × 1-inch baking pan. In large bowl, combine all base ingredients at low speed until crumbly. Press in bottom of greased pan. Bake at 350°F. for 10 minutes. Cool completely.

Dissolve gelatin in water; cool slightly. In large bowl, combine dissolved gelatin and 2 cups of the powdered sugar; mix well. Add 1/2 cup margarine, shortening, peppermint extract and food coloring; beat 1 minute at medium speed until smooth. Blend in remaining 2 cups powdered sugar at low speed until well mixed. Spread filling mixture evenly over cooled base.

In small saucepan over low heat, melt 3 tablespoons margarine and chocolate chips, stirring until smooth. Spoon frosting evenly over filling, carefully spreading to cover. Refrigerate until firm. Cut into bars. Let stand at room temperature about 20 minutes before serving. Store in refrigerator. **48 bars.**

HIGH ALTITUDE — Above 3500 Feet: No change.

NUTRIENTS PER 1 BAR

Calories	160	Protein	<2% U.S. RDA
Protein	1g	Vitamin A	2% U.S. RDA
Carbohydrate	18g	Vitamin C	<2% U.S. RDA
Fat	9g	Thiamine	<2% U.S. RDA
Cholesterol	6mg	Riboflavin	<2% U.S. RDA
Sodium	135mg	Niacin	<2% U.S. RDA
Potassium	35mg	Calcium	2% U.S. RDA
Dietary Fiber	<1g	Iron	<2% U.S. RDA

Chocolate Mint Parfait Bars

Layers of chocolate frosting, refreshing mint filling, and devil's food cake make this bar one of the most requested Bake-Off® recipes.

Treasure Chest Bars

Marie Hammons, Kansas
Bake-Off® 14, 1962

BARS

2 cups all purpose or unbleached flour
½ cup sugar
½ cup firmly packed brown sugar
1½ teaspoons baking powder
    Dash salt
¾ cup milk
½ cup margarine or butter, softened
1 teaspoon vanilla
2 eggs
3 (1.45-ounce) bars milk chocolate candy, cut into small pieces
1 cup maraschino cherries, drained, halved
1 cup coarsely chopped mixed nuts

ICING

¼ cup butter
2 cups powdered sugar
½ teaspoon vanilla
2 to 3 tablespoons milk

Heat oven to 350°F. Grease and flour 15×10×1-inch baking pan. Lightly spoon flour into measuring cup; level off. In large bowl, combine flour and remaining ingredients except chocolate, cherries and nuts. Blend 2 minutes at medium speed or until smooth. By hand, stir in chocolate, cherries and nuts. Spread in greased and floured pan. Bake at 350°F. for 25 to 30 minutes or until light golden brown.

In small heavy saucepan over medium heat, brown butter until light golden brown, stirring constantly. Remove from heat. Blend in powdered sugar, ½ teaspoon vanilla and enough milk for desired spreading consistency. Spread over warm bars. Cool completely. Cut into bars. **48 bars.**

HIGH ALTITUDE—Above 3500 Feet: No change.

NUTRIENTS PER 1 BAR

Calories	120	Protein	2% U.S. RDA
Protein	2g	Vitamin A	2% U.S. RDA
Carbohydrate	15g	Vitamin C	<2% U.S. RDA
Fat	6g	Thiamine	2% U.S. RDA
Cholesterol	15mg	Riboflavin	2% U.S. RDA
Sodium	55mg	Niacin	2% U.S. RDA
Potassium	55mg	Calcium	2% U.S. RDA
Dietary Fiber	<1g	Iron	2% U.S. RDA

Quick Crescent Baklava

This ingenious contestant borrowed an idea from the Greeks, simplified it by using refrigerated crescent roll dough and created a delightful dessert bar.

Quick Crescent Baklava

Annette Erbeck, Ohio
Bake-Off® 29, 1980

2 (8-ounce) cans refrigerated crescent dinner rolls
3 to 4 cups walnuts, finely chopped
½ cup sugar
1 teaspoon cinnamon

GLAZE

¼ cup sugar
½ cup honey
2 tablespoons margarine or butter
2 teaspoons lemon juice

Heat oven to 350°F. Unroll 1 can of dough into 2 long rectangles. Place in ungreased 13×9-inch pan; press over bottom and ½ inch up sides to form crust. Seal perforations. Bake at 350°F. for 5 minutes.

In large bowl, combine walnuts, ½ cup sugar and cinnamon; mix well. Spoon walnut mixture evenly over partially baked crust. Unroll remaining can of dough into 2 long rectangles. Place over walnut mixture; press out to edges of pan. With tip of sharp knife and using dough edges and perforations as a guide, score dough with 5 lengthwise and 7 diagonal markings to form 28 diamond-shaped pieces.

In small saucepan, combine all glaze ingredients. Bring to a boil; remove from heat. Spoon half of glaze evenly over dough. Bake an additional 25 to 30 minutes or until golden brown. Spoon remaining glaze evenly over hot baklava. Cool completely. Refrigerate until thoroughly chilled. Cut into diamond-shaped pieces. **28 servings.**

NUTRIENTS PER 1/28 OF RECIPE

Calories	230	Protein	4% U.S. RDA
Protein	3g	Vitamin A	<2% U.S. RDA
Carbohydrate	20g	Vitamin C	<2% U.S. RDA
Fat	15g	Thiamine	6% U.S. RDA
Cholesterol	0mg	Riboflavin	2% U.S. RDA
Sodium	140mg	Niacin	2% U.S. RDA
Potassium	125mg	Calcium	2% U.S. RDA
Dietary Fiber	1g	Iron	4% U.S. RDA

Quick Crescent Baklava

Rocky Road Fudge Bars

Rocky Road Fudge Bars

Mary Wilson, Georgia
Bake-Off® 23, 1972

BASE
- 1/2 cup margarine or butter
- 1 ounce (1 square) unsweetened chocolate, chopped
- 1 cup all purpose or unbleached flour
- 1 cup sugar
- 3/4 cup chopped nuts
- 1 teaspoon baking powder
- 1 teaspoon vanilla
- 2 eggs

FILLING
- 8-ounce package cream cheese, softened, reserving 2 ounces for frosting
- 1/4 cup margarine or butter, softened
- 1/2 cup sugar
- 2 tablespoons flour
- 1/2 teaspoon vanilla
- 1 egg
- 1/4 cup chopped nuts
- 6-ounce package (1 cup) semi-sweet chocolate chips

FROSTING
- 2 cups miniature marshmallows
- 1/4 cup margarine or butter
- 1/4 cup milk
- 1 ounce (1 square) unsweetened chocolate, chopped
- 3 cups powdered sugar, sifted
- 1 teaspoon vanilla

Heat oven to 350°F. Grease and flour 13 × 9-inch pan. In large saucepan over low heat, melt 1/2 cup margarine and 1 ounce unsweetened chocolate, stirring until smooth. Lightly spoon flour into measuring cup; level off. Add 1 cup flour and remaining base ingredients; mix well. Spread in greased and floured pan.

In small bowl, combine all filling ingredients except 1/4 cup nuts and chocolate chips. Beat 1 minute at medium speed until smooth and fluffy. By hand, stir in nuts. Spread over chocolate mixture; sprinkle evenly with chocolate chips. Bake at 350°F. for 25 to 35 minutes or until toothpick inserted in center comes out clean.

Immediately sprinkle marshmallows over top. Bake an additional 2 minutes. In large saucepan over low heat, combine 1/4 cup margarine, milk, 1 ounce unsweetened chocolate and reserved 2 ounces cream cheese; stir until well blended. Remove from heat. Stir in powdered sugar and 1 teaspoon vanilla; blend until smooth. Immediately spoon warm frosting over marshmallows. To marble, lightly pull knife through frosting and marshmallows in wide curves. Refrigerate until firm. Cut into bars. **48 bars.**

HIGH ALTITUDE—Above 3500 Feet: No change.

Grand Prize Winner

Chocolate Cherry Bars

Frances Jerzak, Minnesota
Bake-Off® 25, 1974

BARS

- 1 package pudding-included devil's food cake mix
- 21-ounce can cherry fruit pie filling
- 1 teaspoon almond extract
- 2 eggs, beaten

FROSTING

- 1 cup sugar
- 1/3 cup milk
- 5 tablespoons margarine or butter
- 6-ounce package (1 cup) semi-sweet chocolate chips

Heat oven to 350°F. Grease and flour 15×10×1-inch baking pan or 13×9-inch pan. In large bowl, combine all bar ingredients; stir until well blended. Pour into greased and floured pan. Bake at 350°F. in 15×10×1-inch pan for 20 to 30 minutes or in 13×9-inch pan for 25 to 30 minutes or until toothpick inserted in center comes out clean.

In small saucepan, combine sugar, milk and margarine. Bring to a boil; boil 1 minute, stirring constantly. Remove from heat; stir in chocolate chips until smooth. Pour and spread over warm bars. Cool completely. **36 to 48 bars.**

HIGH ALTITUDE—Above 3500 Feet: Bake at 375°F. in 15×10×1-inch pan for 20 to 30 minutes or in 13×9-inch pan for 25 to 30 minutes.

Grand Prize Winner

Pecan Pie Surprise Bars

Pearl Hall, Washington
Bake-Off® 22, 1971

BASE

- 1 package pudding-included yellow or butter flavor cake mix
- 1/3 cup margarine or butter, softened
- 1 egg

FILLING

- 1/2 cup firmly packed brown sugar
- 1 1/2 cups dark corn syrup
- 1 teaspoon vanilla
- 3 eggs
- 1 cup chopped pecans

Heat oven to 350°F. Grease 13×9-inch pan. Reserve 2/3 cup of the dry cake mix for filling. In large bowl, combine remaining dry cake mix, margarine and 1 egg at low speed until well blended. Press in bottom of greased pan. Bake at 350°F. for 15 to 20 minutes or until light golden brown.

In large bowl, combine reserved 2/3 cup dry cake mix, brown sugar, corn syrup, vanilla and 3 eggs at low speed until moistened. Beat 1 minute at medium speed until well blended. Pour filling mixture over warm base; sprinkle with pecans. Bake an additional 30 to 35 minutes or until filling is set. Cool completely. Cut into bars. Store in refrigerator. **36 bars.**

HIGH ALTITUDE—Above 3500 Feet: Add 1/3 cup flour to dry cake mix. Decrease dark corn syrup to 1 1/4 cups. Bake as directed above.

Pecan Pie Surprise Bars

The surprise is pecan pie in a convenient bar cookie.

Pictured top to bottom: Orange Kiss-Me Cake, page 153; Caramel Apple Cake, page 153; Double Lemon Streusel Cake, page 152

Cakes and Tortes

❧

It's been said that a great meal without dessert is a contradiction in terms. And what could be a more fitting mealtime finale than a taste-tempting cake or torte, especially if it ranks among the best of Bake-Off® recipes. In fact, cakes have won more Grand Prizes than any other type of food since the beginning of the Bake-Off® Contest.

Although this category has remained ever popular, it has undergone tremendous change over the years. Fancy, elaborately decorated cakes made up the largest category of entries in the 1950s. And several gorgeous multilayered productions of that time, including "My Inspiration" Cake and Mardi Gras Party Cake, have become Bake-Off® classics.

During the ensuing years, cake and frosting mixes came into the limelight. The emphasis on shortcut baking resulted in simple sensations like self-frosted cakes and others with no topping at all. Ring-of-Coconut Fudge Cake and Banana Crunch Cake were typical of those featuring multiple baked-in layers. And with the famous Tunnel of Fudge Cake, a soft, fudgy center "magically" appeared after baking.

Sweets lovers today are showing renewed interest in glamorous desserts. Traditional from-scratch ideas are often coupled with the convenience of mixes to create special occasion desserts, such as Chocolate Orange Cream Torte and Chocolate Praline Layer Cake.

Imaginative toppings, fillings and garnishes create eye-catching presentations. One cake is topped with fruit preserves and then cream cheese frosting. Another features chocolate curls and pecan halves, artistically arranged on whipped cream topping. Still another is carefully drizzled with glaze to create a complex lattice-work design.

Other special touches include baking in pans that add glamour and sophistication. Nutty Graham Picnic Cake, Very Berry Lemon Cake and others bake in a fluted tube pan, while the Swiss Almond Apple Cake recipe calls for a springform pan. Liqueur in Almond Mocha Cake and the fruit filling of Heavenly Hawaiian Cake Roll are among the special ingredients featured in this chapter's artistic centerpiece desserts.

For all those occasions when nothing but the most wonderful dessert will do, these cakes and tortes say it all!

Chocolate Praline Layer Cake

Julie Konecne, Minnesota
Bake-Off® 33, 1988

NUTRIENTS PER 1/12 OF RECIPE

Calories	610	Protein	8% U.S. RDA
Protein	5g	Vitamin A	20% U.S. RDA
Carbohydrate	56g	Vitamin C	<2% U.S. RDA
Fat	41g	Thiamine	10% U.S. RDA
Cholesterol	140mg	Riboflavin	10% U.S. RDA
Sodium	470mg	Niacin	4% U.S. RDA
Potassium	230mg	Calcium	15% U.S. RDA
Dietary Fiber	1g	Iron	10% U.S. RDA

Chocolate Praline Layer Cake

Created by a university professor of music, this easy-to-prepare cake is spectacular to serve and marvelous to eat. It's best if made a few hours ahead and refrigerated before serving.

CAKE
- ½ cup butter or margarine
- ¼ cup whipping cream
- 1 cup firmly packed brown sugar
- ¾ cup coarsely chopped pecans
- 1 package pudding-included devil's food cake mix
- 1¼ cups water
- ⅓ cup oil
- 3 eggs

TOPPING
- 1¾ cups whipping cream
- ¼ cup powdered sugar
- ¼ teaspoon vanilla
- Whole pecans, if desired
- Chocolate curls, if desired

Heat oven to 325°F. In small heavy saucepan, combine butter, ¼ cup whipping cream and brown sugar. Cook over low heat just until butter is melted, stirring occasionally. Pour into two 9 or 8-inch round cake pans; sprinkle evenly with chopped pecans. In large bowl, combine cake mix, water, oil and eggs at low speed until moistened; beat 2 minutes at *highest* speed. Carefully spoon batter over pecan mixture in pans. Bake at 325°F. for 35 to 45 minutes or until top springs back when touched lightly in center. Cool 5 minutes; remove from pans. Cool completely.

In small bowl, beat 1¾ cups whipping cream until soft peaks form. Add powdered sugar and vanilla; beat until stiff peaks form.

To assemble cake, place 1 cake layer praline side up on serving plate. Spread top with ½ of whipped cream mixture. Top with remaining layer, praline side up. Spread top with remaining whipped cream. Garnish top of cake with whole pecans and chocolate curls. Store in refrigerator. **12 servings.**

HIGH ALTITUDE—Above 3500 Feet: Add 2 tablespoons flour to dry cake mix. Increase water to 1⅓ cups. Bake at 350°F. for 30 to 35 minutes. Remove from pans immediately.

Very Berry Lemon Cake

Alice Wyman, North Dakota
Bake-Off® 20, 1969

Very Berry Lemon Cake

Bake-Off® recipes have inspired new Pillsbury products. Among them is the line of Bundt-style cake mixes. The refreshing flavor combination of this cake was the first flavor to be introduced in this line of mixes.

CAKE
- 16½-ounce can blueberries, drained, reserving 1 cup liquid for sauce
- 1 package pudding-included lemon cake mix
- 8-ounce carton (1 cup) plain yogurt or dairy sour cream
- 4 eggs
- Powdered sugar

BLUEBERRY SAUCE
- ¼ cup sugar
- 1 tablespoon cornstarch
- Reserved 1 cup blueberry liquid

Heat oven to 350°F. Grease and flour 12-cup fluted tube pan or 10-inch tube pan. Rinse blueberries with cold water; drain on paper towel. In large bowl, blend cake mix, yogurt and eggs at low speed until moistened; beat 2 minutes at *medium* speed. Carefully fold in blueberries. Pour batter into greased and floured pan. Bake at 350°F. for 35 to 45 minutes or until toothpick inserted in center comes out clean. Cool upright in pan 15 minutes; remove from pan. Cool completely. Sprinkle with powdered sugar.

In small saucepan, blend sugar and cornstarch. If necessary, add enough water to reserved blueberry liquid to make 1 cup. Gradually stir blueberry liquid into sugar mixture. Bring to a boil. Reduce heat to low; cook until mixture thickens, stirring constantly. Serve sauce with cake. **16 servings.**

HIGH ALTITUDE—Above 3500 Feet: Add ¼ cup flour to dry cake mix.

NUTRIENTS PER 1/16 OF RECIPE

Calories	200	Protein	6% U.S. RDA
Protein	4g	Vitamin A	<2% U.S. RDA
Carbohydrate	37g	Vitamin C	<2% U.S. RDA
Fat	4g	Thiamine	6% U.S. RDA
Cholesterol	70mg	Riboflavin	8% U.S. RDA
Sodium	230mg	Niacin	2% U.S. RDA
Potassium	70mg	Calcium	6% U.S. RDA
Dietary Fiber	<1g	Iron	4% U.S. RDA

Chocolate Praline Layer Cake

Kentucky Butter Cake

Kentucky Butter Cake

Nell Lewis, Missouri
Bake-Off® 15, 1963

CAKE

    3 cups all purpose or unbleached
      flour
    2 cups sugar
    1 teaspoon baking powder
    1 teaspoon salt
    ½ teaspoon baking soda
    1 cup buttermilk*
    1 cup butter or margarine,
      softened
    2 teaspoons vanilla or rum extract
    4 eggs

BUTTER SAUCE

    ¾ cup sugar
    ⅓ cup butter or margarine
    3 tablespoons water
    1 to 2 teaspoons vanilla or rum
      extract
    Powdered sugar
    Whipped cream, if desired

Heat oven to 325°F. Generously grease
and lightly flour 12-cup fluted tube pan
or 10-inch tube pan. Lightly spoon
flour into measuring cup; level off. In
large bowl, combine flour and all remaining cake ingredients at low speed
until moistened; beat 3 minutes at medium speed. Pour batter into greased
and floured pan. Bake at 325°F. for 55

to 70 minutes or until toothpick inserted in center comes out clean. Do not remove cake from pan.

In small saucepan, combine all sauce ingredients; cook over low heat until butter melts, stirring occasionally. *Do not boil.* Using long-tined fork, pierce hot cake in pan 10 to 12 times. Slowly pour hot sauce over cake. Remove cake from pan immediately after sauce has been absorbed, 5 to 10 minutes. Cool completely. Just before serving, sprinkle with powdered sugar. Serve with whipped cream. **12 to 16 servings.**

TIP: *To substitute for buttermilk, use 1 tablespoon vinegar or lemon juice plus milk to make 1 cup.

HIGH ALTITUDE—Above 3500 Feet: Decrease sugar to 1¾ cups; increase buttermilk to 1 cup plus 2 tablespoons. Bake at 350°F. for 60 to 70 minutes.

NUTRIENTS PER 1/16 OF RECIPE

Calories	410	Protein	6% U.S. RDA
Protein	5g	Vitamin A	15% U.S. RDA
Carbohydrate	54g	Vitamin C	<2% U.S. RDA
Fat	20g	Thiamine	10% U.S. RDA
Cholesterol	120mg	Riboflavin	10% U.S. RDA
Sodium	380mg	Niacin	6% U.S. RDA
Potassium	75mg	Calcium	4% U.S. RDA
Dietary Fiber	<1g	Iron	8% U.S. RDA

Grand Prize Winner

Nutty Graham Picnic Cake

Esther V. Tomich, California
Bake-Off® 28, 1978

CAKE

2 cups all purpose or unbleached flour

1 cup (14 squares) finely crushed graham crackers or graham cracker crumbs

1 cup firmly packed brown sugar

½ cup sugar

1 teaspoon baking powder

1 teaspoon baking soda

1 teaspoon salt

½ teaspoon cinnamon

1 cup margarine or butter, softened

1 cup orange juice

1 tablespoon grated orange peel

3 eggs

1 cup chopped nuts

GLAZE

2 tablespoons brown sugar

5 teaspoons milk

1 tablespoon margarine or butter

¾ cup powdered sugar

¼ cup chopped nuts

Heat oven to 350°F. Generously grease and flour 12-cup fluted tube pan or 10-inch tube pan. Lightly spoon flour into measuring cup; level off. In large bowl, combine flour and remaining cake ingredients except nuts at low speed until moistened; beat 3 minutes at medium speed. By hand, stir in 1 cup nuts. Pour batter into greased and floured pan. Bake at 350°F. for 40 to 60 minutes or until toothpick inserted in center comes out clean. Cool upright in pan 15 minutes; invert onto serving plate. Cool completely.

In small saucepan over low heat, combine 2 tablespoons brown sugar, milk and 1 tablespoon margarine; heat just until sugar is dissolved, stirring constantly. Remove from heat. Stir in powdered sugar; blend until smooth. Drizzle over cake; sprinkle with ¼ cup nuts. **12 to 16 servings.**

HIGH ALTITUDE—Above 3500 Feet: Bake at 350°F. for 50 to 55 minutes.

NUTRIENTS PER 1/16 OF RECIPE

Calories	380	Protein	6% U.S. RDA
Protein	5g	Vitamin A	10% U.S. RDA
Carbohydrate	46g	Vitamin C	8% U.S. RDA
Fat	20g	Thiamine	10% U.S. RDA
Cholesterol	50mg	Riboflavin	8% U.S. RDA
Sodium	420mg	Niacin	6% U.S. RDA
Potassium	190mg	Calcium	4% U.S. RDA
Dietary Fiber	1g	Iron	10% U.S. RDA

A new cake shape sweeps the country!

In 1966, the 17th Bake-Off® Contest, the chocolate beauty, Tunnel of Fudge Cake, popularized the little-known Bundt-shaped cake pan into kitchen prominence. The Pillsbury Company received over 200,000 consumer requests for help in locating the 12-cup fluted tube pan following the contest. More than twenty years later Tunnel of Fudge Cake continues to be a recipe most frequently requested. It was also a recipe that stimulated the development of a new line of Bundt cake mixes featuring tempting fillings.

Swiss Almond Apple Cake

Swiss Almond Apple Cake

Stephen Hill, California
Bake-Off® 33, 1988

CAKE
- ²/₃ cup sugar
- ½ cup butter or margarine, softened
- 2 eggs
- 2 tablespoons lemon juice
- 2 cups all purpose or unbleached flour
- 2 teaspoons baking powder
- ¼ teaspoon salt
- ¼ cup raspberry preserves
- 3½ cups (about 4 medium) thinly sliced peeled apples

TOPPING
- 1 cup ground almonds
- ½ cup sugar
- 2 tablespoons flour
- ½ cup dairy sour cream
- 1 teaspoon grated lemon peel
- 2 eggs, beaten

GLAZE
- ¼ cup powdered sugar
- 1 to 2 teaspoons lemon juice

Heat oven to 350°F. Grease and flour 9 or 10-inch springform pan. In large bowl, beat ²/₃ cup sugar and butter until light and fluffy. Add 2 eggs and 2 tablespoons lemon juice; beat until well blended. Lightly spoon flour into measuring cup; level off. In small bowl, combine 2 cups flour, baking powder and salt; mix well. Add to sugar mixture; beat at low speed until well blended. Spread batter in greased and floured pan. Spoon preserves over batter; carefully spread to cover. Top with apple slices; slightly press into batter. In medium bowl, combine all topping ingredients; blend well. Pour over apples.

Bake at 350°F. for 55 to 65 minutes or until apples are tender, edges of cake are light golden brown and toothpick inserted in center comes out clean. Cool 10 minutes; carefully remove sides of pan. In small bowl, blend powdered sugar and enough lemon juice for desired drizzling consistency. Drizzle over warm cake. Serve warm or cold. **16 servings.**

HIGH ALTITUDE—Above 3500 Feet: No change.

NUTRIENTS PER 1/16 OF RECIPE

Calories	280	Protein	6% U.S. RDA
Protein	5g	Vitamin A	6% U.S. RDA
Carbohydrate	39g	Vitamin C	4% U.S. RDA
Fat	12g	Thiamine	8% U.S. RDA
Cholesterol	90mg	Riboflavin	8% U.S. RDA
Sodium	150mg	Niacin	6% U.S. RDA
Potassium	125mg	Calcium	6% U.S. RDA
Dietary Fiber	2g	Iron	6% U.S. RDA

Ring-of-Coconut Fudge Cake

Rita Glomb, Pennsylvania
Bake-Off® 22, 1971

FILLING
- 8-ounce package cream cheese, softened
- ¼ cup sugar
- 1 teaspoon vanilla
- 1 egg
- ½ cup flaked coconut
- 6-ounce package (1 cup) semi-sweet or milk chocolate chips

CAKE
- 3 cups all purpose, unbleached or self-rising flour*
- ¾ cup unsweetened cocoa
- 2 teaspoons baking soda
- 2 teaspoons baking powder
- 1½ teaspoons salt
- 2 cups sugar
- 1 cup cooking oil
- 2 eggs
- 1 cup hot coffee or water
- 1 cup buttermilk**
- 1 teaspoon vanilla
- ½ cup chopped nuts

GLAZE
- 1 cup powdered sugar
- 3 tablespoons unsweetened cocoa
- 2 tablespoons margarine or butter, softened
- 2 teaspoons vanilla
- 1 to 3 tablespoons hot water

Heat oven to 350°F. Generously grease and lightly flour 12-cup fluted tube pan or 10-inch tube pan. In small bowl, beat cream cheese, ¼ cup sugar, 1 teaspoon vanilla and 1 egg until smooth. By hand, stir in coconut and chocolate chips; set aside.

Lightly spoon flour into measuring cup; level off. In medium bowl, combine flour, ¾ cup cocoa, baking soda, baking powder and salt; mix well. In large bowl, combine 2 cups sugar, oil and 2 eggs; beat 1 minute at high speed. Add flour mixture, coffee, buttermilk and 1 teaspoon vanilla to sugar mixture. Blend at low speed until moistened; beat 3 minutes at medium speed. By hand, stir in nuts. Pour half of batter into greased and floured pan. Carefully spoon cream cheese filling over batter. (Filling should not touch sides or center of pan.) Spoon remaining batter over filling. Bake at 350°F. for 70 to 75 minutes or until top springs back when touched lightly in center. Cool upright in pan 15 minutes; invert onto serving plate. Cool completely.

In small bowl, blend powdered sugar, 3 tablespoons cocoa, margarine, 2 teaspoons vanilla and enough water for desired glaze consistency. Spoon over cake, allowing some to run down sides. Store in refrigerator. **16 servings.**

TIPS: *If using self-rising flour, decrease baking soda to 1 teaspoon; omit baking powder and salt.

**To substitute for buttermilk, use 1 tablespoon vinegar or lemon juice plus milk to make 1 cup.

HIGH ALTITUDE—Above 3500 Feet: Increase flour to 3½ cups. Decrease sugar in cake to 1⅔ cups.

NUTRIENTS PER 1/16 OF RECIPE

Calories	510	Protein	10% U.S. RDA
Protein	7g	Vitamin A	4% U.S. RDA
Carbohydrate	57g	Vitamin C	<2% U.S. RDA
Fat	28g	Thiamine	10% U.S. RDA
Cholesterol	70mg	Riboflavin	10% U.S. RDA
Sodium	480mg	Niacin	6% U.S. RDA
Potassium	170mg	Calcium	6% U.S. RDA
Dietary Fiber	3g	Iron	10% U.S. RDA

Ring-of-Coconut Fudge Cake

This chocolate cake with its macaroon-like tunnel of cream cheese, coconut and chocolate chips has certainly made its mark. Its popularity encouraged Pillsbury to add a pudding-filled version to its line of Bundt-style cake mixes.

Swiss Almond Apple Cake

Serve this European-style cake for dessert or anytime with coffee or tea. Sliced apples, a rippling of raspberry preserves and ground almonds make this an extra-special cake.

Golden Apricot Cake

Dale P. Grant, Texas
Bake-Off® 32, 1986

CAKE

1 package pudding-included
   yellow cake mix
1 cup apricot nectar
1/3 cup oil
1/4 cup honey
3 eggs

FILLING AND FROSTING

10-ounce jar apricot preserves
3-ounce package cream cheese,
   softened
1/4 cup margarine or butter,
   softened
2 1/2 cups powdered sugar
1/3 cup chopped pecans or walnuts

Heat oven to 350°F. Grease and flour two 8 or 9-inch round cake pans. In large bowl, combine all cake ingredients at low speed until moistened; beat 2 minutes at *highest* speed. Pour batter into greased and floured pans. Bake at 350°F. for 25 to 35 minutes or until toothpick inserted in center comes out clean. Cool 10 minutes; remove from pans. Cool completely.

Reserve 2/3 cup of the preserves. In small saucepan, heat remaining preserves until melted, stirring occasionally. Set aside.

In small bowl, beat cream cheese and margarine until smooth. Add powdered sugar; beat at low speed until well blended. Add enough warm preserves to cream cheese mixture for desired spreading consistency. Stir in pecans.

To assemble cake, place 1 cake layer on serving plate. Spread top with reserved 2/3 cup preserves. Top with remaining layer. Frost sides and top of cake with frosting mixture. Refrigerate before serving. Store in refrigerator.
12 servings.

HIGH ALTITUDE—Above 3500 Feet: Add 5 tablespoons flour to dry cake mix. Decrease apricot nectar to 1/2 cup and honey to 1 tablespoon. Add 1/2 cup water. Bake at 375°F. for 30 to 40 minutes.

NUTRIENTS PER 1/12 OF RECIPE

Calories	520	Protein	6% U.S. RDA
Protein	4g	Vitamin A	10% U.S. RDA
Carbohydrate	80g	Vitamin C	20% U.S. RDA
Fat	21g	Thiamine	10% U.S. RDA
Cholesterol	80mg	Riboflavin	8% U.S. RDA
Sodium	360mg	Niacin	4% U.S. RDA
Potassium	105mg	Calcium	6% U.S. RDA
Dietary Fiber	<1g	Iron	8% U.S. RDA

Grand Prize Winner

"My Inspiration" Cake

Lois Kanago, South Dakota
Bake-Off® 5, 1953

CAKE

1 cup finely chopped pecans
1 package pudding-included white
   cake mix
1 1/4 cups water
1/3 cup oil
3 egg whites
2 ounces (2 squares) semi-sweet
   chocolate, grated

FROSTING

1/2 cup sugar
2 ounces (2 squares) unsweetened
   chocolate
1/4 cup water
1/2 cup margarine or butter,
   softened
1 teaspoon vanilla
2 1/4 cups powdered sugar

Heat oven to 350°F. Grease and flour two 8 or 9-inch round cake pans. Sprinkle pecans evenly over bottom of both greased and floured pans. In large bowl, combine cake mix, 1 1/4 cups water, oil and egg whites at low speed until moistened; beat 2 minutes at *highest* speed. Carefully spoon 1/4 of batter into each nut-lined pan; sprinkle with grated chocolate. Spoon remaining batter over grated chocolate; spread carefully. Bake at 350°F. for 20 to 28 minutes or until toothpick inserted in center comes out clean. Cool 15 minutes; remove from pans. Cool completely.

In small saucepan over low heat, melt

Golden Apricot Cake

This golden layer cake, filled with tangy apricot preserves and frosted with a cream cheese frosting, was a winning recipe for a retired lieutenant commander in the U.S. Navy.

"My Inspiration" Cake

This cake could inspire a party! Each layer has a ribbon of chocolate running through it and a toasted nut topping baked right in. The layers are attractively put together with buttery chocolate and white frostings. The bonus is that the recipe is even easier to make now, using a cake mix.

"My Inspiration" Cake

sugar and unsweetened chocolate in ¼ cup water, stirring until smooth. Remove from heat; cool. In small bowl, beat margarine and vanilla until smooth. Gradually add powdered sugar at low speed until well blended. Reserve ⅓ cup of frosting mixture. Add cooled chocolate mixture to remaining frosting; beat until smooth.

To assemble cake, place 1 cake layer nut side up on serving plate. Spread top with ⅓ (about ½ cup) of chocolate frosting. Top with remaining layer, nut side up. Frost sides and ½ inch around top edge of cake with remaining chocolate frosting. Pipe reserved white frosting around edge of chocolate frosting and nuts on top of cake.*
12 servings.

TIP: *If necessary, add water, 1 drop at a time, to white frosting for desired piping consistency.

HIGH ALTITUDE—Above 3500 Feet: Add 3 tablespoons flour to dry cake mix and increase water to 1⅓ cups.

NUTRIENTS PER 1/12 OF RECIPE

Calories	530	Protein	6% U.S. RDA
Protein	4g	Vitamin A	6% U.S. RDA
Carbohydrate	68g	Vitamin C	<2% U.S. RDA
Fat	29g	Thiamine	8% U.S. RDA
Cholesterol	0mg	Riboflavin	4% U.S. RDA
Sodium	390mg	Niacin	4% U.S. RDA
Potassium	170mg	Calcium	4% U.S. RDA
Dietary Fiber	2g	Iron	4% U.S. RDA

Tunnel of Fudge Cake

Tunnel of Fudge Cake

—∻∻—

The popularity of Bundt[†] shaped fluted tube pans was heightened after this recipe won Bake-Off® judges' approval. The original recipe called for dry frosting mix that is no longer available. Updated and revised, this version still has a soft tunnel of fudge surrounded by delicious chocolate cake.

† Registered trademark of Northland Aluminum Products, Inc., Minneapolis, MN

Tunnel of Fudge Cake

—∻∻—

Ella Helfrich, Texas
Bake-Off® 17, 1966

CAKE
1³⁄₄ **cups sugar**
1³⁄₄ **cups margarine or butter, softened**
6 **eggs**
2 **cups powdered sugar**
2¹⁄₄ **cups all purpose or unbleached flour**
2 **cups chopped walnuts***
³⁄₄ **cup unsweetened cocoa**

GLAZE
³⁄₄ **cup powdered sugar**
¹⁄₄ **cup unsweetened cocoa**
1¹⁄₂ **to 2 tablespoons milk**

Heat oven to 350°F. Grease and flour 12-cup fluted tube pan or 10-inch tube pan. In large bowl, beat sugar and margarine until light and fluffy. Add eggs, 1 at a time, beating well after each addition. Gradually add 2 cups powdered sugar; blend well. Lightly spoon flour into measuring cup; level off. By hand, stir in flour and remaining cake ingredients until well blended. Spoon batter into greased and floured pan; spread evenly. Bake at 350°F. for 58 to 62 minutes.** Cool upright in pan on wire rack 1 hour; invert onto serving plate. Cool completely.

In small bowl, blend ³⁄₄ cup powdered sugar, ¹⁄₄ cup cocoa and enough milk for desired drizzling consistency. Spoon over cake, allowing some to run down sides. Store tightly covered.
16 servings.

TIPS: *Nuts are essential for the success of this recipe.

**Since this cake has a soft tunnel of fudge, an ordinary doneness test cannot be used. Accurate oven temperature and baking time are essential.

HIGH ALTITUDE—Above 3500 Feet: Increase flour to 2¹⁄₄ cups plus 3 tablespoons. Bake as directed above.

NUTRIENTS PER 1/16 OF RECIPE

Calories	560	Protein	10% U.S. RDA
Protein	7g	Vitamin A	20% U.S. RDA
Carbohydrate	58g	Vitamin C	<2% U.S. RDA
Fat	33g	Thiamine	10% U.S. RDA
Cholesterol	100mg	Riboflavin	10% U.S. RDA
Sodium	300mg	Niacin	6% U.S. RDA
Potassium	170mg	Calcium	4% U.S. RDA
Dietary Fiber	2g	Iron	10% U.S. RDA

Almond Mocha Cake

Debbie Russell, Colorado
Bake-Off® 33, 1988

1/2 cup chopped almonds
1 1/4 cups strong coffee
1/2 cup margarine or butter
12-ounce package (2 cups) semi-
  sweet chocolate chips
1 cup sugar
1/4 cup amaretto*
2 cups all purpose or unbleached
  flour**
1 teaspoon baking soda
1 teaspoon vanilla
2 eggs
  Powdered sugar

Heat oven to 325°F. Generously grease 12-cup fluted tube pan or 10-inch tube pan. Press almonds in bottom and half-way up sides of greased pan. In medium saucepan over low heat, warm coffee. Add margarine and chocolate chips; cook until mixture is smooth, stirring constantly. Remove from heat; stir in sugar and amaretto. Place in large bowl; cool 5 minutes.

Lightly spoon flour into measuring cup; level off. Gradually blend flour and baking soda into chocolate mixture at low speed until moistened. Add vanilla and eggs; beat at medium speed about 30 seconds or just until well blended. Pour batter over almonds in greased pan.

Bake at 325°F. for 60 to 75 minutes or until toothpick inserted in center comes out clean. Cool upright in pan 25 minutes; invert onto serving plate. Cool completely. Sprinkle with powdered sugar. **16 servings.**

TIPS: *Two teaspoons almond extract can be substituted for amaretto. Increase coffee to 1 1/2 cups.

**Self-rising flour is not recommended.

HIGH ALTITUDE—Above 3500 Feet: No change.

NUTRIENTS PER 1/16 OF RECIPE

Calories	320	Protein	6% U.S. RDA
Protein	4g	Vitamin A	4% U.S. RDA
Carbohydrate	41g	Vitamin C	<2% U.S. RDA
Fat	16g	Thiamine	8% U.S. RDA
Cholesterol	35mg	Riboflavin	8% U.S. RDA
Sodium	50mg	Niacin	4% U.S. RDA
Potassium	130mg	Calcium	2% U.S. RDA
Dietary Fiber	2g	Iron	8% U.S. RDA

Banana Crunch Cake

Bonnie Brooks, Maryland
Bake-Off® 24, 1973

1/2 cup all purpose or unbleached
  flour
1 cup coconut
1 cup rolled oats
3/4 cup firmly packed brown sugar
1/2 cup chopped pecans
1/2 cup margarine or butter
1 1/2 cups (2 large) sliced *very ripe*
  bananas
1/2 cup dairy sour cream
4 eggs
1 package pudding-included
  yellow cake mix

Heat oven to 350°F. Grease and flour 10-inch tube pan. Lightly spoon flour into measuring cup; level off. In medium bowl, combine flour, coconut, rolled oats, brown sugar and pecans; mix well. Using pastry blender or fork, cut in margarine until mixture is crumbly; set aside.

In large bowl, combine bananas, sour cream and eggs; blend until smooth. Add cake mix; beat 2 minutes at *highest* speed. Spread 1/3 of batter in greased and floured pan; sprinkle with 1/3 of coconut mixture. Repeat layers twice, using remaining batter and coconut mixture and ending with coconut mixture. Bake at 350°F. for 50 to 60 minutes or until toothpick inserted in center comes out clean. Cool upright in pan 15 minutes; remove from pan. Place on serving plate, coconut side up. **16 servings.**

HIGH ALTITUDE—Above 3500 Feet: Add 3 tablespoons flour to dry cake mix. Bake at 375°F. for 45 to 55 minutes.

NUTRIENTS PER 1/16 RECIPE

Calories	360	Protein	6% U.S. RDA
Protein	5g	Vitamin A	8% U.S. RDA
Carbohydrate	50g	Vitamin C	<2% U.S. RDA
Fat	16g	Thiamine	10% U.S. RDA
Cholesterol	70mg	Riboflavin	8% U.S. RDA
Sodium	310mg	Niacin	6% U.S. RDA
Potassium	220mg	Calcium	6% U.S. RDA
Dietary Fiber	2g	Iron	8% U.S. RDA

Almond Mocha Cake

"It melts in your mouth" describes the texture of this brownie-like chocolate cake. Coffee and amaretto enhance its deep dark chocolate flavor.

Banana Crunch Cake

This recipe originally used a dry frosting mix that is no longer available for the streusel layer. Now that crunchy layer is made from scratch to create the same great winning taste.

Banana Split Cake

❧❦❧

Sally Kraywiecki, Michigan
Bake-Off® 11, 1959

Banana Split Cake

❧❦❧

An impressive dessert is created with three layers of milk chocolate banana cake filled with banana-pecan pudding and topped with a chocolate glaze. Use fully ripened bananas that have skins with brown flecks for the best flavor and texture.

CAKE
4-ounce bar sweet cooking chocolate
1/4 cup water
2 1/2 cups all purpose or unbleached flour
1 teaspoon baking soda
1 teaspoon salt
3/4 cup shortening
1 1/2 cups sugar
2 eggs
2 eggs, separated, reserving yolks for filling
1 cup mashed ripe bananas
1 teaspoon vanilla
1 cup buttermilk*
3/4 cup chopped pecans or nuts

FILLING
3/4 cup sugar
3/4 cup evaporated milk
3 tablespoons butter or margarine
Reserved 2 egg yolks
3/4 cup chopped pecans or nuts
1/4 cup mashed ripe banana
1 teaspoon vanilla

GLAZE
1 ounce (1 square) unsweetened chocolate
2 tablespoons butter or margarine
1 cup powdered sugar
1/2 teaspoon vanilla
3 to 4 tablespoons milk
Chopped pecans, if desired

Heat oven to 375°F. Grease and flour three 8 or 9-inch round cake pans. In small saucepan over low heat, melt sweet cooking chocolate in water, stirring until smooth. Remove from heat; set aside. Lightly spoon flour into measuring cup; level off. In medium bowl, combine flour, baking soda and salt; mix well. In large bowl, beat shortening and 1 1/2 cups sugar until light and fluffy. Beat in 2 whole eggs, 1 at a time, beating well after each addition. Beat in 2 egg whites. Blend in melted chocolate, 1 cup mashed bananas and 1 teaspoon vanilla. Add flour mixture and buttermilk alternately to chocolate mixture, beginning and ending with flour mixture. Blend well after each

addition. By hand, stir in 3/4 cup pecans. Pour batter evenly into greased and floured pans. Bake at 375°F. for 25 to 30 minutes or until toothpick inserted in center comes out clean. Cool 5 minutes; remove from pan. Cool completely.

In medium saucepan, combine 3/4 cup sugar, evaporated milk, 3 tablespoons butter and reserved egg yolks; mix well. Cook over medium heat 10 to 14 minutes or until mixture thickens, stirring constantly. Stir in 3/4 cup pecans, 1/4 cup mashed bananas and 1 teaspoon vanilla. Cool to spreading consistency, stirring occasionally.

In small saucepan over low heat, melt unsweetened chocolate and 2 tablespoons butter, stirring until smooth. Remove from heat. Blend in powdered sugar, 1/2 teaspoon vanilla and enough milk for desired glaze consistency.

To assemble cake, place 1 cake layer on serving plate. Spread top with half of filling mixture. Repeat with second layer and remaining filling. Top with third layer. Spoon glaze over top of cake, allowing some to run down sides. Sprinkle pecans over top of cake. Store in refrigerator. **16 servings.**

TIP: *To substitute for buttermilk, use 1 tablespoon vinegar or lemon juice plus enough milk to make 1 cup.

HIGH ALTITUDE—Above 3500 Feet: Add 3 tablespoons flour to cake ingredients.

NUTRIENTS PER 1/16 OF RECIPE

Calories	510	Protein	10% U.S. RDA
Protein	7g	Vitamin A	6% U.S. RDA
Carbohydrate	63g	Vitamin C	2% U.S. RDA
Fat	26g	Thiamine	10% U.S. RDA
Cholesterol	80mg	Riboflavin	10% U.S. RDA
Sodium	290mg	Niacin	6% U.S. RDA
Potassium	250mg	Calcium	8% U.S. RDA
Dietary Fiber	2g	Iron	10% U.S. RDA

❧❦❧

Banana Split Cake

Apricot Fantasia Cake

Marge Walker, Indiana
Bake-Off® 32, 1986

Apricot Fantasia Cake

Sweet orange cream sauce tops a tart and tangy apricot "steamed pudding" cake that's easily made in the microwave.

CAKE
- ¾ to 1 cup chopped dried apricots
- 1½ cups apricot nectar
- ½ cup margarine or butter, cut into pieces
- 1¾ cups all purpose, unbleached or self-rising flour*
- 1 cup firmly packed brown sugar
- ¼ cup whole wheat flour
- 1½ teaspoons baking powder
- ½ teaspoon baking soda
- ½ teaspoon salt
- ½ teaspoon cinnamon
- ½ teaspoon nutmeg
- ¼ teaspoon ginger
- 1 teaspoon vanilla
- 2 eggs

SAUCE
- 1 cup ready-to-spread cream cheese frosting
- 2 tablespoons orange juice
- 2 teaspoons grated orange peel

MICROWAVE DIRECTIONS: Grease 4-cup microwave-safe measuring cup; line bottom with waxed paper and grease again.** In medium microwave-safe bowl, combine apricots, apricot nectar and margarine. Cover loosely with waxed paper; microwave on HIGH for 3 minutes. Let stand 3 minutes.

Lightly spoon flour into measuring cup; level off. In large bowl, combine all purpose flour, brown sugar, whole wheat flour and all remaining cake ingredients; mix well. Add warm apricot mixture; mix until well blended. Pour half of batter, about 2½ cups, into greased measuring cup; cover tightly with microwave-safe plastic wrap.

Microwave on MEDIUM for 9 to 11 minutes, rotating measuring cup once halfway through cooking. Cake is done when toothpick inserted in center comes out clean and bottom of cake is no longer wet. Uncover; let stand on flat surface 5 minutes. Loosen cake from sides of measuring cup; invert onto serving plate. Remove waxed paper. Repeat cooking steps with remaining batter.

In small bowl, combine all sauce ingredients; mix well. Spoon over warm cakes. Garnish as desired. Cut into wedges to serve. Serve with remaining sauce. Store in refrigerator.
2 (6-serving) cakes.

TIPS: *If using self-rising flour, omit baking powder and salt. Reduce baking soda to ¼ teaspoon.

**A 12-cup microwave-safe fluted tube pan can be substituted for measuring cup; omit lining with waxed paper. *Grease and sugar pan.* Prepare cake batter as directed above; pour *all of batter* into greased and sugared pan. Cover tightly with microwave-safe plastic wrap. Microwave on MEDIUM for 10 minutes. Rotate pan ½ turn. Microwave on HIGH for 5 to 6 minutes or until toothpick inserted in center comes out clean, rotating pan once halfway through cooking. Continue as directed above.

HIGH ALTITUDE—Above 3500 Feet: No change.

NUTRIENTS PER 1/12 OF RECIPE

Calories	360	Protein	6% U.S. RDA
Protein	4g	Vitamin A	30% U.S. RDA
Carbohydrate	59g	Vitamin C	2% U.S. RDA
Fat	12g	Thiamine	10% U.S. RDA
Cholesterol	45mg	Riboflavin	8% U.S. RDA
Sodium	340mg	Niacin	8% U.S. RDA
Potassium	310mg	Calcium	6% U.S. RDA
Dietary Fiber	2g	Iron	10% U.S. RDA

Apricot Fantasia Cake

Spicy Raisin Brunch Cake

Spicy Raisin Brunch Cake

◦°◦ 26

Shirley Domeier, Minnesota
Bake-Off® 32, 1986

¹/₄ cup graham cracker crumbs
1¹/₂ cups all purpose or unbleached
    flour
¹/₂ cup raisins
¹/₂ cup chopped walnuts
¹/₂ teaspoon baking soda
1¹/₂ teaspoons pumpkin pie spice
¹/₄ to ¹/₂ teaspoon cloves
 1 cup firmly packed brown sugar
¹/₂ cup apricot preserves
¹/₂ cup margarine or butter,
    softened
 2 tablespoons rum or ¹/₂ teaspoon
    rum extract
 4 eggs
²/₃ cup buttermilk*

GLAZE
 1 cup powdered sugar
 1 teaspoon margarine or butter
¹/₂ teaspoon rum, if desired
 5 to 6 teaspoons milk

MICROWAVE DIRECTIONS: Grease
12-cup microwave-safe fluted tube
pan; sprinkle with graham cracker
crumbs. Lightly spoon flour into measuring cup; level off. In medium bowl,
combine flour, raisins, walnuts, baking
soda, pumpkin pie spice and cloves;
mix well. Set aside. In large bowl, combine brown sugar, preserves, ¹/₂ cup
margarine, 2 tablespoons rum and eggs;
beat well. Alternately add flour mixture and buttermilk to brown sugar
mixture, beating well after each addition. Pour batter carefully over crumbs
in greased pan.

Microwave on MEDIUM for 10 minutes, rotating pan once halfway

through cooking. Microwave on HIGH for 4 to 8 minutes, rotating pan once halfway through cooking. Cake is done when toothpick inserted in center comes out clean and cake begins to pull away from sides of pan. Cool upright in pan on flat surface 5 minutes. Invert onto serving plate. Cool completely. In small bowl, blend powdered sugar, 1 teaspoon margarine, ½ teaspoon rum and enough milk for desired drizzling consistency. Drizzle over cake. Store cake loosely covered. **16 servings.**

TIP: *To substitute for buttermilk, use 2 teaspoons vinegar or lemon juice plus milk to make ⅔ cup.

HIGH ALTITUDE — Above 3500 Feet: No change.

NUTRIENTS PER 1/16 OF RECIPE

Calories	270	Protein	6% U.S. RDA
Protein	4g	Vitamin A	6% U.S. RDA
Carbohydrate	42g	Vitamin C	<2% U.S. RDA
Fat	10g	Thiamine	8% U.S. RDA
Cholesterol	70mg	Riboflavin	6% U.S. RDA
Sodium	150mg	Niacin	4% U.S. RDA
Potassium	170mg	Calcium	6% U.S. RDA
Dietary Fiber	<1g	Iron	8% U.S. RDA

Japanese Fruit Marble Cake

Flora H. Grantham, Maryland
Bake-Off® 31, 1984

2 cups sugar

1 cup margarine or butter, softened

1 teaspoon vanilla

1 teaspoon lemon extract

4 eggs

3 cups all purpose or unbleached flour

3 teaspoons baking powder

⅛ teaspoon salt

1 cup milk

2 teaspoons cinnamon

2 teaspoons nutmeg

1 teaspoon lemon extract

1 tablespoon flour

½ cup chopped pecans or walnuts

½ cup raisins

¼ cup coconut

GLAZE

1 cup powdered sugar

4 to 6 teaspoons lemon juice

Heat oven to 350°F. Grease and flour 10-inch tube pan or 12-cup fluted tube pan. In large bowl, beat sugar, margarine, vanilla and 1 teaspoon lemon extract until light and fluffy. Add eggs, 1 at a time, beating well after each addition. Lightly spoon flour into measuring cup; level off. In medium bowl, combine 3 cups flour, baking powder and salt; mix well. Add flour mixture and milk to egg mixture. Blend at low speed until moistened; beat 2 minutes at medium speed. Pour ⅔ of batter into greased and floured pan. To remaining batter, stir in cinnamon, nutmeg and 1 teaspoon lemon extract until well blended. In small bowl, combine 1 tablespoon flour, pecans, raisins and coconut; mix well. Fold pecan mixture into spice batter. Spoon spice batter over batter in pan. To marble, pull knife through batter in folding motion, turning pan while folding.

Bake at 350°F. for 50 to 60 minutes or until toothpick inserted in center comes out clean. Cool upright in pan 10 minutes; remove from pan. Place on serving plate, top side up. In small bowl, blend powdered sugar and enough lemon juice for desired drizzling consistency. Drizzle over warm cake. Cool completely. **16 servings.**

HIGH ALTITUDE — Above 3500 Feet: Increase flour to 3 cups plus 3 tablespoons. Bake at 375°F. for 45 to 55 minutes.

NUTRIENTS PER 1/16 OF RECIPE

Calories	390	Protein	8% U.S. RDA
Protein	5g	Vitamin A	10% U.S. RDA
Carbohydrate	56g	Vitamin C	<2% U.S. RDA
Fat	16g	Thiamine	10% U.S. RDA
Cholesterol	70mg	Riboflavin	10% U.S. RDA
Sodium	230mg	Niacin	6% U.S. RDA
Potassium	125mg	Calcium	8% U.S. RDA
Dietary Fiber	1g	Iron	8% U.S. RDA

Japanese Fruit Marble Cake

Regional American foods continue their popularity as a part of the Bake-Off® Contests. This pleasant lemon-and-spice-flavored cake is a variation of fruitcake traditionally served during the holidays in Southeastern United States.

Caramel Pear Upside-Down Cake

We've added new-fashioned ease to this old-fashioned cake by using a cake mix. The unique upside-down layer is a yummy combination of pears and caramel.

Caramel Pear Upside-Down Cake

Margaret Faxon, Missouri
Bake-Off® 5, 1953

29-ounce can pear halves, drained, reserving ¹⁄₂ cup liquid
28 caramels
2 tablespoons margarine or butter
1 package pudding-included yellow cake mix
1 cup water
¹⁄₃ cup oil
3 eggs
¹⁄₄ cup chopped nuts
Whipped cream, if desired

Heat oven to 350°F. Generously grease 13 × 9-inch pan. Slice pear halves; arrange over bottom of greased pan. In small saucepan over medium heat, melt caramels in reserved pear liquid, stirring until smooth. Stir in margarine; blend well. Pour mixture evenly over pears. In large bowl, combine cake mix, water, oil and eggs at low speed until moistened; beat 2 minutes at *highest* speed. Carefully pour batter evenly over pear mixture.

Bake at 350°F. for 35 to 55 minutes or until toothpick inserted in center comes out clean. Cool 5 minutes; invert onto cookie sheet or large serving plate. Sprinkle with nuts. Serve warm or cold with whipped cream. **12 servings.**

HIGH ALTITUDE—Above 3500 Feet: Add 3 tablespoons flour to dry cake mix. Bake at 375°F. for 35 to 45 minutes.

NUTRIENTS PER 1/12 OF RECIPE

Calories	440	Protein	6% U.S. RDA
Protein	5g	Vitamin A	4% U.S. RDA
Carbohydrate	58g	Vitamin C	<2% U.S. RDA
Fat	21g	Thiamine	10% U.S. RDA
Cholesterol	80mg	Riboflavin	10% U.S. RDA
Sodium	370mg	Niacin	4% U.S. RDA
Potassium	130mg	Calcium	8% U.S. RDA
Dietary Fiber	2g	Iron	8% U.S. RDA

Double Lemon Streusel Cake

Betty Engles, Michigan
Bake-Off® 28, 1978

CAKE
1 package pudding-included lemon cake mix
¹⁄₃ cup margarine or butter, softened
¹⁄₂ cup milk
2 eggs

TOPPING
8-ounce package cream cheese, softened
¹⁄₄ cup sugar
4 teaspoons lemon juice
¹⁄₂ teaspoon grated lemon peel
¹⁄₂ cup chopped nuts

Heat oven to 350°F. Generously grease and flour 13 × 9-inch pan. In large bowl, combine cake mix and margarine at low speed until crumbly. Reserve 1 cup of crumb mixture for topping. Add remaining cake ingredients; beat 2 minutes at *highest* speed. Pour batter into greased and floured pan.

In small bowl, combine all topping ingredients except nuts; beat until smooth. Drop by teaspoonfuls onto batter; carefully spread evenly to cover. In second small bowl, blend reserved 1 cup crumb mixture and nuts. Sprinkle over cream cheese mixture. Bake at 350°F. for 30 to 40 minutes or until top springs back when touched lightly in center. Cool completely. **15 servings.**

HIGH ALTITUDE—Above 3500 Feet: Add 4 tablespoons flour to dry cake mix. Bake at 375°F. for 30 to 40 minutes.

NUTRIENTS PER 1/15 OF RECIPE

Calories	280	Protein	6% U.S. RDA
Protein	4g	Vitamin A	8% U.S. RDA
Carbohydrate	32g	Vitamin C	<2% U.S. RDA
Fat	16g	Thiamine	8% U.S. RDA
Cholesterol	50mg	Riboflavin	8% U.S. RDA
Sodium	320mg	Niacin	4% U.S. RDA
Potassium	75mg	Calcium	6% U.S. RDA
Dietary Fiber	<1g	Iron	4% U.S. RDA

Orange Kiss-Me Cake

Lily Wuebel, California
Bake-Off® 2, 1950

CAKE
- 1 orange
- 1 cup raisins
- 1/3 cup walnuts
- 2 cups all purpose or unbleached flour
- 1 cup sugar
- 1 teaspoon baking soda
- 1 teaspoon salt
- 1 cup milk
- 1/2 cup shortening
- 2 eggs

TOPPING
- 1/3 cup sugar
- 1 teaspoon cinnamon
- 1/4 cup finely chopped walnuts

Heat oven to 350°F. Grease and flour 13×9-inch pan. Squeeze orange, reserving 1/3 cup juice. Grind together orange peel and pulp, raisins and 1/3 cup walnuts; set aside.* Lightly spoon flour into measuring cup; level off. In large bowl, combine flour, 1 cup sugar, baking soda, salt, milk, shortening and eggs at low speed until moistened; beat 3 minutes at medium speed. Stir in orange-raisin mixture. Pour batter into greased and floured pan. Bake at 350°F. for 35 to 45 minutes or until toothpick inserted in center comes out clean.

Drizzle reserved 1/3 cup orange juice over warm cake in pan. In small bowl, combine 1/3 cup sugar and cinnamon; mix well. Stir in 1/4 cup walnuts; sprinkle over cake. Cool completely. **12 to 16 servings.**

TIP: *A blender or food processor can be used to grind orange-raisin mixture.

HIGH ALTITUDE—Above 3500 Feet: Increase flour to 2 cups plus 2 tablespoons. Bake at 375°F. for 35 to 40 minutes.

NUTRIENTS PER 1/16 OF RECIPE
Calories	260	Protein	6% U.S. RDA
Protein	4g	Vitamin A	<2% U.S. RDA
Carbohydrate	38g	Vitamin C	4% U.S. RDA
Fat	10g	Thiamine	10% U.S. RDA
Cholesterol	35mg	Riboflavin	6% U.S. RDA
Sodium	220mg	Niacin	4% U.S. RDA
Potassium	150mg	Calcium	4% U.S. RDA
Dietary Fiber	1g	Iron	6% U.S. RDA

Caramel Apple Cake

Josephine DeMarco, Illinois
Bake-Off® 27, 1976

- 1 3/4 cups all purpose or unbleached flour
- 1 1/2 cups firmly packed brown sugar
- 1/2 teaspoon baking powder
- 1/2 teaspoon baking soda
- 1/2 teaspoon salt
- 1 1/2 teaspoons cinnamon
- 3/4 cup margarine or butter, softened
- 1 teaspoon vanilla
- 3 eggs
- 1 1/2 cups finely chopped peeled apples
- 1/2 to 1 cup chopped nuts
- 1/2 cup raisins, if desired

FROSTING
- 2 cups powdered sugar
- 1/4 teaspoon cinnamon
- 1/4 cup margarine or butter, melted
- 1/2 teaspoon vanilla
- 4 to 5 teaspoons milk

Heat oven to 350°F. Grease and flour 13×9-inch pan. Lightly spoon flour into measuring cup; level off. In large bowl, combine flour, brown sugar, baking powder, baking soda, salt, 1 1/2 teaspoons cinnamon, 3/4 cup margarine, 1 teaspoon vanilla and eggs at low speed until moistened; beat 3 minutes at medium speed. By hand, stir in apples, nuts and raisins. Pour batter into greased and floured pan. Bake at 350°F. for 30 to 40 minutes or until toothpick inserted in center comes out clean. Cool completely. In small bowl, blend powdered sugar, 1/4 teaspoon cinnamon, 1/4 cup margarine, 1/2 teaspoon vanilla and enough milk for desired spreading consistency. Frost cooled cake. **15 servings.**

HIGH ALTITUDE—Above 3500 Feet: Decrease brown sugar to 1 cup. Bake at 375°F. for 25 to 35 minutes.

NUTRIENTS PER 1/15 OF RECIPE
Calories	390	Protein	6% U.S. RDA
Protein	4g	Vitamin A	10% U.S. RDA
Carbohydrate	53g	Vitamin C	<2% U.S. RDA
Fat	18g	Thiamine	10% U.S. RDA
Cholesterol	60mg	Riboflavin	6% U.S. RDA
Sodium	280mg	Niacin	4% U.S. RDA
Potassium	210mg	Calcium	8% U.S. RDA
Dietary Fiber	1g	Iron	10% U.S. RDA

Orange Kiss-Me Cake

Time-proven and "classic" in status, this moist, fresh orange-tasting cake is as popular today as when it won top honors more than thirty-five years ago. It continues to be one of the most requested Bake-Off® recipes.

Black Bottom Cups

Black Bottom Cups

Doris Geisert, California
Bake-Off® 13, 1961

**2 (3-ounce) packages cream
cheese, softened**
¹/₃ cup sugar
1 egg
**6-ounce package (1 cup) semi-
sweet chocolate chips**
**1¹/₂ cups all purpose or unbleached
flour**
1 cup sugar
¹/₄ cup unsweetened cocoa
1 teaspoon baking soda
¹/₂ teaspoon salt
1 cup water
¹/₃ cup oil
1 tablespoon vinegar
1 teaspoon vanilla
**¹/₂ cup chopped almonds, if
desired**
2 tablespoons sugar, if desired

Heat oven to 350°F. Line 18 muffin
cups with paper baking cups. In small
bowl, beat cream cheese, ¹/₃ cup sugar
and egg until smooth. By hand, stir in
chocolate chips; set aside. Lightly
spoon flour into measuring cup; level
off. In large bowl, combine flour, 1 cup
sugar, cocoa, baking soda and salt; mix
well. Add water, oil, vinegar and
vanilla; beat 2 minutes at medium
speed. Fill paper-lined muffin cups
¹/₂ full. Top each with tablespoonful of
cream cheese mixture. In small bowl,
combine almonds and 2 tablespoons of
sugar; sprinkle evenly over cream
cheese mixture. Bake at 350°F. for 20
to 30 minutes or until cream cheese
mixture is light golden brown. Cool
15 minutes; remove from pans. Cool
completely. Store in refrigerator.
18 cupcakes.

HIGH ALTITUDE—Above 3500 Feet:
No change.

NUTRIENTS PER 1 CUPCAKE

Calories	250	Protein	4% U.S. RDA
Protein	3g	Vitamin A	2% U.S. RDA
Carbohydrate	31g	Vitamin C	<2% U.S. RDA
Fat	13g	Thiamine	4% U.S. RDA
Cholesterol	25mg	Riboflavin	6% U.S. RDA
Sodium	160mg	Niacin	4% U.S. RDA
Potassium	90mg	Calcium	2% U.S. RDA
Dietary Fiber	2g	Iron	6% U.S. RDA

Mardi Gras Party Cake

❧

Eunice Surles, Louisiana
Bake-Off® 11, 1959

CAKE

    6-ounce package (1 cup)
      butterscotch chips
  ¼ cup water
2¼ cups all purpose or unbleached
    flour
1¼ cups sugar
  1 teaspoon baking soda
  1 teaspoon salt
  ½ teaspoon baking powder
  1 cup buttermilk*
  ½ cup shortening
  3 eggs

FILLING

  ½ cup sugar
  1 tablespoon cornstarch
  ½ cup half-and-half or evaporated
    milk
  ⅓ cup water
  1 egg, slightly beaten
  2 tablespoons margarine or butter
  1 cup coconut
  1 cup chopped nuts

SEAFOAM CREAM

  1 cup whipping cream
  ¼ cup firmly packed brown sugar
  ½ teaspoon vanilla

Heat oven to 350°F. Generously grease and flour two 9-inch round cake pans.** In small saucepan over low heat, melt ⅔ cup of the butterscotch chips in ¼ cup water, stirring until smooth. Cool. Lightly spoon flour into measuring cup; level off. In large bowl, combine flour, all remaining cake ingredients and cooled butterscotch mixture at low speed until moistened; beat 3 minutes at medium speed. Pour batter into greased and floured pans. Bake at 350°F. for 20 to 30 minutes or until toothpick inserted in center comes out clean. Cool 10 minutes; remove from pans. Cool completely.

In medium saucepan, combine ½ cup sugar and cornstarch; stir in half-and-half, ⅓ cup water, 1 egg and remaining ⅓ cup butterscotch chips. Cook over medium heat until mixture thickens, stirring constantly. Remove from heat. Stir in margarine, coconut and nuts; cool.

In small bowl, beat whipping cream until soft peaks form. Gradually add brown sugar and vanilla, beating until stiff peaks form.

To assemble cake, place 1 cake layer on serving plate. Spread top with half of filling mixture. Top with remaining layer; spread remaining filling on top to within ½ inch of edge. Frost sides and top edge of cake with seafoam cream. Refrigerate at least 1 hour before serving. Store in refrigerator. **16 servings.**

TIPS: *To substitute for buttermilk, use 1 tablespoon vinegar or lemon juice plus milk to make 1 cup.

**Cake can be baked in 13 × 9-inch pan; grease bottom of pan only. Bake at 350°F. for 30 to 35 minutes or until toothpick inserted in center comes out clean. Cool completely. Spread top of cooled cake with filling mixture. Serve topped with seafoam cream.

HIGH ALTITUDE—Above 3500 Feet: Bake at 350°F. for 30 to 35 minutes. Cool 7 minutes; remove from pans. Cool completely.

NUTRIENTS PER 1/16 OF RECIPE

Calories	450	Protein	8% U.S. RDA
Protein	6g	Vitamin A	8% U.S. RDA
Carbohydrate	50g	Vitamin C	<2% U.S. RDA
Fat	25g	Thiamine	10% U.S. RDA
Cholesterol	90mg	Riboflavin	10% U.S. RDA
Sodium	270mg	Niacin	4% U.S. RDA
Potassium	140mg	Calcium	6% U.S. RDA
Dietary Fiber	<1g	Iron	8% U.S. RDA

Mardi Gras Party Cake

❧

A delicate butterscotch-flavored cake with a scrumptious coconut-butterscotch-nut filling and fluffy brown sugar frosting. This recipe reflects the longtime Southern tradition of serving foods rich in flavor and especially appealing in appearance.

❧

Chocolate Orange Cream Torte

Dorine K. Firestone, Ohio
Bake-Off® 32, 1986

CAKE

1 package pudding-included
   devil's food cake mix
1/2 cup water
1/2 cup orange juice
1/3 cup oil
3 eggs

FILLING

8-ounce package cream cheese,
   softened
1/3 cup whipping cream
2 tablespoons powdered sugar
8-ounce bar milk chocolate,
   chopped

FROSTING

2 cups whipping cream
1 teaspoon powdered sugar
2 teaspoons orange marmalade
1/2 teaspoon orange extract

Heat oven to 350°F. Grease and flour two 8 or 9-inch round cake pans. In large bowl, combine all cake ingredients at low speed until moistened; beat 2 minutes at *highest* speed. Pour batter into greased and floured pans. Bake at 350°F. for 25 to 35 minutes or until toothpick inserted in center comes out clean. Cool 10 minutes; remove from pans. Cool completely.

In small bowl, combine cream cheese, 1/3 cup whipping cream and 2 tablespoons powdered sugar at low speed until smooth and fluffy. Fold in chocolate.

In large bowl, beat 2 cups whipping cream and 1 teaspoon powdered sugar until thickened. Add orange marmalade and orange extract; beat until stiff peaks form.

To assemble torte, slice each cake layer in half horizontally to make 4 layers. Place 1 layer on serving plate. Spread top with 1/3 of filling mixture. Repeat with 2 more layers and remaining filling. Top with fourth layer; frost sides and top of cake with frosting mixture. Refrigerate until serving time. Store in refrigerator. **16 servings.**

HIGH ALTITUDE—Above 3500 Feet: Add 5 tablespoons flour to dry cake mix. Increase water to 2/3 cup. Bake at 375°F. for 25 to 35 minutes.

NUTRIENTS PER 1/16 OF RECIPE

Calories	450	Protein	8% U.S. RDA
Protein	6g	Vitamin A	15% U.S. RDA
Carbohydrate	36g	Vitamin C	4% U.S. RDA
Fat	31g	Thiamine	4% U.S. RDA
Cholesterol	120mg	Riboflavin	10% U.S. RDA
Sodium	340mg	Niacin	2% U.S. RDA
Potassium	210mg	Calcium	15% U.S. RDA
Dietary Fiber	<1g	Iron	8% U.S. RDA

Streamlined Hungarian Torte

(Sidebar, left column:)

Streamlined Hungarian Torte

Feather-light meringue tops flaky pastry layers filled with nuts and apricot preserves in this torte. It is not as time-consuming as it looks!

Rose Manske, Wisconsin
Bake-Off® 18, 1967

1 package active dry yeast
1/4 cup warm water
3 1/2 cups all purpose, unbleached, or
   self-rising flour
1 1/3 cups margarine or butter
1/2 cup dairy sour cream
4 eggs, separated
1 3/4 cups chopped walnuts
3/4 cup sugar
1 teaspoon cinnamon
10-ounce jar (3/4 cup) apricot
   preserves*
1/2 cup sugar

Heat oven to 350°F. Grease 13 × 9-inch pan. In small bowl, dissolve yeast in warm water (105 to 115°F.). Lightly spoon flour into measuring cup; level off. In large bowl, using pastry blender or fork, cut margarine into flour until mixture resembles coarse crumbs. Stir in sour cream, egg yolks and dissolved yeast just until a soft dough forms.

Shape dough into a ball; divide into 3 equal parts. On well-floured surface, roll each part to 13 × 9-inch rectangle. Place 1 rectangle in bottom of greased pan. Reserve 1/4 cup of the walnuts. In small bowl, combine remaining 1 1/2 cups walnuts, 3/4 cup sugar and cinnamon; sprinkle over rectangle in pan. Top with second rectangle; spread evenly with preserves. Top with remaining rectangle. Bake at 350°F. for 40 to 50 minutes or until light golden brown.

In large bowl, beat egg whites until foamy. Gradually add 1/2 cup sugar;

beat until stiff peaks form, about 3 minutes. Spread egg white mixture over baked pastry, covering completely. Sprinkle with reserved 1/4 cup walnuts. Bake an additional 10 to 15 minutes or until egg white mixture is golden brown. Cool. **16 servings.**

TIP: *Other flavors of preserves can be substituted for apricot preserves.

HIGH ALTITUDE—Above 3500 Feet: No change.

NUTRIENTS PER 1/16 OF RECIPE

Calories	480	Protein	10% U.S. RDA
Protein	7g	Vitamin A	15% U.S. RDA
Carbohydrate	52g	Vitamin C	<2% U.S. RDA
Fat	27g	Thiamine	15% U.S. RDA
Cholesterol	70mg	Riboflavin	10% U.S. RDA
Sodium	200mg	Niacin	8% U.S. RDA
Potassium	150mg	Calcium	4% U.S. RDA
Dietary Fiber	1g	Iron	10% U.S. RDA

Raspberry Ribbon Torte

Frances A. Neilsen, California
Bake-Off® 6, 1954

PASTRY
2 cups all purpose or unbleached flour
1/4 teaspoon salt
1 cup margarine or butter, softened
4 to 6 tablespoons cold water
2 to 4 tablespoons sugar

FILLINGS
1 1/2 cups milk
3 1/2-ounce package instant vanilla pudding and pie filling mix
2 tablespoons cornstarch
1/4 cup water
10-ounce package frozen raspberries with syrup, thawed, undrained
1/4 cup finely ground almonds

FROSTING
1 cup whipping cream
2 tablespoons powdered sugar
1/4 teaspoon almond extract

Lightly spoon flour into measuring cup; level off. In medium bowl, blend flour and salt. Using pastry blender or fork, cut margarine into flour mixture until mixture resembles coarse crumbs. Sprinkle flour mixture with water, 1 tablespoon at a time, while tossing and mixing lightly with fork. Add water until dough is just moist enough to hold together. Shape dough into a ball; wrap in plastic wrap. Cover and refrigerate 30 minutes or until dough is easy to handle.

Heat oven to 450°F. Divide dough into 6 equal parts. Shape each into a ball; flatten and smooth edges. On well-floured surface, roll 1 ball lightly from center to edge into 9-inch circle; cut around an inverted 9-inch pie pan to even edges. Place on ungreased *cool* cookie sheet; prick generously with fork. Sprinkle with 1 to 2 teaspoons of the sugar. Bake at 450°F. for 5 to 7 minutes or until light golden brown. (Watch carefully, as pastry browns quickly.) Remove from cookie sheet. Cool completely. Repeat with remaining balls of dough.

In small bowl, combine milk and pudding mix at low speed until slightly thickened; cover and refrigerate. In medium saucepan, blend cornstarch and water; add raspberries. Cook over medium heat until mixture becomes thick and clear, stirring constantly. Cool slightly; refrigerate.

Assemble torte 2 to 4 hours before serving. Place 1 pastry layer on serving plate; spread thinly with 1/3 of the raspberry filling. Top with second pastry layer; spread thinly with 1/3 of the vanilla filling. Repeat with remaining 4 layers, ending with vanilla filling. Sprinkle almonds over top of torte. In small bowl, beat whipping cream until soft peaks form. Blend in powdered sugar and almond extract; beat until stiff peaks form. Frost sides of torte with whipped cream mixture. If desired, pipe rim or rosettes of whipped cream around top edge of cake. Refrigerate until serving time. **16 servings.**

HIGH ALTITUDE—Above 3500 Feet: No change.

NUTRIENTS PER 1/16 OF RECIPE

Calories	290	Protein	4% U.S. RDA
Protein	3g	Vitamin A	15% U.S. RDA
Carbohydrate	30g	Vitamin C	4% U.S. RDA
Fat	18g	Thiamine	8% U.S. RDA
Cholesterol	20mg	Riboflavin	8% U.S. RDA
Sodium	210mg	Niacin	4% U.S. RDA
Potassium	105mg	Calcium	6% U.S. RDA
Dietary Fiber	1g	Iron	6% U.S. RDA

Raspberry Ribbon Torte

When making this stunning dessert, prepare everything early in the day. Then assemble the six baked pastry layers, raspberries and creamy vanilla filling two hours before serving.

Mocha Cream Chocolate Torte

Mocha Cream Chocolate Torte

Natalie C. Glomb, Pennsylvania
Bake-Off® 32, 1986

CAKE
- 1 package pudding-included German chocolate cake mix
- 1¼ cups water
- ⅓ cup oil
- 3 eggs

FROSTING
- ½ cup sugar
- ¼ cup cornstarch
- 2 tablespoons instant coffee granules or crystals
- 1¼ cups milk
- 1 cup margarine or butter, softened
- ¼ powdered sugar
  Chocolate sprinkles, if desired
  Whole blanched almonds, if desired

Heat oven to 350°F. Grease and flour 13 × 9-inch pan. In large bowl, combine all cake ingredients at low speed until moistened; beat 2 minutes at *highest* speed. Pour batter into greased and floured pan. Bake at 350°F. for 30 to 40 minutes or until toothpick inserted in center comes out clean. Cool 15 minutes; remove from pan. Cool completely.

Meanwhile, in heavy saucepan combine sugar, cornstarch and instant coffee; blend well. Gradually stir in milk. Cook over medium heat until mixture thickens and boils, stirring constantly. Remove from heat; cover with plastic wrap. Refrigerate 30 minutes or until cool. (Mixture will be very thick.) In large bowl, beat margarine and powdered sugar until well blended. Gradually add cooled coffee mixture; beat until light and fluffy.

To assemble torte, cut cooled cake in half lengthwise. Slice each half in half horizontally to make 4 layers. Place 1 layer on serving tray. Spread top with frosting mixture. Repeat with remaining layers and frosting. Frost sides and top of cake. Sprinkle top of torte with chocolate sprinkles; garnish with almonds. Store in refrigerator. **12 servings.**

HIGH ALTITUDE—Above 3500 Feet: Add 2 tablespoons flour to dry cake mix. Bake at 375°F. for 25 to 35 minutes.

NUTRIENTS PER 1/12 OF RECIPE

Calories	470	Protein	6% U.S. RDA
Protein	5g	Vitamin A	15% U.S. RDA
Carbohydrate	50g	Vitamin C	<2% U.S. RDA
Fat	28g	Thiamine	8% U.S. RDA
Cholesterol	70mg	Riboflavin	10% U.S. RDA
Sodium	530mg	Niacin	6% U.S. RDA
Potassium	140mg	Calcium	8% U.S. RDA
Dietary Fiber	<1g	Iron	6% U.S. RDA

Heavenly Hawaiian Cake Roll

Judy Merritt, New York
Bake-Off® 33, 1988

FILLING

Powdered sugar
⅓ cup butter or margarine, melted
½ cup firmly packed brown sugar
1 cup coconut
2 tablespoons chopped maraschino cherries
8-ounce can crushed pineapple in its own juice, well drained, reserving ½ cup liquid for cake

CAKE

3 eggs
1 cup sugar
1 cup all purpose, unbleached or self-rising flour*
1 teaspoon baking powder
¼ teaspoon salt

TOPPING

½ cup whipping cream
½ teaspoon vanilla
2 tablespoons powdered sugar
¼ cup chopped macadamia nuts, toasted**

Heat oven to 375°F. Line 15 × 10 × 1-inch baking pan with foil. Lightly sprinkle clean towel with powdered sugar. Spread butter evenly in bottom of foil-lined pan; sprinkle with brown sugar.

Sprinkle coconut, maraschino cherries and pineapple evenly over brown sugar; press down lightly. Set aside.

In small bowl, beat eggs at high speed until thick and lemon-colored, about 5 minutes. Gradually add sugar; beat well. If necessary, add enough water to reserved pineapple liquid to make ½ cup. Blend reserved pineapple liquid into egg mixture at low speed. Lightly spoon flour into measuring cup; level off. Add flour, baking powder and salt; beat at medium speed until smooth. Spread batter evenly over coconut mixture in pan.

Bake at 375°F. for 13 to 18 minutes or until top springs back when touched lightly in center. Immediately invert cake onto powdered-sugared towel; remove pan. Gently lift sides of foil from hot cake; carefully remove foil. Starting with shortest side and using towel to guide cake, roll up. (Do not roll towel into cake.) Wrap towel around rolled cake; cool completely on wire rack.

In small bowl, combine whipping cream, vanilla and 2 tablespoons powdered sugar; beat until stiff peaks form. Place cake roll seam side down on serving plate. Spread topping over sides and top of cake roll; sprinkle with nuts. Store in refrigerator. **12 servings.**

TIPS: *If using self-rising flour, omit baking powder and salt.

**To toast macadamia nuts, spread on cookie sheet; bake at 375°F. for about 3 minutes or until light golden brown, stirring occasionally.

Chopped toasted almonds or pecans can be substituted for macadamia nuts.

HIGH ALTITUDE—Above 3500 Feet: No change.

NUTRIENTS PER 1/12 OF RECIPE

Calories	300	Protein	4% U.S. RDA
Protein	3g	Vitamin A	8% U.S. RDA
Carbohydrate	41g	Vitamin C	2% U.S. RDA
Fat	14g	Thiamine	6% U.S. RDA
Cholesterol	100mg	Riboflavin	6% U.S. RDA
Sodium	140mg	Niacin	2% U.S. RDA
Potassium	120mg	Calcium	4% U.S. RDA
Dietary Fiber	1g	Iron	6% U.S. RDA

Heavenly Hawaiian Cake Roll

The cake and filling bake together in this easy-to-make jelly roll. Heavenly to eat!

Chocolate Silk Pecan Pie, page 170

Pies, Pastries and Other Desserts

Early Bake-Off® finalists were depicted as homemakers who served made-from-scratch pies and other desserts with everyday regularity. But as time pressures have mounted, good cooks have turned to more streamlined methods to speed preparation.

Today the fancy pies, pastries and desserts of yesterday can be made with remarkable ease and equally delicious results. A pat-in-the-pan crust allows even the most inexperienced baker to present a lovely pie for dessert. Versatile refrigerated crescent rolls form the crust for many delicious sweets. The latest advancement, all ready pie crusts, takes the worry and work out of pastry making altogether so that anyone can prepare favorite heirloom Bake-Off® desserts like Cherry-Berry Pie and Peacheesy Pie.

Instead of fussing over the crust, today's creative Bake-Off® entrants spend their time dreaming up "designer" fillings—a tart flavored with tangy lemon and hazelnuts, a cherry pie with an almond-coconut topping, a deliciously rich dessert featuring whipped cream, caramel and pecan filling drizzled with chocolate. Complex, traditional recipes for flans and cheesecakes are turned into quick modern-day versions. And indulgent new treats like Italian Crescent Crostata are gilded with ethnic touches of faraway places and times gone by.

At the same time, certain ingredients are cherished for their time-tested appeal. Among the favorite flavors are apple, cherry, lemon, pumpkin and chocolate teamed ever so skillfully with sweet spices, nuts, coconut and caramel as well as the creamy goodness of sour cream and whipping cream.

So, when it's time for a reward, turn to these pies, pastries and desserts. They offer sweetly satisfying answers for all types of special dessert occasions—even when preparation time is limited.

Cherry-Berry Pie

Eva Carter, Wisconsin
Bake-Off® 7, 1955

15-ounce package refrigerated pie crusts
1 teaspoon flour

FILLING
¾ cup sugar
2 tablespoons quick-cooking tapioca
2 tablespoons cornstarch
¼ teaspoon salt
16-ounce can pitted tart red cherries, drained, reserving liquid
10-ounce package frozen strawberries with syrup, thawed, drained, reserving syrup
1 tablespoon lemon juice
Sugar

Prepare pie crust according to package directions for *two-crust pie* using 9-inch pie pan. Heat oven to 400°F.

In medium saucepan, combine ¾ cup sugar, tapioca, cornstarch and salt; mix well. Stir in reserved cherry and strawberry liquids. Cook over medium heat 5 to 10 minutes or until mixture becomes thick and clear, stirring constantly. Remove from heat. Stir in cherries, strawberries and lemon juice. Spoon fruit mixture into pie crust-lined pan. Top with second crust; seal and flute. Sprinkle with sugar. Cut slits in several places. Bake at 400°F. for 30 minutes or until golden brown. Cool.
8 servings.

NUTRIENTS PER 1/8 OF RECIPE

Calories	430	Protein	2% U.S. RDA
Protein	2g	Vitamin A	8% U.S. RDA
Carbohydrate	69g	Vitamin C	20% U.S. RDA
Fat	16g	Thiamine	<2% U.S. RDA
Cholesterol	15mg	Riboflavin	2% U.S. RDA
Sodium	390mg	Niacin	2% U.S. RDA
Potassium	115mg	Calcium	<2% U.S. RDA
Dietary Fiber	2g	Iron	6% U.S. RDA

Topsy Turvy Apple Pie

This is a fun-to-serve upside-down pie. Traditional apple filling is baked between two flaky crusts and topped off with a rich pecan glaze. Preparation is simplified by using refrigerated pie crusts.

Topsy Turvy Apple Pie

Ronelva Gaard, Minnesota
Bake-Off® 3, 1951

GLAZE AND CRUST
¼ cup firmly packed brown sugar
1 tablespoon margarine or butter, melted
1 tablespoon corn syrup
¼ cup pecan halves
15-ounce package refrigerated pie crusts
1 teaspoon flour

FILLING
⅔ cup sugar
2 tablespoons flour
½ teaspoon cinnamon
4 cups sliced peeled apples

Whipped cream, if desired

In 9-inch pie pan, combine brown sugar, margarine and corn syrup; spread evenly over bottom of pan. Arrange pecans over mixture in pan. Prepare pie crust according to package directions for *two-crust pie*; place bottom crust over mixture in pan. Heat oven to 425°F.

In small bowl, combine sugar, 2 tablespoons flour and cinnamon; mix well. Arrange half of apple slices in pie crust-lined pan; sprinkle with half of sugar mixture. Repeat with remaining apple slices and sugar mixture. Top with second crust; seal and flute. Cut slits in several places. Bake at 425°F. for 8 minutes. Reduce oven temperature to 375°F. Bake an additional 25 to 35 minutes or until apples are tender and crust is golden brown. (Place pan on foil or cookie sheet during baking to catch any spillage.) Loosen edge of pie; carefully invert onto serving plate. Serve warm or cold with whipped cream.
8 servings.

NUTRIENTS PER 1/8 OF RECIPE

Calories	440	Protein	2% U.S. RDA
Protein	2g	Vitamin A	4% U.S. RDA
Carbohydrate	59g	Vitamin C	2% U.S. RDA
Fat	22g	Thiamine	4% U.S. RDA
Cholesterol	25mg	Riboflavin	2% U.S. RDA
Sodium	350mg	Niacin	<2% U.S. RDA
Potassium	130mg	Calcium	2% U.S. RDA
Dietary Fiber	2g	Iron	2% U.S. RDA

Topsy Turvy Apple Pie

Almond Macaroon Cherry Pie

Almond Macaroon Cherry Pie

Rose Anne LeMon, Arizona
Bake-Off® 32, 1986

15-ounce package refrigerated pie crusts
1 teaspoon flour

FILLING
21-ounce can cherry fruit pie filling
¼ to ½ teaspoon cinnamon
⅛ teaspoon salt, if desired
1 teaspoon lemon juice

TOPPING
1 cup coconut
½ cup sliced almonds
¼ cup sugar
⅛ teaspoon salt, if desired
¼ cup milk
1 tablespoon margarine or butter, melted
¼ teaspoon almond extract
1 egg, beaten

Prepare pie crust according to package directions for *filled one-crust pie* using 9-inch pie pan. (Refrigerate remaining crust for later use.) Heat oven to 400°F.

In large bowl, combine all filling ingredients; mix lightly. Spoon into pie crust-lined pan. Bake at 400°F. for 20 minutes.

Meanwhile, in medium bowl combine all topping ingredients; mix well. Spread evenly over partially baked pie. Bake an additional 15 to 30 minutes or until crust and topping are golden brown. Store in refrigerator. **8 servings.**

TIP: Cover pie with foil during last 5 to 10 minutes of baking if necessary to prevent excessive browning.

NUTRIENTS PER 1/8 OF RECIPE

Calories	400	Protein	6% U.S. RDA
Protein	4g	Vitamin A	6% U.S. RDA
Carbohydrate	58g	Vitamin C	4% U.S. RDA
Fat	17g	Thiamine	2% U.S. RDA
Cholesterol	35mg	Riboflavin	6% U.S. RDA
Sodium	260mg	Niacin	2% U.S. RDA
Potassium	170mg	Calcium	4% U.S. RDA
Dietary Fiber	3g	Iron	4% U.S. RDA

Peacheesy Pie

❧
Janis Boykin, Florida
Bake-Off® 16, 1964

15-ounce package refrigerated pie crusts
1 teaspoon flour

FILLING
½ cup sugar
2 tablespoons cornstarch
1 to 2 teaspoons pumpkin pie spice
2 tablespoons light corn syrup
2 teaspoons vanilla
28-ounce can peach slices, drained, reserving 3 tablespoons liquid

TOPPING
⅓ cup sugar
1 tablespoon lemon juice
2 eggs, slightly beaten
3-ounce package cream cheese, softened
½ cup dairy sour cream
2 tablespoons margarine or butter

Allow both crust pouches to stand at room temperature for 15 to 20 minutes. Meanwhile, in medium bowl combine all filling ingredients except reserved peach liquid; mix well. Set aside.

In small saucepan, combine 2 tablespoons of the reserved peach liquid, ⅓ cup sugar, lemon juice and eggs; mix well. Cook over medium heat until mixture thickens, stirring constantly. Remove from heat. In small bowl, beat cream cheese and sour cream until smooth. Gradually beat in hot egg mixture until well blended. Heat oven to 425°F.

Prepare 1 pie crust according to package directions for *filled one-crust pie* using 9-inch pie pan. Unfold remaining pie crust; remove plastic sheets. Press out fold lines from crust. Using floured 3-inch round cutter, cut out 8 circles from crust. Brush tops with remaining 1 tablespoon peach liquid. Spoon peach filling into pie crust-lined pan; dot with margarine. Spoon cream cheese topping over filling. Arrange pie crust circles over topping. Bake at 425°F. for 10 minutes. Reduce oven temperature to 350°F. Bake an addi-tional 35 to 40 minutes or until crust is golden brown. Cool. Store in refrigerator. **8 servings.**

NUTRIENTS PER 1/8 OF RECIPE

Calories	530	Protein	8% U.S. RDA
Protein	5g	Vitamin A	15% U.S. RDA
Carbohydrate	70g	Vitamin C	2% U.S. RDA
Fat	26g	Thiamine	<2% U.S. RDA
Cholesterol	100mg	Riboflavin	6% U.S. RDA
Sodium	310mg	Niacin	2% U.S. RDA
Potassium	190mg	Calcium	4% U.S. RDA
Dietary Fiber	2g	Iron	6% U.S. RDA

Lemon Luscious Pie

❧
Helen Gorsuch, California
Bake-Off® 14, 1962

15-ounce package refrigerated pie crusts
1 teaspoon flour

FILLING
1 cup sugar
3 tablespoons cornstarch
1 cup milk
¼ cup lemon juice
3 egg yolks, slightly beaten
¼ cup margarine or butter
1 tablespoon grated lemon peel
1 cup dairy sour cream
Whipped cream, if desired
Chopped walnuts, if desired

Heat oven to 450°F. Prepare pie crust according to package directions for *unfilled one-crust pie* using 9-inch pie pan. (Refrigerate remaining pie crust for later use.) Bake at 450°F. for 9 to 11 minutes or until light golden brown. Cool completely.

In medium saucepan, combine sugar and cornstarch; mix well. Stir in milk, lemon juice and beaten egg yolks; cook over medium heat until mixture thickens, stirring constantly. Remove from heat. Add margarine and lemon peel; stir until margarine is melted. Cool. Fold in sour cream. Spoon filling mixture into cooled baked crust; spread evenly. Refrigerate about 2 hours or until firm. Just before serving, garnish with whipped cream and walnuts.
8 servings.

NUTRIENTS PER 1/8 OF RECIPE

Calories	430	Protein	6% U.S. RDA
Protein	4g	Vitamin A	15% U.S. RDA
Carbohydrate	44g	Vitamin C	6% U.S. RDA
Fat	27g	Thiamine	2% U.S. RDA
Cholesterol	130mg	Riboflavin	8% U.S. RDA
Sodium	270mg	Niacin	<2% U.S. RDA
Potassium	135mg	Calcium	8% U.S. RDA
Dietary Fiber	<1g	Iron	2% U.S. RDA

Peacheesy Pie

❧

It isn't often that a $25,000 prize rewards homework well done. Yet that's just what happened in September 1964 for seventeen-year-old Janis Boykin of Melbourne, Florida. Her Home Economics assignment was to develop a new recipe at home.

"It's a new creation," she said proudly. Her five brothers liked it . . . and her Home Economics teacher, Mrs. Newman, wholeheartedly agreed and encouraged Janis to enter the recipe in the Bake-Off®. Hardly expecting to win, but daring to dream, Janis entered—and won.

Janis, now Mrs. Michael F. Risley, was the youngest contestant ever to win the top prize. Refrigerated pie crusts update this spiced peach and cheesecake pie for today's bakers.

Chocolate Caramel Satin Pie

Phelles Friedenauer, Illinois
Bake-Off® 33, 1988

15-ounce package refrigerated pie crusts
1 teaspoon flour

FILLING
24 caramels
1/3 cup water
2/3 cup firmly packed brown sugar
1/2 cup chopped walnuts
2/3 cup dairy sour cream
1 teaspoon vanilla
2 eggs, beaten
1 1/2 ounces (1/3 cup) grated sweet cooking chocolate, reserving 2 tablespoons for topping

TOPPING
1 cup vanilla milk chips*
1/4 cup milk
1 cup whipping cream
Reserved 2 tablespoons grated sweet cooking chocolate

Heat oven to 450°F. Prepare pie crust according to package directions for *unfilled one-crust pie* using 9-inch pie pan. (Refrigerate remaining pie crust for later use.) Bake at 450°F. for 8 to 9 minutes or until light golden brown. Cool slightly.

Meanwhile, in medium heavy saucepan over low heat, melt caramels in water, stirring until smooth. Remove from heat. Stir in brown sugar, walnuts, sour cream, vanilla and eggs; blend well. Pour into baked crust. Reduce oven temperature to 350°F. *Immediately* return pie to oven. Bake an additional 30 to 40 minutes or until edges of filling are set. Cool 15 minutes. Sprinkle chocolate over pie. Refrigerate until firm, about 2 hours.

In small heavy saucepan over low heat, melt vanilla milk chips in milk, stirring until smooth. Remove from heat; cool. In small bowl, beat whipping cream until stiff peaks form. Fold in cooled chip mixture. Spread over cooled filling. Sprinkle top of pie with reserved

2 tablespoons chocolate. Refrigerate until serving time. Store in refrigerator. **10 servings.**

TIP: *Do not substitute almond bark or vanilla-flavored candy coating.

NUTRIENTS PER 1/10 OF RECIPE

Calories	540	Protein	8% U.S. RDA
Protein	6g	Vitamin A	10% U.S. RDA
Carbohydrate	57g	Vitamin C	<2% U.S. RDA
Fat	32g	Thiamine	4% U.S. RDA
Cholesterol	100mg	Riboflavin	10% U.S. RDA
Sodium	240mg	Niacin	<2% U.S. RDA
Potassium	260mg	Calcium	10% U.S. RDA
Dietary Fiber	1g	Iron	8% U.S. RDA

Caramel Candy Pie

Florence Ries, Minnesota
Bake-Off® 4, 1952

15-ounce package refrigerated pie crusts
1 teaspoon flour

FILLING
1 envelope unflavored gelatin
1/4 cup cold water
1 cup milk
14-ounce package caramels
1 1/2 cups whipping cream, whipped

TOPPING
2 tablespoons sugar
1/4 cup slivered almonds

Heat oven to 450°F. Prepare pie crust according to package directions for *unfilled one-crust pie* using 9-inch pie pan. (Refrigerate remaining pie crust for later use.) Bake at 450°F. for 9 to 11 minutes or until light golden brown. Cool completely.

In small bowl, soften gelatin in water; set aside. In medium heavy saucepan, combine milk and caramels; cook over low heat until caramels are melted and mixture is smooth, stirring frequently. Add softened gelatin; stir until gelatin is dissolved. Refrigerate about 1 hour or until mixture is slightly thickened but not set, stirring occasionally. Fold caramel mixture into whipped cream. Pour into cooled baked crust; spread evenly. Refrigerate 2 hours or until firm.

In small skillet, combine sugar and almonds; cook over low heat until sugar is melted and almonds are golden brown, stirring constantly. Immediately spread on foil or greased cookie sheet. Cool; break apart. Just before serving, garnish pie with caramelized almonds. **8 servings.**

NUTRIENTS PER 1/8 OF RECIPE

Calories	530	Protein	8% U.S. RDA
Protein	6g	Vitamin A	15% U.S. RDA
Carbohydrate	56g	Vitamin C	<2% U.S. RDA
Fat	32g	Thiamine	2% U.S. RDA
Cholesterol	60mg	Riboflavin	10% U.S. RDA
Sodium	310mg	Niacin	<2% U.S. RDA
Potassium	210mg	Calcium	15% U.S. RDA
Dietary Fiber	<1g	Iron	4% U.S. RDA

Grand Prize Winner

Open Sesame Pie

Mrs. B. A. Koteen, Washington, D.C.
Bake-Off® 6, 1954

PASTRY
1 cup all purpose, unbleached or self-rising flour*
2 tablespoons sesame seed, toasted**
1/2 teaspoon salt
1/3 cup shortening
3 to 4 tablespoons cold water

FILLING
1 envelope unflavored gelatin
1/4 cup cold water
1 cup chopped dates
1/4 cup sugar
1/4 teaspoon salt
1 cup milk
2 eggs, separated
1 teaspoon vanilla
1 cup whipping cream, whipped
2 tablespoons sugar
Nutmeg

Heat oven to 450°F. Lightly spoon flour into measuring cup; level off. In medium bowl, combine flour, sesame seed and 1/2 teaspoon salt. Using pastry blender or fork, cut shortening into flour mixture until mixture resembles coarse crumbs. Sprinkle flour mixture with water, 1 tablespoon at a time, while tossing and mixing lightly with fork. Add water until dough is just moist enough to hold together. Shape dough into a ball. Flatten ball; smooth edges. On floured surface, roll lightly from center to edge into 10½-inch circle. Fold dough in half; fit evenly in 9-inch pie pan. Do not stretch. Turn edges under; flute. Prick bottom and sides of pastry generously with fork. Bake at 450°F. for 9 to 15 minutes or until light golden brown. Cool completely.

In small bowl, soften gelatin in 1/4 cup water; set aside. In medium saucepan, combine dates, 1/4 cup sugar, 1/4 teaspoon salt, milk and egg yolks. Cook over medium heat 6 to 10 minutes or until mixture is slightly thickened, stirring constantly. Remove from heat. Add softened gelatin and vanilla; stir until gelatin is dissolved. Refrigerate until date mixture is thickened and partially set, stirring occasionally. Fold whipped cream into date mixture. In small bowl, beat egg whites until soft peaks form. Gradually add 2 tablespoons sugar, beating until stiff peaks form. Fold into date mixture. Spoon filling into cooled baked pie shell; sprinkle with nutmeg. Refrigerate at least 2 hours before serving. Store in refrigerator. **8 servings.**

TIPS: *If using self-rising flour, omit salt.

**To toast sesame seed, spread on cookie sheet; bake at 375°F. for 3 to 5 minutes or until light golden brown, stirring occasionally. Or, spread in small skillet; stir over medium heat for about 5 minutes or until light golden brown.

HIGH ALTITUDE—Above 3500 Feet: No change.

NUTRIENTS PER 1/8 OF RECIPE

Calories	390	Protein	10% U.S. RDA
Protein	7g	Vitamin A	10% U.S. RDA
Carbohydrate	40g	Vitamin C	<2% U.S. RDA
Fat	23g	Thiamine	10% U.S. RDA
Cholesterol	110mg	Riboflavin	10% U.S. RDA
Sodium	250mg	Niacin	6% U.S. RDA
Potassium	250mg	Calcium	8% U.S. RDA
Dietary Fiber	2g	Iron	8% U.S. RDA

Open Sesame Pie

This recipe created a profitable rush to the country's supermarkets. It wasn't the date chiffon filling but the sesame seed crust that caused such commotion. Within hours after this pie was announced as the winning Bake-Off® recipe, a virtual "out of stock" was declared on sesame seed. And from that time on, it has been a regularly stocked item on most supermarket shelves.

Cookie Crust Pecan Pie

Ever-popular pecan pie is baked in a 13 × 9-inch pan for a new shape. Refrigerated cookie dough makes a quick-to-prepare crust.

Lemon Fudge Ribbon Pie

Harriet Mason, California
Bake-Off® 32, 1986

CRUST
15-ounce package refrigerated pie crusts
1 teaspoon flour
½ teaspoon unsweetened cocoa

FILLING
8-ounce package cream cheese, cut into 2 pieces
1 cup sugar
¼ cup lemon juice
1 teaspoon vanilla
3 eggs, beaten
½ ounce (½ square) unsweetened chocolate or 1 ounce (1 square) semi-sweet chocolate

TOPPING
1 cup whipping cream*
1 tablespoon powdered sugar*
Grated sweet cooking or semi-sweet chocolate, if desired

MICROWAVE DIRECTIONS: Prepare pie crust according to package directions for *unfilled one-crust pie* using 9-inch microwave-safe pie pan. (Refrigerate remaining crust for later use.) Sprinkle edge of crust with cocoa; rub in gently with finger tips before fluting. Generously prick crust with fork. Microwave on HIGH for 6 to 8 minutes, rotating pan ½ turn every 2 minutes. Crust is done when surface appears dry and flaky. Cool completely.

In medium microwave-safe bowl, microwave cream cheese on HIGH for 1 to 1½ minutes to soften. Stir in sugar until smooth. Add lemon juice, vanilla and eggs; blend well. Microwave on HIGH for 5 to 7 minutes, stirring every 2 minutes until smooth and thickened.

In small microwave-safe bowl, microwave unsweetened chocolate on HIGH for 2 minutes or until melted; blend in ½ cup of lemon filling. Pour into cooled cooked crust; spread evenly. Carefully spread remaining lemon filling over chocolate filling. Cover with waxed paper; refrigerate 3 to 4 hours or until firm. In small bowl, beat whip-

ping cream until soft peaks form. Blend in powdered sugar; beat until stiff peaks form. Spoon or pipe over filling. Garnish with grated chocolate. Store in refrigerator. **8 servings.**

TIP: *One and one-half cups frozen whipped topping, thawed, can be substituted for whipping cream and powdered sugar.

NUTRIENTS PER 1/8 OF RECIPE

Calories	490	Protein	8% U.S. RDA
Protein	6g	Vitamin A	20% U.S. RDA
Carbohydrate	43g	Vitamin C	4% U.S. RDA
Fat	33g	Thiamine	2% U.S. RDA
Cholesterol	180mg	Riboflavin	8% U.S. RDA
Sodium	290mg	Niacin	<2% U.S. RDA
Potassium	130mg	Calcium	6% U.S. RDA
Dietary Fiber	<1g	Iron	4% U.S. RDA

Cookie Crust Pecan Pie

Louise Schlinkert, California
Bake-Off® 20, 1969

20-ounce package refrigerated sliceable sugar cookie dough
3¾-ounce package instant butterscotch pudding and pie filling mix
Dash salt
¾ cup dark corn syrup
⅔ cup milk
½ teaspoon vanilla, if desired
1 egg
1½ cups pecan halves or pieces
Whipped cream or ice cream, if desired

Heat oven to 350°F. Slice cookie dough into ¼-inch slices; place in ungreased 13 × 9-inch pan. With lightly floured hands, press dough over bottom and 1 inch up sides to form crust. pressing dough as thin as possible on sides of pan. In medium bowl, combine pudding mix, salt, corn syrup, milk, vanilla and egg; mix well. Fold in pecans. Pour into crust-lined pan. Bake at 350°F. for 25 to 35 minutes or until edges are deep golden brown and filling is set. Cool completely; cut into squares. Serve with whipped cream or ice cream. **12 servings.**

NUTRIENTS PER 1/12 OF RECIPE

Calories	440	Protein	6% U.S. RDA
Protein	4g	Vitamin A	2% U.S. RDA
Carbohydrate	57g	Vitamin C	<2% U.S. RDA
Fat	22g	Thiamine	15% U.S. RDA
Cholesterol	35mg	Riboflavin	15% U.S. RDA
Sodium	270mg	Niacin	6% U.S. RDA
Potassium	170mg	Calcium	6% U.S. RDA
Dietary Fiber	1g	Iron	10% U.S. RDA

Lemon Fudge Ribbon Pie

Mystery
Pecan Pie

Mary McClain, Arkansas
Bake-Off® 16, 1964

15-ounce package refrigerated pie
  crusts
1 teaspoon flour

FILLING
  8-ounce package cream cheese,
    softened
  1 teaspoon vanilla
  1 egg
  ¹/₃ cup sugar
  ¹/₄ teaspoon salt
  3 eggs
  ¹/₄ cup sugar
  1 cup corn syrup
  1 teaspoon vanilla
  1¹/₄ cups chopped pecans

Prepare pie crust according to package directions for *filled one-crust pie* using 9-inch pie pan. (Refrigerate remaining crust for later use.) Heat oven to 375°F.

In small bowl, beat cream cheese, 1 teaspoon vanilla, 1 egg, ¹/₃ cup sugar and salt at low speed until smooth and well blended; set aside. In second small bowl, beat 3 eggs. Stir in ¹/₄ cup sugar, corn syrup and 1 teaspoon vanilla; mix well.

Spread cream cheese mixture in bottom of pie crust-lined pan. Sprinkle with pecans. Gently pour corn syrup mixture over pecans. Bake at 375°F. for 35 to 45 minutes or until center is set. Cool. Store in refrigerator. **8 servings.**

TIP: Cover edge of pie crust with strip of foil during last 10 to 15 minutes of baking if necessary to prevent excessive browning.

NUTRIENTS PER 1/8 OF RECIPE

Calories	570	Protein	10% U.S. RDA
Protein	8g	Vitamin A	10% U.S. RDA
Carbohydrate	63g	Vitamin C	<2% U.S. RDA
Fat	32g	Thiamine	6% U.S. RDA
Cholesterol	180mg	Riboflavin	8% U.S. RDA
Sodium	320mg	Niacin	<2% U.S. RDA
Potassium	150mg	Calcium	6% U.S. RDA
Dietary Fiber	1g	Iron	15% U.S. RDA

Chocolate Silk
Pecan Pie

Leonard Thompson, California
Bake-Off® 32, 1986

CRUST
  15-ounce package refrigerated pie
    crusts
  1 teaspoon flour
  ¹/₃ cup sugar
  ¹/₈ teaspoon salt, if desired
  ¹/₂ cup dark corn syrup
  3 tablespoons margarine or butter,
    melted
  2 eggs
  ¹/₂ cup chopped pecans

FILLING
  1 cup hot milk
  ¹/₄ teaspoon vanilla
  1¹/₃ cups (8 ounces) semi-sweet
    chocolate chips

TOPPING
  1 cup whipping cream
  2 tablespoons powdered sugar
  ¹/₄ teaspoon vanilla
  Chocolate curls, if desired

Prepare pie crust according to package directions for *filled one-crust pie* using 9-inch pie pan. (Refrigerate remaining crust for later use.) Heat oven to 350°F. In small bowl, beat sugar, salt, corn syrup, margarine and eggs 1 minute at medium speed. Fold in pecans. Pour into pie crust-lined pan. Bake at 350°F. for 40 to 55 minutes or until center of pie is puffed and golden brown. Cool on wire rack 1 hour.

While filled crust is cooling, in blender container or food processor bowl with metal blade, combine all filling ingredients; blend 1 minute or until smooth. Refrigerate about 1¹/₂ hours or until filling mixture is slightly thickened but not set. Gently stir mixture; pour into cooled filled crust; spread evenly. Refrigerate 1 hour or until firm.

In small bowl, beat whipping cream until soft peaks form. Blend in powdered sugar and ¹/₄ teaspoon vanilla; beat until stiff peaks form. Spoon or

---

Mystery
Pecan Pie

Solve the mystery when you taste the smooth cream cheese filling hiding under the rich pecan filling in this extra-special pie.

Chocolate Silk
Pecan Pie

In this luscious pie, smooth-as-silk chocolate crowns rich-flavored pecan pie. It is one of our favorites! For best results, be sure to measure ingredients accurately.

pipe over filling. Garnish with chocolate curls. Store in refrigerator. **8 to 10 servings.**

TIP: Cover pie with foil during last 15 to 20 minutes of baking if necessary to prevent excessive browning.

NUTRIENTS PER 1/10 OF RECIPE

Calories	490	Protein	6% U.S. RDA
Protein	5g	Vitamin A	10% U.S. RDA
Carbohydrate	46g	Vitamin C	<2% U.S. RDA
Fat	32g	Thiamine	4% U.S. RDA
Cholesterol	90mg	Riboflavin	6% U.S. RDA
Sodium	240mg	Niacin	<2% U.S. RDA
Potassium	180mg	Calcium	6% U.S. RDA
Dietary Fiber	2g	Iron	8% U.S. RDA

Raspberry Angel Cream Pie

Kay Bare, Idaho
Bake-Off® 33, 1988

15-ounce package refrigerated pie
   crusts
1 teaspoon flour
¼ cup chopped walnuts or pecans

FILLING
½ cup milk
25 large marshmallows
1 cup whipping cream, whipped

TOPPING
⅓ cup sugar
2 tablespoons cornstarch
¾ cup water
1 teaspoon lemon juice
1 teaspoon orange-flavored
   liqueur, if desired
1 teaspoon red food coloring, if
   desired
2 cups fresh or frozen raspberries
   without syrup, thawed, drained
   Whipped cream
   Whole raspberries

Heat oven to 450°F. Prepare pie crust according to package directions for *unfilled one-crust pie* using 9-inch pie pan. (Refrigerate remaining pie crust for later use.) Press walnuts into bottom of pie crust-lined pan. Bake at 450°F. for 9 to 11 minutes or until light golden brown. Cool completely.*

MICROWAVE DIRECTIONS: In 2-quart microwave-safe bowl, combine milk and marshmallows. Microwave on HIGH for 2 to 3 minutes or until marshmallows are melted, stirring once halfway through cooking.** With wire whisk, beat mixture until smooth. Cover; refrigerate 35 to 45 minutes or until mixture is thickened but not set. Fold in whipped cream. Spread filling mixture in cooled baked crust. Cover; refrigerate.

In medium microwave-safe bowl, combine sugar, cornstarch, water, lemon juice, liqueur and food coloring; blend well. Stir in 1 cup of the raspberries. Microwave on HIGH for 2 minutes; stir. Microwave on HIGH 2 to 5 minutes or until mixture becomes thick and clear, stirring once halfway through cooking. Refrigerate 30 to 45 minutes or until set. Fold in remaining 1 cup raspberries. Spoon topping mixture over cooled filling. Refrigerate 1 to 2 hours or until firm. Garnish with whipped cream and whole raspberries. Refrigerate before serving. Store in refrigerator. **8 servings.**

TIPS: *To microwave pie crust, prepare crust as directed above. Microwave on HIGH for 6 to 8 minutes, rotating pan once halfway through cooking. Crust is done when surface appears dry and flaky. Cool completely.

**Marshmallows puff up and do not appear melted. Stir to melt; additional cooking can toughen them.

NUTRIENTS PER 1/8 OF RECIPE

Calories	400	Protein	4% U.S. RDA
Protein	3g	Vitamin A	10% U.S. RDA
Carbohydrate	44g	Vitamin C	10% U.S. RDA
Fat	25g	Thiamine	2% U.S. RDA
Cholesterol	50mg	Riboflavin	6% U.S. RDA
Sodium	190mg	Niacin	2% U.S. RDA
Potassium	140mg	Calcium	6% U.S. RDA
Dietary Fiber	1g	Iron	2% U.S. RDA

Beginner's luck?

A woman who expressed frustration to her husband about never becoming a finalist after entering for many years found her spouse trying on his own to perfect a winning recipe. Sure enough, his creation not only took him to the Bake-Off® (along with his wife, who coached from the visitors' gallery), it gave him the distinction of becoming the first man ever to win a major prize. A U.S. Navy submarine steward, he aptly named his dessert Sub Meringue Pie.

Frost-on-the-Pumpkin Pie

Kathleen S. Johnson, Ohio
Bake-Off® 29, 1980

Tangy Crescent Nut Tart

Refrigerated crescent roll dough forms the easy flaky crust for this tart. Coconut and hazelnuts give texture and subtle flavor to the lemony filling.

CRUST
1¼ cups (18 squares) finely crushed graham crackers or graham cracker crumbs
3 tablespoons sugar
½ teaspoon cinnamon
¼ teaspoon nutmeg
⅛ teaspoon cloves
⅓ cup margarine or butter, melted

FILLING
1 can ready-to-spread vanilla frosting
1 cup dairy sour cream
1 cup canned pumpkin
1 teaspoon cinnamon
½ teaspoon ginger
¼ teaspoon cloves
8-ounce container (3¼ cups) frozen whipped topping, thawed

Heat oven to 350°F. In small bowl, combine all crust ingredients; stir until blended. Reserve 2 tablespoons of crust mixture for topping. Press remaining crust mixture in bottom and up sides of 9 or 10-inch pie pan. Bake at 350°F. for 6 minutes. Cool.

In large bowl, combine all filling ingredients except whipped topping; beat 2 minutes at medium speed. Fold in 1 cup of the whipped topping; pour into cooled baked crust; spread evenly. Refrigerate until firm. Spread remaining whipped topping over filling; sprinkle with reserved 2 tablespoons crust mixture. Refrigerate at least 4 hours before serving.* Store in refrigerator. **8 servings.**

TIP: *Refrigerate 6 hours or overnight before serving if substituting non-frozen whipped topping or whipped cream.

NUTRIENTS PER 1/8 OF RECIPE

Calories	560	Protein	4% U.S. RDA
Protein	3g	Vitamin A	150% U.S. RDA
Carbohydrate	64g	Vitamin C	2% U.S. RDA
Fat	32g	Thiamine	2% U.S. RDA
Cholesterol	10mg	Riboflavin	8% U.S. RDA
Sodium	320mg	Niacin	2% U.S. RDA
Potassium	190mg	Calcium	6% U.S. RDA
Dietary Fiber	1g	Iron	6% U.S. RDA

Tangy Crescent Nut Tart

Debi Wolf, Oregon
Bake-Off® 32, 1986

8-ounce can refrigerated crescent dinner rolls
1 cup sugar
¼ cup all purpose or unbleached flour
3 to 4 tablespoons lemon juice
2 to 3 teaspoons grated lemon peel
1 teaspoon vanilla
4 eggs
1 cup coconut
1 cup finely chopped hazelnuts (filberts) or walnuts
1 to 2 tablespoons powdered sugar

Heat oven to 350°F. Lightly grease 10-inch tart pan.* Separate dough into 8 triangles. Place triangles in greased pan; press over bottom and up sides to form crust. Seal perforations. Bake at 350°F. for 5 minutes. Cool 5 minutes; gently press sides of warm crust to top of pan.

In large bowl, combine sugar, flour, lemon juice, lemon peel, vanilla and eggs; beat 3 minutes at medium speed. By hand, stir in coconut and hazelnuts. Pour hazelnut mixture into cooled partially baked crust. Bake an additional 25 to 30 minutes or until filling is set and crust is golden brown. Cool. Sprinkle with powdered sugar. Store in refrigerator. **8 to 12 servings.**

TIP: *A 10-inch pizza pan can be substituted for the tart pan. Bake filled crust 20 to 25 minutes.

NUTRIENTS PER 1/12 OF RECIPE

Calories	270	Protein	8% U.S. RDA
Protein	5g	Vitamin A	<2% U.S. RDA
Carbohydrate	32g	Vitamin C	2% U.S. RDA
Fat	14g	Thiamine	8% U.S. RDA
Cholesterol	90mg	Riboflavin	6% U.S. RDA
Sodium	180mg	Niacin	4% U.S. RDA
Potassium	135mg	Calcium	2% U.S. RDA
Dietary Fiber	2g	Iron	6% U.S. RDA

Tangy Crescent Nut Tart

Caramel Pear Pecan Flan

Caramel Pear
Pecan Flan

※

Tillie A. Astorino, Massachusetts
Bake-Off® 32, 1986

15-ounce package refrigerated pie
  crusts
1 teaspoon flour
½ cup chopped pecans

FILLING
  8-ounce package cream cheese,
    softened
¾ to 1 cup caramel ice cream
    topping
  2 eggs
29-ounce can pear halves, well
    drained, sliced*
1½ cups frozen whipped topping,
    thawed
  3 tablespoons chopped pecans

MICROWAVE DIRECTIONS: Prepare
pie crust according to package directions for *unfilled one-crust pie* using 10-
inch microwave-safe tart pan or 9-inch
microwave-safe pie pan. (Refrigerate
remaining crust for later use.) Place
prepared crust in pan; press in bottom
and up sides of pan. Trim edges if necessary. Press ½ cup pecans into bottom
and sides of pie crust-lined pan. Generously prick crust with fork. Microwave on HIGH for 6 to 8 minutes,
rotating pan ½ turn every 2 minutes.
Crust is done when surface appears dry
and flaky. Cool completely.

In small bowl, beat cream cheese,
½ cup of the ice cream topping and
eggs until smooth. Pour into cooled
cooked pie crust; spread evenly. Arrange pear slices in single layer over
cream cheese mixture. Microwave on
HIGH for 6 to 9 minutes for tart pan

or 9 to 11 minutes for pie pan, rotating pan 1/4 turn every 3 minutes. Pie is done when center is almost set. (Cream cheese mixture will firm as it sets and cools.) Cover loosely with waxed paper; cool on flat surface 1 hour. Refrigerate 2 hours before serving. Just before serving, top with whipped topping; drizzle with remaining 1/4 to 1/2 cup ice cream topping. Sprinkle with 3 tablespoons pecans. Store in refrigerator. **6 to 10 servings.**

TIP: *Six to 10 canned pear halves, drained, arranged with rounded sides up and narrow ends pointing toward center, can be substituted for sliced pears. If desired, for decorative garnish, score pear halves by making 1/8-inch-deep decorative cuts on rounded side.

NUTRIENTS PER 1/10 OF RECIPE

Calories	400	Protein	10% U.S. RDA
Protein	6g	Vitamin A	10% U.S. RDA
Carbohydrate	43g	Vitamin C	<2% U.S. RDA
Fat	23g	Thiamine	2% U.S. RDA
Cholesterol	90mg	Riboflavin	4% U.S. RDA
Sodium	240mg	Niacin	<2% U.S. RDA
Potassium	130mg	Calcium	2% U.S. RDA
Dietary Fiber	2g	Iron	4% U.S. RDA

Grand Prize Winner

Apple Nut Lattice Tart

Mary Lou Warren, Colorado
Bake-Off® 32, 1986

15-ounce package refrigerated pie crusts
1 teaspoon flour

FILLING
  3 to 3 1/2 cups (3 to 4 medium) thinly sliced peeled apples
  1/2 cup sugar
  3 tablespoons chopped walnuts or pecans
  3 tablespoons golden raisins
  1/2 teaspoon cinnamon
  2 teaspoons lemon juice
  1/4 to 1/2 teaspoon grated lemon peel
  1 egg yolk, beaten
  1 teaspoon water

GLAZE
  1/4 cup powdered sugar
  1 to 2 teaspoons lemon juice

Prepare pie crust according to package directions for *two-crust pie* using 10-inch tart pan with removable bottom or 9-inch pie pan. Place 1 prepared crust in pan; press in bottom and up sides of pan. Trim edges if necessary. Heat oven to 400°F.

In large bowl, combine apples, sugar, walnuts, raisins, cinnamon, 2 teaspoons lemon juice and lemon peel; mix lightly. Spoon into pie crust-lined pan.

To make lattice top, cut remaining crust into 1/2-inch wide strips. Arrange strips in lattice design over apple mixture. Trim and seal edges. In small bowl, blend egg yolk and water; gently brush over lattice. Bake at 400°F. for 40 to 60 minutes or until golden brown and apples are tender. Cool 1 hour.

In small bowl, blend powdered sugar and enough lemon juice for desired drizzling consistency. Drizzle over slightly warm tart. Cool; remove sides of pan. **8 servings.**

TIP: Cover tart with foil during last 15 to 20 minutes of baking if necessary to prevent excessive browning.

NUTRIENTS PER 1/8 OF RECIPE

Calories	380	Protein	2% U.S. RDA
Protein	2g	Vitamin A	<2% U.S. RDA
Carbohydrate	50g	Vitamin C	4% U.S. RDA
Fat	19g	Thiamine	2% U.S. RDA
Cholesterol	35mg	Riboflavin	<2% U.S. RDA
Sodium	330mg	Niacin	<2% U.S. RDA
Potassium	125mg	Calcium	<2% U.S. RDA
Dietary Fiber	2g	Iron	2% U.S. RDA

Apple Nut Lattice Tart

A distinctive lattice top, golden raisins, and walnuts make this updated apple pie special enough to win the top prize.

Caramel Pear Pecan Flan

The subtle flavor of pears and the rich flavor of caramel combine in a microwave cheesecake pie.

Pecan Caramel Tart

Kathy Specht, California
Bake-Off® 33, 1988

15-ounce package refrigerated pie crusts
1 teaspoon flour

FILLING
½ cup whipping cream
36 caramels
3½ cups pecan halves

TOPPING
¼ cup semi-sweet chocolate chips
1 teaspoon margarine or butter
1 tablespoon whipping cream

Pecan Caramel Tart
——— ⸎ ———

Turtle candy in a crust! So unbelievably easy and so irresistibly delicious!

Heat oven to 450°F. Prepare pie crust according to package directions for *unfilled one-crust pie* using 10-inch tart pan with removable bottom or 9-inch pie pan. (Refrigerate remaining crust for later use.) Place prepared crust in pan; press in bottom and up sides of pan. Trim edges if necessary. Generously prick crust with fork. Bake at 450°F. for 9 to 11 minutes or until light golden brown. Cool completely.

In medium heavy saucepan, combine ½ cup whipping cream and caramels; cook over low heat until caramels are melted and mixture is smooth, stirring frequently. Remove from heat. Add pecans; stir until well coated. Spread evenly over cooled baked crust.

In small saucepan over low heat, melt chocolate chips and margarine, stirring until smooth. Stir in 1 tablespoon whipping cream until well blended. Drizzle over pecan filling. Refrigerate 1 hour or until filling is firm. If desired, garnish with sweetened whipped cream. **12 servings.**

NUTRIENTS PER 1/12 OF RECIPE

Calories	480	Protein	6% U.S. RDA
Protein	4g	Vitamin A	4% U.S. RDA
Carbohydrate	37g	Vitamin C	<2% U.S. RDA
Fat	35g	Thiamine	20% U.S. RDA
Cholesterol	15mg	Riboflavin	6% U.S. RDA
Sodium	180mg	Niacin	2% U.S. RDA
Potassium	210mg	Calcium	6% U.S. RDA
Dietary Fiber	3g	Iron	6% U.S. RDA

Praline Crescent Dessert

Marjorie Hooper, Florida
Bake-Off® 30, 1982

⅓ cup margarine or butter
½ cup firmly packed brown sugar
3 tablespoons dairy sour cream
1 cup crisp rice cereal
½ cup chopped pecans or nuts
½ cup coconut
8-ounce can refrigerated crescent dinner rolls
3-ounce package cream cheese, softened
2 tablespoons powdered sugar
Whipping cream, whipped, if desired

Heat oven to 375°F. In medium saucepan over low heat, melt margarine. Stir in brown sugar; cook 2 minutes, stirring constantly. Stir in sour cream; cook 4 minutes, stirring occasionally. Remove from heat. Add cereal, pecans and coconut; stir until evenly coated.

Separate dough into 8 triangles. Place 1 triangle in each ungreased muffin cup; press dough to cover bottom and sides, forming ¼-inch rim. In small bowl, beat cream cheese and powdered sugar until smooth. Spoon rounded teaspoonful into each dough-lined cup; spread over bottom. Spoon brown sugar mixture evenly over cream cheese mixture. Bake at 375°F. for 11 to 16 minutes or until edges of crust are deep golden brown. Cool 1 minute; remove from pan. Serve warm or cold topped with whipped cream. Store in refrigerator. **8 servings.**

TIP: To make ahead, prepare, cover and refrigerate up to 2 hours; bake as directed above.

NUTRIENTS PER 1/8 OF RECIPE

Calories	390	Protein	6% U.S. RDA
Protein	4g	Vitamin A	15% U.S. RDA
Carbohydrate	33g	Vitamin C	2% U.S. RDA
Fat	27g	Thiamine	10% U.S. RDA
Cholesterol	25mg	Riboflavin	10% U.S. RDA
Sodium	400mg	Niacin	6% U.S. RDA
Potassium	190mg	Calcium	4% U.S. RDA
Dietary Fiber	2g	Iron	8% U.S. RDA

Italian Crescent Crostata

Italian Crescent Crostata

—◦○◦—

Ann Mehl, Minnesota
Bake-Off® 31, 1984

2 (8-ounce) cans refrigerated crescent dinner rolls
1½ cups raspberry preserves
¾ cup chopped walnuts or pecans
½ cup raisins or currants
Beaten egg, if desired
Powdered sugar

Heat oven to 350°F. Separate dough into 8 rectangles; separate 5 of the rectangles into 10 triangles. Place the 10 triangles in ungreased 12-inch pizza pan or 13 × 9-inch pan; press over bottom and ½ inch up sides to form crust. Seal perforations. Bake at 350°F. for 12 to 15 minutes or until light golden brown.

In medium bowl, combine preserves, walnuts and raisins. Spread over partially baked crust. To make lattice top, seal perforations of remaining 3 rectangles; cut each lengthwise into 5 strips to make 15 strips of dough. Arrange strips in lattice design over preserve mixture, pinching strips together where necessary. Gently brush beaten egg over lattice. Bake an additional 17 to 22 minutes or until golden brown. Cool; sprinkle with powdered sugar.
10 to 12 servings.

NUTRIENTS PER 1/12 OF RECIPE

Calories	330	Protein	6% U.S. RDA
Protein	4g	Vitamin A	<2% U.S. RDA
Carbohydrate	49g	Vitamin C	2% U.S. RDA
Fat	13g	Thiamine	10% U.S. RDA
Cholesterol	25mg	Riboflavin	6% U.S. RDA
Sodium	320mg	Niacin	6% U.S. RDA
Potassium	210mg	Calcium	2% U.S. RDA
Dietary Fiber	1g	Iron	8% U.S. RDA

Almond Filled Cookie Cake

Elizabeth Meijer, Connecticut
Bake-Off® 30, 1982

Almond Filled Cookie Cake

This special recipe is a rich almond dessert adapted from a Dutch pastry. Thinly slice this tempting dessert to serve.

CRUST

2²/₃ cups all purpose or unbleached flour

1¹/₃ cups sugar

1¹/₃ cups unsalted or regular butter or margarine, softened*

¹/₂ teaspoon salt

1 egg

FILLING

1 cup grated or finely chopped almonds

¹/₂ cup sugar

1 teaspoon grated lemon peel

1 egg, slightly beaten

Whole almonds

Powdered sugar, if desired

Heat oven to 325°F. Grease 10 or 9-inch springform pan.** Lightly spoon flour into measuring cup; level off. In large bowl, blend flour and remaining crust ingredients at low speed until a soft dough forms. Refrigerate for easier handling, if desired. Divide dough in half; spread half in bottom of greased pan.

In small bowl, blend all filling ingredients except whole almonds and powdered sugar; spread over crust to within ¹/₂ inch of sides of pan. Between waxed paper, press out remaining half of dough to 10 or 9-inch circle. Remove top layer of waxed paper; invert dough over filling. Remove bottom layer of waxed paper; press dough into place. Garnish with whole almonds.

Bake at 325°F. for 55 to 65 minutes or until light golden brown. (Place foil on rack below pan during baking to catch any spillage.) Cool 15 minutes; remove sides of pan. Cool completely. Sprinkle with powdered sugar.

24 to 32 servings.

TIPS: *If using regular butter or margarine, omit ¹/₂ teaspoon salt.

**A 9-inch round cake pan can be used. Line bottom with waxed paper; grease. Continue as directed above. Cool 30 minutes; remove from pan.

HIGH ALTITUDE—Above 3500 Feet: No change.

NUTRIENTS PER 1/32 OF RECIPE

Calories	190	Protein	4% U.S. RDA
Protein	3g	Vitamin A	6% U.S. RDA
Carbohydrate	21g	Vitamin C	<2% U.S. RDA
Fat	11g	Thiamine	4% U.S. RDA
Cholesterol	40mg	Riboflavin	6% U.S. RDA
Sodium	40mg	Niacin	4% U.S. RDA
Potassium	60mg	Calcium	2% U.S. RDA
Dietary Fiber	<1g	Iron	4% U.S. RDA

Peaches and Cream Crescent Dessert

Marilyn Blankschien, Wisconsin
Bake-Off® 28, 1978

8-ounce can refrigerated crescent dinner rolls

8-ounce package cream cheese, softened

¹/₂ cup sugar

¹/₄ to ¹/₂ teaspoon almond extract

21-ounce can peach fruit pie filling*

¹/₂ cup all purpose or unbleached flour

¹/₄ cup firmly packed brown sugar

3 tablespoons margarine, softened

¹/₂ cup sliced almonds or chopped nuts

Heat oven to 375°F. Unroll dough into 2 long rectangles. Place in ungreased 13 × 9-inch pan; press over bottom to form crust. Seal perforations. Bake at 375°F. for 5 minutes.

Meanwhile, in small bowl beat cream cheese, sugar and almond extract until smooth. Spread over partially baked crust. Spoon fruit filling evenly over cream cheese mixture. Lightly spoon flour into measuring cup; level off. In second small bowl, blend flour, brown sugar and margarine at low speed until crumbly. Stir in almonds; sprinkle crumb mixture over fruit filling. Bake an additional 25 to 30 minutes or until golden brown. Cool completely. Cut into squares. Store in refrigerator.

12 servings.

NUTRIENTS PER 1/12 OF RECIPE

Calories	310	Protein	6% U.S. RDA
Protein	4g	Vitamin A	15% U.S. RDA
Carbohydrate	37g	Vitamin C	2% U.S. RDA
Fat	16g	Thiamine	6% U.S. RDA
Cholesterol	25mg	Riboflavin	8% U.S. RDA
Sodium	250mg	Niacin	4% U.S. RDA
Potassium	115mg	Calcium	2% U.S. RDA
Dietary Fiber	1g	Iron	15% U.S. RDA

Spicy Apple Twists

Dorothy DeVault, Ohio
Bake-Off® 10, 1958

2 large baking apples, cored
1½ cups all purpose, unbleached or self rising flour*
½ teaspoon salt
½ cup shortening
4 to 6 tablespoons cold water
1 tablespoon margarine or butter, softened

TOPPING
¼ cup margarine or butter, melted
½ cup sugar
1 teaspoon cinnamon
1 cup water

Heat oven to 425°F. Cut each apple into 8 wedges. Lightly spoon flour into measuring cup; level off. In medium bowl, blend flour and salt. Using pastry blender or fork, cut shortening into flour mixture until mixture resembles coarse crumbs. Sprinkle flour mixture with water, 1 tablespoon at a time, while tossing and mixing lightly with fork. Add water until dough is just moist enough to hold together. Shape dough into a ball. Flatten ball; smooth edges. On floured surface, roll lightly from center to edge into 12-inch square. Spread with 1 tablespoon softened margarine. Fold 2 sides to center. Roll into 16×10-inch rectangle. Cut crosswise into sixteen 10-inch strips. Wrap one strip around each apple wedge. Place ½ inch apart in ungreased 13×9-inch pan. Brush each wrapped apple wedge with melted margarine.

In small bowl, blend sugar and cinnamon; sprinkle over wrapped apples. Bake at 425°F. for 20 minutes. Pour water into pan. Bake an additional 12 to 17 minutes or until golden brown. Serve warm or cold, plain or with whipped cream. **16 servings.**

TIP: *If using self-rising flour, omit salt.

NUTRIENTS PER 1/16 OF RECIPE

Calories	170	Protein	2% U.S. RDA
Protein	1g	Vitamin A	2% U.S. RDA
Carbohydrate	18g	Vitamin C	<2% U.S. RDA
Fat	10g	Thiamine	4% U.S. RDA
Cholesterol	0mg	Riboflavin	2% U.S. RDA
Sodium	110mg	Niacin	2% U.S. RDA
Potassium	40mg	Calcium	<2% U.S. RDA
Dietary Fiber	<1g	Iron	2% U.S. RDA

Almond Brickle Dessert

Louise Bork, Ohio
Bake-Off® 18, 1967

½ cup slivered almonds
⅓ cup sugar
½ cup margarine or butter
¼ cup honey
1 tablespoon milk
1¾ cups all purpose, unbleached or self-rising flour*
⅔ cup sugar
2 teaspoons baking powder
½ cup margarine or butter, softened
⅓ cup milk
1 teaspoon almond extract
2 eggs

Heat oven to 350°F. Grease 9-inch square pan. In small saucepan, combine almonds, ⅓ cup sugar, ½ cup margarine, honey and 1 tablespoon milk. Cook over medium heat 9 to 11 minutes or until mixture comes to a boil, stirring constantly. Boil 2 minutes. Remove from heat; set aside.

Lightly spoon flour into measuring cup; level off. In large bowl, combine 1 cup flour, ⅔ cup sugar, baking powder, ½ cup margarine, ⅓ cup milk, almond extract and eggs. Blend at low speed until moistened; beat 3 minutes at medium speed. By hand, stir in remaining ¾ cup flour; mix well. Spread batter in greased pan. Spoon almond mixture over batter; spread evenly to cover. Bake at 350°F. for 25 to 35 minutes or until toothpick inserted in center comes out clean. **9 servings.**

TIP: *If using self-rising flour, omit baking powder.

HIGH ALTITUDE—Above 3500 feet: No change.

NUTRIENTS PER 1/9 OF RECIPE

Calories	440	Protein	8% U.S. RDA
Protein	6g	Vitamin A	20% U.S. RDA
Carbohydrate	51g	Vitamin C	<2% U.S. RDA
Fat	25g	Thiamine	10% U.S. RDA
Cholesterol	60mg	Riboflavin	10% U.S. RDA
Sodium	330mg	Niacin	8% U.S. RDA
Potassium	125mg	Calcium	15% U.S. RDA
Dietary Fiber	2g	Iron	8% U.S. RDA

Almond Brickle Dessert

Honey almond topping and a rich almond-flavored base create a small-sized dessert with homemade goodness.

Fudge Marble Cheesecake

Fudge Marble Cheesecake

Wanda Bierbaum, Illinois
Bake-Off® 32, 1986

1 package pudding-included fudge marble cake mix
¹/₃ cup oil
3 eggs
¹/₂ cup sugar
2 (8-ounce) packages cream cheese, softened
1 cup ricotta cheese or small curd cottage cheese
¹/₂ cup dairy sour cream
¹/₂ cup whipping cream

Heat oven to 350°F. Grease 13 × 9-inch pan. Reserve 1 cup of the dry cake mix and marble pouch; set aside. In large bowl, combine remaining cake mix, oil and 1 egg at low speed until a soft dough forms. Press in bottom and 1¹/₂ inches up sides of greased pan. Bake at 350°F. for 10 minutes.

In large bowl, combine reserved 1 cup cake mix, remaining 2 eggs, sugar, cream cheese, ricotta cheese, sour cream and whipping cream at low speed until blended; beat 3 minutes at medium speed. Reserve 1¹/₂ cups of cheese mixture. Spoon remaining cheese mixture over partially baked crust. Add reserved marble pouch to reserved cheese mixture; blend well. Spoon chocolate mixture randomly over cheese mixture. To marble, pull knife through mixture in wide curves; turn pan and repeat.

Bake an additional 30 to 40 minutes or until top springs back when touched lightly in center. *Do not overbake. To prevent cracking, immediately run knife around edge of pan.* Cool completely. Refrigerate until serving time. Store in refrigerator. **15 servings or 36 bars.**

HIGH ALTITUDE—Above 3500 feet: No change.

NUTRIENTS PER 1/15 OF RECIPE

Calories	410	Protein	10% U.S. RDA
Protein	7g	Vitamin A	15% U.S. RDA
Carbohydrate	38g	Vitamin C	<2% U.S. RDA
Fat	26g	Thiamine	8% U.S. RDA
Cholesterol	110mg	Riboflavin	10% U.S. RDA
Sodium	360mg	Niacin	4% U.S. RDA
Potassium	120mg	Calcium	10% U.S. RDA
Dietary Fiber	<1g	Iron	8% U.S. RDA

Peanut Chocolate Parfait Dessert

Karen Everly, Oregon
Bake-Off® 32, 1986

BASE
1 package pudding-included
   devil's food cake mix
1/2 cup margarine or butter, melted
1/4 cup milk
1 egg
3/4 cup peanuts

FILLING
1 1/2 cups powdered sugar
3/4 cup peanut butter
8-ounce package cream cheese,
   softened
2 1/2 cups milk
8-ounce container (3 1/4 cups)
   frozen whipped topping, thawed
5 1/4-ounce package instant vanilla
   pudding and pie filling mix (6-
   serving size)

TOPPING
1/2 cup peanuts
1.45-ounce bar milk chocolate,
   chilled, grated

Heat oven to 350°F. Grease and flour bottom only of 13 × 9-inch pan. In large bowl, combine all base ingredients except 3/4 cup peanuts; beat at medium speed until well blended. By hand, stir in 3/4 cup peanuts. Spread evenly in greased and floured pan. Bake at 350°F. for 20 to 25 minutes. *Do not overbake.* Cool completely.

In small bowl, combine powdered sugar and peanut buter at low speed until crumbly; set aside. In large bowl, beat cream cheese until smooth. Add milk, whipped topping and pudding mix; beat 2 minutes at low speed until well blended. Pour half of cream cheese mixture over cooled base; spread evenly. Sprinkle with half of peanut butter mixture. Repeat layers with remaining cream cheese and peanut butter mixtures. Sprinkle with 1/2 cup peanuts; gently press into filling. Sprinkle grated chocolate over peanuts.

Cover; refrigerate or freeze until serving time. Store in refrigerator or freezer. **16 servings.**

HIGH ALTITUDE—Above 3500 Feet: No change.

NUTRIENTS PER 1/16 OF RECIPE

Calories	540	Protein	20% U.S. RDA
Protein	11g	Vitamin A	10% U.S. RDA
Carbohydrate	53g	Vitamin C	<2% U.S. RDA
Fat	32g	Thiamine	10% U.S. RDA
Cholesterol	35mg	Riboflavin	10% U.S. RDA
Sodium	500mg	Niacin	20% U.S. RDA
Potassium	330mg	Calcium	20% U.S. RDA
Dietary Fiber	2g	Iron	8% U.S. RDA

Peanut Chocolate Parfait Dessert

Fudgy cake crust and fluffy peanut cream filling team up to make this heavenly dessert. Make it ahead and store in the freezer.

Microwave Honey Apple Cobbler

James Sloboden, Washington
Bake-Off® 32, 1986

4 cups thinly sliced apples
1/2 cup firmly packed brown sugar
1 teaspoon cornstarch
1/2 teaspoon cinnamon
2 tablespoons water
1 tablespoon lemon juice

CAKE
1/2 cup buttermilk*
1/4 cup honey
2 tablespoons oil
1 egg
1 cup all purpose, unbleached or self-rising flour**
1/4 cup firmly packed brown sugar
1/2 teaspoon baking soda
1/2 teaspoon ginger
1/4 teaspoon baking powder
1/4 teaspoon salt
1/4 teaspoon nutmeg

MICROWAVE DIRECTIONS: In 8-inch (1 1/2-quart) round microwave-safe dish or 2-quart round microwave-safe casserole, combine apples, 1/2 cup brown sugar, cornstarch, cinnamon, water and lemon juice; mix well. Cover with microwave-safe plastic wrap. Microwave on HIGH for 4 minutes or until apples are tender, stirring once halfway through cooking. Spread apples evenly over bottom of pan.

In small bowl, combine buttermilk, honey, oil and egg; blend until smooth. Lightly spoon flour into measuring cup; level off. Add flour and all remaining cake ingredients to buttermilk mixture. Blend at low speed until well combined; beat 2 minutes at medium speed. Pour batter over cooked apples; tap dish on counter so batter settles evenly over apples.

Elevate dish on inverted microwave-safe dish or on shelf provided. Microwave on HIGH for 6 to 10 minutes, rotating dish 1/4 turn every 2 minutes. Cake is done when toothpick inserted in center comes out clean and cake pulls away from sides of pan. Let stand on flat surface 5 minutes before serving. Serve warm or cold. If desired, top with whipped cream. Store in refrigerator. **6 to 8 servings.**

TIPS: *To substitute for buttermilk, use 1 1/2 teaspoons vinegar or lemon juice plus milk to make 1/2 cup.

**If using self-rising flour, omit baking soda, baking powder and salt.

HIGH ALTITUDE—Above 3500 Feet: No change.

NUTRIENTS PER 1/8 OF RECIPE

Calories	260	Protein	4% U.S. RDA
Protein	3g	Vitamin A	<2% U.S. RDA
Carbohydrate	50g	Vitamin C	4% U.S. RDA
Fat	5g	Thiamine	8% U.S. RDA
Cholesterol	35mg	Riboflavin	6% U.S. RDA
Sodium	180mg	Niacin	4% U.S. RDA
Potassium	190mg	Calcium	4% U.S. RDA
Dietary Fiber	2g	Iron	10% U.S. RDA

Sour Cream Apple Squares

Grand Prize Winner

Sour Cream Apple Squares

Luella Maki, Minnesota
Bake-Off® 26, 1975

2 cups all purpose or unbleached flour
2 cups firmly packed brown sugar
½ cup margarine or butter, softened
1 cup chopped nuts
1 teaspoon baking soda
1 to 2 teaspoons cinnamon
½ teaspoon salt
1 cup dairy sour cream
1 teaspoon vanilla
1 egg
2 cups finely chopped peeled apples

Heat oven to 350°F. Lightly spoon flour into measuring cup; level off. In large bowl, combine flour, brown sugar and margarine at low speed until crumbly. Stir in nuts. Press 2¾ cups of crumb mixture into ungreased 13 × 9-inch pan. To remaining crumb mixture, add baking soda, cinnamon, salt, sour cream, vanilla and egg; blend well. Stir in apples. Spoon apple mixture evenly over crumb mixture in pan. Bake at 350°F. for 30 to 40 minutes or until toothpick inserted in center comes out clean. Cut into squares. If desired, serve with whipped cream or ice cream.
12 servings.

HIGH ALTITUDE—Above 3500 Feet: Bake at 375°F. for 25 to 35 minutes.

NUTRIENTS PER 1/12 OF RECIPE

Calories	420	Protein	6% U.S. RDA
Protein	5g	Vitamin A	10% U.S. RDA
Carbohydrate	58g	Vitamin C	2% U.S. RDA
Fat	19g	Thiamine	10% U.S. RDA
Cholesterol	30mg	Riboflavin	8% U.S. RDA
Sodium	300mg	Niacin	6% U.S. RDA
Potassium	270mg	Calcium	10% U.S. RDA
Dietary Fiber	1g	Iron	15% U.S. RDA

Ruby Razz Crunch

⚜

Achsa Myers, Colorado
Bake-Off® 8, 1956

Ruby Razz Crunch

⚜

Frozen rhubarb and raspberries bake into a delectable dessert garnished with a frozen raspberry-flavored whipped cream topping.

FILLING
- 10-ounce package frozen raspberries with syrup, thawed, drained, reserving syrup
- 16-ounce package frozen rhubarb, thawed, drained, reserving liquid
- ½ cup sugar
- 3 tablespoons cornstarch

TOPPING
- ½ cup whipping cream, whipped
- 2 tablespoons sugar
- 1 to 3 drops red food coloring, if desired

CRUST
- 1¼ cups all purpose or unbleached flour
- 1 cup quick-cooking rolled oats
- 1 cup firmly packed brown sugar
- 1 teaspoon cinnamon
- ½ cup margarine or butter, melted

Heat oven to 325°F. In measuring cup, combine reserved raspberry and rhubarb liquids. If necessary, add water to make 1 cup. In medium saucepan, combine ½ cup sugar and cornstarch; mix well. Stir in 1 cup reserved liquids. Cook over medium heat until mixture becomes thick and clear, stirring constantly. Remove from heat. Reserve 2 tablespoons of the raspberries for topping. Stir remaining raspberries and rhubarb into cornstarch mixture. Set aside.

Line cookie sheet with waxed paper. In small bowl, combine all topping ingredients and reserved 2 tablespoons raspberries; blend well. Make 9 mounds of topping mixture on waxed-paper-lined cookie sheet; freeze until firm.*

Lightly spoon flour into measuring cup; level off. In large bowl, combine flour, rolled oats, brown sugar and cinnamon; mix well. Add margarine; mix until crumbly. Press ⅔ of crumb mixture in bottom of ungreased 9-inch square pan. Spoon filling mixture over crumb mixture in pan; spread evenly. Sprinkle with remaining crumb mixture. Bake at 325°F. for 45 to 55 minutes or until crust is golden brown and filling bubbles around edges. Cool slightly. To serve, cut into squares; top each serving with mound of frozen topping.
9 servings.

MICROWAVE DIRECTIONS: In 4-cup microwave-safe measuring cup, combine ½ cup sugar and cornstarch; mix well. Measure reserved liquids as directed above; stir into cornstarch mixture. Microwave on HIGH for 4 to 4½ minutes or until thick and bubbly, stirring once halfway through cooking. Reserve 2 tablespoons of the raspberries for topping. Stir remaining raspberries and rhubarb into cornstarch mixture. Set aside. Prepare topping as directed above.* Place margarine in medium microwave-safe bowl. Microwave on HIGH for 45 to 60 seconds or until melted. Add remaining crust ingredients; mix until crumbly. Press ⅔ of crumb mixture in bottom of 8-inch (2-quart) square microwave-safe dish. Spoon filling mixture over crumb mixture in pan; spread evenly. Sprinkle with remaining crumb mixture. Microwave on MEDIUM for 10 minutes, turning dish ¼ turn halfway through cooking. Turn ¼ turn; microwave on HIGH for 4 to 5 minutes or until filling bubbles around edges. Let cool at least 20 minutes before serving. Serve as directed above.

TIP: *If desired, topping can be prepared and served without freezing.

NUTRIENTS PER 1/9 OF RECIPE

Calories	440	Protein	6% U.S. RDA
Protein	4g	Vitamin A	25% U.S. RDA
Carbohydrate	70g	Vitamin C	8% U.S. RDA
Fat	16g	Thiamine	20% U.S. RDA
Cholesterol	20mg	Riboflavin	10% U.S. RDA
Sodium	220mg	Niacin	15% U.S. RDA
Potassium	240mg	Calcium	20% U.S. RDA
Dietary Fiber	3g	Iron	20% U.S. RDA

Ruby Razz Crunch

Chocolate Almond Frozen Mousse

·ₒ·ₒ·

Adelaide B. Shaw, New York
Bake-Off® 29, 1980

CRUST
1 cup all purpose or unbleached flour
1/2 cup ground almonds
1/2 cup firmly packed brown sugar
1/2 cup margarine or butter, melted

FILLING
4 eggs, separated
1/4 cup milk
1/2 to 1 teaspoon almond extract
1 can ready-to-spread chocolate fudge frosting
1 cup whipping cream, whipped

Heat oven to 350°F. Lightly spoon flour into measuring cup; level off. In medium bowl, combine flour and all remaining crust ingredients; mix until crumbly. Spread in bottom of ungreased 13 × 9-inch pan. Bake at 350°F. for 10 to 15 minutes or until light golden brown, stirring once. Cool. Press 2 cups of crumb mixture in bottom of ungreased 9 or 10-inch springform pan or 9-inch square pan. Reserve remaining crumb mixture.

In small saucepan, slightly beat egg yolks; add milk. Cook over medium heat until thickened, stirring constantly. Remove from heat; stir in almond extract. In large bowl, fold egg yolk mixture into frosting. In small bowl, beat egg whites until stiff peaks form. Fold beaten egg whites and whipped cream into frosting mixture; pour over crumb mixture in pan.

Freeze 1 hour; sprinkle with reserved crumb mixture. Freeze an additional 3 to 4 hours or until firm. If desired, serve with whipped cream. **12 servings.**

NUTRIENTS PER 1/12 OF RECIPE

Calories	410	Protein	8% U.S. RDA
Protein	5g	Vitamin A	15% U.S. RDA
Carbohydrate	42g	Vitamin C	<2% U.S. RDA
Fat	25g	Thiamine	6% U.S. RDA
Cholesterol	120mg	Riboflavin	8% U.S. RDA
Sodium	210mg	Niacin	4% U.S. RDA
Potassium	210mg	Calcium	4% U.S. RDA
Dietary Fiber	1g	Iron	10% U.S. RDA

·ₒ·ₒ·

No Dancing in This Ballroom!

For its first eight years, the Bake-Off® was held in the Grand Ballroom of New York's Waldorf-Astoria Hotel. Chosen because it symbolized New York's glamour, had an established reputation for gracious weekend entertaining, and had space and facilities for the world's biggest contemporary kitchen, the Waldorf was a happy choice. Finalists reveled in the carefree atmosphere of a weekend at the Waldorf. Pillsbury personnel, working at a dead-run behind the scenes, found the efficient personnel a big help in staging the production.

European Almond Crescent Cups

·ₒ·ₒ·

Debi Wolf, Oregon
Bake-Off® 31, 1984

1/4 cup sugar
1/4 cup ground almonds
3 tablespoons margarine or butter, softened
1/2 teaspoon almond extract
1/4 teaspoon vanilla
1 egg, slightly beaten
8-ounce can refrigerated crescent dinner rolls
3 tablespoons apricot preserves or orange marmalade

GLAZE
1/2 cup powdered sugar
2 to 3 tablespoons orange-flavored liqueur or 3 to 4 teaspoons orange juice
8 candied cherry halves or whole almonds, if desired

Heat oven to 375°F. Grease 8 muffin cups. In small bowl, combine sugar, almonds, margarine, almond extract, vanilla and egg; blend well. Separate dough into 8 triangles. Place 1 triangle in each greased muffin cup; press dough to cover bottom and sides forming 1/4-inch rim. Spoon about 1 tablespoonful of almond mixture into each dough-lined cup; spoon scant 1 teaspoonful of the preserves over almond mixture. Bake at 375°F. for 10 to 18 minutes or until edges of crust are deep golden brown. Cool 1 minute; remove from pan. In small bowl, blend powdered sugar and enough liqueur for desired drizzling consistency. Drizzle over cups. Garnish each with cherry half. **8 servings.**

NUTRIENTS PER 1/8 OF RECIPE

Calories	260	Protein	4% U.S. RDA
Protein	3g	Vitamin A	4% U.S. RDA
Carbohydrate	35g	Vitamin C	<2% U.S. RDA
Fat	12g	Thiamine	6% U.S. RDA
Cholesterol	35mg	Riboflavin	6% U.S. RDA
Sodium	300mg	Niacin	4% U.S. RDA
Potassium	100mg	Calcium	2% U.S. RDA
Dietary Fiber	1g	Iron	4% U.S. RDA

Appendix

Nutrition Information

To assist in planning healthful, wholesome meals, specific nutritional information is provided with each recipe. This unique NUTRI-CODED system, a computerized method designed by Pillsbury research scientists, utilizes information compiled by the U.S. Department of Agriculture in the revised Agriculture Handbook No. 8, and represents Pillsbury's strong, continuing commitment to nutrition education for the consumer. Every effort has been made to ensure accuracy of information; however, The Pillsbury Company does not guarantee its suitability for specific medically imposed diets.

The NUTRI-CODES for each recipe provide information on a per serving basis about:

calories, protein, carbohydrates, fat, cholesterol, sodium, potassium, dietary fiber, calcium, iron, and vitamins.

Protein, carbohydrates, fats, and dietary fiber are expressed in grams; cholesterol, sodium and potassium in milligrams. The amounts of vitamins, calcium, and iron are expressed as percentages needed by the body on a daily basis (U.S. Recommended Daily Allowance).

Guidelines to Use Nutrition Information:

SERVING SIZE: This has been determined as a typical serving for each recipe. If more or less is eaten, adjust nutrition information accordingly.

CALORIES: The amount of calories a person needs is determined by age, size and activity level. The recommended daily allowances generally are: 1800 to 2400 for women and children 4 to 10 years of age and 2400 to 2800 for men.

PROTEIN: The amount of protein needed daily is determined by age and size; the general U.S. RDA is 65 grams for adults and children of at least 4 years of age.

CARBOHYDRATE, FAT, CHOLESTEROL, SODIUM, AND POTASSIUM: Recommended Daily Allowances (RDA) for these nutrients have not been determined. The amounts of carbohydrates and fat needed in the daily diet are dependent upon daily caloric requirements. The amounts should be adequate so the body does not burn protein for energy. The American Heart Association recommendation for those who wish to restrict dietary cholesterol is for a daily intake that is less than 100 milligrams per 1000 calories and not exceeding a total of 300 milligrams.

DIETARY FIBER: Nutritionists recommend a dietary fiber intake of 20 to 35 grams per day from a variety of foods.

PERCENT U.S. RDA PER SERVING: For a nutritionally balanced diet, choose recipes which will provide 100% of the U.S. Recommended Daily Allowance for each nutrient.

Guidelines Used in Calculating Nutrition Information:

- When the ingredient listing gives one or more options, the first ingredient listed is the one analyzed.
- When a range is given for an ingredient, the larger amount is analyzed.
- When ingredients are listed as "if desired," these ingredients are included in the nutrition information.
- Serving suggestions listed in the ingredients are calculated in the nutrition information.
- When each bread recipe is analyzed, a serving of yeast-leavened bread is a 1-oz. slice and a quick bread serving is $1/16$ of the loaf. Recipes that vary are indicated.
- Symbols used in relation to nutrition data:

  <   Less than 2% of the nutrient
  <1   Less than one gram (or milligram) of the nutrient

Any questions regarding nutrition information in this book should be addressed to:

The Pillsbury Company
Pillsbury Center—Suite 2866
Minneapolis, Minnesota 55402

Pillsbury Products Used in Bake-Off® Contest Recipes

DRY GROCERY PRODUCTS:

Canned Vegetables

Green Giant® Cut Green Beans
Green Giant® Mexicorn® Whole Kernel Golden
  Sweet Corn with Red and Green Sweet Peppers
Green Giant® Niblets® Whole Kernel
  Golden Sweet Corn
Green Giant® Sliced Mushrooms
Green Giant® Sweet Peas
Green Giant® Whole Kernel Golden Sweet Corn
Green Giant® Whole Mushrooms
Le Sueur® Early Peas

Flour

Pillsbury's BEST® All Purpose Flour
Pillsbury's BEST® Bread Flour
Pillsbury's BEST® Self-Rising Flour
Pillsbury's BEST® Unbleached All Purpose Flour
Pillsbury's BEST® Whole Wheat Flour

Frosting

Pillsbury Ready to Spread Chocolate Fudge
  Frosting Supreme
Pillsbury Ready to Spread Cream Cheese
  Frosting Supreme
Pillsbury Ready to Spread Milk Chocolate
  Frosting Supreme
Pillsbury Ready to Spread Vanilla Frosting Supreme

Mixes

Cake:

Pillsbury Plus Butter Recipe Cake Mix
Pillsbury Plus Dark Chocolate Cake Mix
Pillsbury Plus Devil's Food Cake Mix
Pillsbury Plus Fudge Marble Cake Mix
Pillsbury Plus German Chocolate Cake Mix
Pillsbury Plus Lemon Cake Mix
Pillsbury Plus White Cake Mix
Pillsbury Plus Yellow Cake Mix

Specialty:

Hungry Jack® Buttermilk Pancake
  and Waffle Mix
Hungry Jack® Buttermilk Complete
  Pancake Mix
Hungry Jack® Extra Lights®
  Complete Pancake Mix
Hungry Jack® Mashed Potato Flakes
Pillsbury Au Gratin Potatoes
Pillsbury Creamy White Sauce
  Scalloped Potatoes
Pillsbury Date Quick Bread Mix
Pillsbury Hot Roll Mix
Pillsbury Real Cheese Sauce Scalloped Potatoes

REFRIGERATED PRODUCTS:

Hungry Jack® Refrigerated Flaky Biscuits
Pillsbury All Ready Pie Crusts
Pillsbury's BEST® Refrigerated Sugar Cookies
Pillsbury Refrigerated Biscuits
Pillsbury Refrigerated Quick Crescent Dinner Rolls

FROZEN PRODUCTS:

Side Dishes

Green Giant® Rice Originals® Frozen Rice Medley

Vegetables

Green Giant® Frozen Broccoli Cuts
Green Giant® Frozen Cut Green Beans
Green Giant® Frozen Mixed Vegetables
Green Giant® Frozen Sweet Peas
Green Giant® Harvest Fresh®
  Frozen Chopped Spinach
Green Giant® Harvest Fresh® Frozen Cut Broccoli
Green Giant® Harvest Fresh®
  Frozen Mixed Vegetables
Green Giant® Harvest Fresh® Frozen Sweet Peas
Green Giant® Niblets® Frozen Corn
Green Giant® Valley Combinations®
  Frozen Broccoli Cauliflower Supreme

Index